Also by Shiva Naipaul

A New World Tragedy

JOURNEY TO NOWHERE

BY Shiva Naipaul

Simon and Schuster
NEW YORK

SIMON AND SCHUSTER and colophon are trademarks of
Simon & Schuster
Designed by Irving Perkins Associates
Originally published in Great Britain in 1980
under the title *Black and White*
Manufactured in the United States of America
1   3   5   7   9   10   8   6   4   2

Library of Congress Cataloging in Publication Data

Naipaul, Shiva, date.
Journey to nowhere.

First published in 1980 under title: Black and white.
Bibliography: p.
Includes index.
1. Peoples Temple.   2. Jones, Jim, 1931-1978.
I. Title.
BP605.P46N34   1980   289.9   80-29138

ISBN 0-671-42471-8

The author gratefully acknowledges permission to quote from the following:

"In Memory of W. B. Yeats" by W. H. Auden from *W. H. Auden: Collected Poems,* edited by Edward Mendelson, copyright © 1940, renewed 1968 by W. H. Auden. Reprinted by permission of Random House, Inc.

"Sitting on the Dock of the Bay" by Otis Redding, copyright © 1968 by East/Memphis & Time Music.

The author wishes to acknowledge the generous help of the Guggenheim Foundation during the writing of this book.

Intellectual disgrace
Stares from every human face,
And the seas of pity lie
Locked and frozen in each eye.
                —W. H. AUDEN

PART
ONE

CHAPTER
1

At Piarco Airport in Trinidad, I all but jumped ship. My wretchedness had been building throughout the long flight from London. I was separated by no more than an hour from the jungly nightmare of Guyana.

It was early afternoon and it was raining hard. The crowded aircraft, invaded by sultry tropical air, steamed with the blended vapors of sweat, tobacco and alcohol. Boxes and bags laden with London-bought treasure crammed the overhead racks and overflowed from under the seats. This treasure was, for the most part, so tawdry, so down-at-heel, that it could only heighten my apprehension of what lay ahead. It consisted, in the main, of food—canned goods, tins of biscuits, confectionery—and the commoner household utensils—cutlery, towel racks, pots and pans. This cargo emphasized the fact that I was on my way to a land of endemic scarcity; a land where, a couple of weeks previously, just over nine hundred Americans, in thrall to a faith healer espousing a mixture of socialism, racial brotherhood and cooperative agricultural enterprise—the stated ideals, in short, of the Guyanese Government—had died in a desolation of murder and suicide: a messianic climax which, in its reliance on Fla-Vor-Aid as a sweetening agent for the cyanide soup administered to the victims, was not without its horrible and deserved bathos. The first Guyanese to arrive on the scene had plundered the encampment. They had also behaved badly at the Kaituma airstrip, not far from Jonestown, where Congressman Leo Ryan's delegation had been ambushed by Jim Jones's assassins. Before the stunned survivors could intervene, the locals had stripped the fallen bodies of cameras, tape recorders and other technical equipment. When water was requested, some had demanded payment.

Still, as one of my fellow passengers (a Guyanese) had pointed out to me, there was some comfort to be drawn from the catastrophe. It had always annoyed him when his English friends asked him where Guyana was located. Mostly, they would place it somewhere in Africa. "This thing," he said, "has put Guyana on the map." He even hoped that the sudden flood of publicity might stimulate some badly needed foreign investment.

Not many weeks before, I had been to another of the Guianas, to neighboring Surinam, the former Dutch colony which had recently been given its political freedom. Surinam was still suffering the aftermath of the panic that had swept over many of its potential citizens (the majority of them Indians—or Hindustanis, as they are called there) on the eve of Independence. Clinging to their still operative Dutch nationality, thousands had fled to Holland. Almost a quarter of the Surinamese population of half a million now live in the Netherlands. This stampede gave rise to a joke which, I suspect, is not unique to Surinam. The Surinamese say that the exodus led to the prominent display of a sign at the airport: "Will The Last Person To Leave Please Turn Off The Lights."

It was a panic with which I could easily sympathize. If Guyana, their immediate neighbor, loosed into the world by the British in 1966, was anything to go by, the Hindustanis, the Chinese and the Javanese—these last an exotic reminder of the Dutch colonies in the East Indies—had every reason to be worried and fearful about the implications of Independence. The excesses of an unrestrained and cynical black supremacy were at hand. All they had to do was peep through the fence and look at what was going on in the yard next door. They packed up and left.

But in 1978 these fears had not yet been realized. Surinam, despite incipient Third World frailties, despite the modish Cuba-inspired affectations of its young black and mulatto intellectuals, was still a reasonably charming and civilized place. The Dutch, in parting, had been generous with their guilders. This, together with the income derived from bauxite mining, was sufficient to create an atmosphere of somewhat raffish prosperity. The shops of Paramaribo, the capital, were well stocked with imported goods. You could buy good cigars, Dutch cheeses, French wines. Whores from Colombia and Santo Domingo crowded the numerous nightclubs—even the vehicles of sin had to be imported—providing competition for the cheaper Guyanese girls. But it was not only adventurous Guyanese girls who were coming to share in the modest largesse supplied by the Dutch and by bauxite. All kinds of Guyanese were trooping illegally across the border hawking minor skills.

As far as it was possible to tell, expression of opinion remained untrammeled. There were probably twenty political parties—one for every 2,500 Surinamese—including five or six with subtly differing interpretations of the Marxist message. There was, for the time being, no Leader. The Surinamese, isolated by language from the lethal resentments and no less lethal visions frothing to the surface everywhere in the English-speaking Caribbean, remained in a state of qualified innocence. Above all, the Chinese, the bellwethers of political and economic stability, continued to be represented in comforting numbers.

One evening, a Chinese acquaintance invited me to his house on the outskirts of Paramaribo: he was giving a small birthday party for his daughter. The two-storied house overlooked the broad, brown Surinam River. When I arrived, the younger people were dancing to records on the veranda. Dishes of steaming food flowed from the kitchen. The older members of the family sat in a row and looked on benignly. Conversation was easy; the scene was intimate and convivial. Everything about the house and the people in it signaled serenity. The times were out of joint, full of alarms and dangers. But they did not know that. They remained innocents. I chatted briefly with one of my host's daughters. She was a student at a Dutch university; she was hoping to become a nurse; she was betrothed to a man with whom she was very much in love; she blushed when her mother mentioned her trousseau. After my recent experiences in Trinidad, I felt as if I had gone back in time. The music played. The young people danced. My host showed me his collection of piranha fish. Then he began to talk of his charitable work with the Lions. His association with that organization kept him busy, involving a great deal of travel about the Caribbean.

"Lionism is service," he said enthusiastically. "Service to those less fortunate than ourselves." He asked if I had ever thought of becoming a Lion.

I said I had not.

"Just the other day," he went on, "I had a letter from *International.* Headquarters itself wrote to me!" He took the letter from his pocket and gave it to me. "Read it."

The letter was addressed to Lion Lee. Lion Lee was informed that he was to receive an award from Lions International in recognition of all his services to the cause and especially of his labors in setting up new Lions clubs in the Caribbean region.

"Both my wife and daughter are Lionesses," he said.

The alarms and dangers were far away at that moment. I congratulated Lion Lee and went out to the veranda. That night, staring at the reflections on the Surinam River, I had never heard of Pastor Jim Jones or the People's Temple. I did not know that somewhere beyond this glistening water, not much more than two hundred miles away, the sentiment of service to humanity was undergoing yet another of its deadly transformations; that Guyana, which had long since progressed from Lionism to Leninism, was soon to astonish the world.

On my way back to London from Surinam, my flight stopped

at Georgetown. The 707 was almost empty when we left Paramaribo. We spent nearly an hour and a half on Guyanese soil. Singly or in little groups of two or three, Guyanese filtered through the exits of the terminal building. It is as difficult to leave Guyana as it is to enter it. Those exits were like trapdoors, opening, closing, opening again. I felt I was looking at animals being let out of a cage. Later, I was to experience at first hand the indignities of the Guyanese emigration process—the insolent searches for jewelry, worthless Guyanese dollars and other, more valuable currencies. Gradually, the aircraft filled up. So many of these people had tight, hunted faces. A young Indian wearing electric blue trousers and a brown, shiny jacket took the seat next to mine. He held himself rigidly, clutching his passport and staring straight ahead. To which imperialist haven was he heading? The U.K.? The U.S.A.? Canada? A Guyanese businessman with whom I had chatted in Paramaribo had told me of the long queues that formed each day outside the British, American and Canadian embassies. Students, doctors, nurses, teachers, technicians, whores—they were all trying to run away. I was gazing at social collapse; I was glad I was only in transit.

Now, less than two months later, I was actually on my way to that nightmare. I stared at the water streaming down the window. Beyond, blurred shapes scuttled about the tarmac. Two middle-aged English expatriates, both Guyanese residents, shared my row. The seats in front of and behind us were occupied by a Russian delegation of some indeterminate variety. Throughout the flight from London they had played cards and smiled fervently at everyone. One of the Englishmen—his name was Walter—was sipping from a bottle of Johnnie Walker. He winked at me.

"Better make hay while the sun shines," he said, offering me a drink from the bottle. "It's not as classy as the Chivas Regal our Comrade Prime Minister likes to drink, but it's better than nothing." Earlier, he had described himself as "demob"-happy: he had managed to find himself a job in Barbados and was now returning to collect his Guyanese wife and family, settle his affairs and depart for good. Like everyone else, he was traveling with a larder of food. He pointed at the cigarette I was surreptitiously smoking. "I would go easy on those if I were you, old chap. You won't find any of those in Georgetown for love or money."

I said I had no objection to using the local brands.

He laughed. "What local brands? You'll be lucky to find any cigarettes at all."

That was bad news.

"We even have shortages of sugar in Guyana. Everywhere you look in the world's first and only Cooperative Socialist Republic you'll see sugar-cane fields. But still we have shortages of sugar. Quite a feat."

"Have you been to the toilets recently?" His companion, who was altogether more sedate in dress and manner, spoke quietly.

"Let me guess," Walter said. "Someone's run off with the toilet bowls and washbasins."

His companion (I did not know his name) smiled. "Nothing quite as drastic as that. But they've taken all the soap and toilet paper and towels."

Looting, it was clear, had become a reflex; a way of life.

My sense of oppression deepened. I could take a taxi to my sister's house, which was not much more than a half-hour's drive from the airport. I could spend a day or two with her. Steel myself. I spoke my thoughts aloud.

"Chicken . . . chicken . . ." Walter grinned at me. "What's so great about Trinidad in any case? It's a mess of a place too."

I remained where I was, staring at the rain.

The sun was low in the sky when the northeastern shoulder of South America appeared below us. An ocean discolored with the silt brought down by the great rivers fringed the coast. It was as if the land were melting, oozing brown blood. Masses of purple cloud were banked on the horizon. The scene was bleak; uninviting. A copy of Newsweek lay open on my lap. Jonestown—"The

Cult Of Death"—supplied its cover story that week. (*Time* maga-zine had chosen the same title for its version of the affair.) I had been glancing at it desultorily all the way from London. For some reason I had not been able to apply myself wholeheartedly to it. I tried again. ". . . Many were not recognizable as human corpses; they had ballooned to nearly twice their size and resembled some sort of grotesque dolls. . . ." Once more my concentration unrav-eled.

There was much talk of "charisma" and "mind control." "It's all so simple," one psychiatrist was reported as saying. "Converts have to believe only what they are told. They don't have to think, and that relieves tremendous tensions." Others talked compla-cently—even indulgently—about "kids" searching for "signifi-cance" and "a sense of belonging." One expert, described as a specialist on death, was no more enlightening. He pointed out that what had occurred at Jonestown "was a mixture of submit-ting to mass suicide and submitting to murder." The Jews who died at Masada rather than surrender to the Romans were dis-cussed. The Japanese were discussed. The ecstatic movements of the Middle Ages were discussed. It was argued that Buddha, Jesus and Muhammad could all be described as leaders of cults. Lists of existing cults were compiled and their creeds summa-rized.

It was all so reflexive. The impression emerged of a culture overrun by taxonomists of all kinds, who, at a moment's notice, could supply tidy printouts that would explain any event. The categories and the labels were to hand. All these technicians had to do was open the correct file. Jonestown and its rotting dead could be swiftly classified, reduced to a few sonorous polysylla-bles. (This uncharitable reaction is not entirely baseless. The au-*thors of a well-known book on mind control concluded not long* ago that there was "nothing really human inside human beings" —only biology, chemistry and machinery.) Within a month or two, the incident would be exhaustively indexed and forgotten. When the next aberration occurred it would be briefly resur-rected for purposes of comparison.

American response was also practical. Congress, alive as ever to fiscal irresponsibility, fretted about the cost to the taxpayer of transporting and storing the bodies. Guyana had turned her back on the pile of corpses. It did not want those nine hundred bodies to enrich its soil. In life they had been hailed by the Guyanese Government as socialist heroes; in death they had become hopelessly American. Nobody wanted them, not even family and friends. Scores of bodies remained unclaimed in the cold-storage chambers of an Air Force base in Delaware.

We were over the estuary of the Essequibo River. Swirling channels of muddy water separated the darkly green, lozenge-shaped islands anchored in it. Fourteen years earlier when I had left Trinidad for England, British Guiana had been caught in the toils of yet another bout of racial warfare between blacks and Indians. The Mighty Sparrow (Trinidad's top calypso singer) was singing: "I don't care if the whole of B.G. burn down/I don't care if the whole of Bookers burn down . . ." But Guyana's troubles had started long before that. I was eight years old in 1953 when, in fear of a Communist takeover by the People's Progressive Party led by Cheddi Jagan, the Constitution was suspended and British troops landed. From then on, the place became indelibly associated with unsavory tumult and drama.

British Guiana was, I knew, very different from Trinidad. In fact, it was so different as to be not completely real. To begin with, it was not an island. By our standards, it was almost unimaginably vast. It contained extensive jungles and savannas, high waterfalls in a remote interior, broad rivers. (I remember a Guyanese friend laughing at our Caroni River. "You call that thing a river? The Essequibo is twenty or thirty times the width of that. We have an island as big as the whole of Barbados in that river.") In a geography book we used at school, the chapter on British Guiana was embellished with a photograph of a near-naked Amerindian standing on the prow of a canoe shooting fish with a bow and arrow. Such exotic people did not exist in Trinidad. For a time, we used to receive free of charge—I am not quite sure why—a monthly newsletter from Georgetown dealing with what nowadays would be called development projects. It carried photographs of tractors drawing logs, tiny health clinics in the bush and the proud owners of little houses built by self-help being given their keys. This newsletter, however, only served to emphasize the backwardness, the poverty and the strangeness. I had a childish feeling of aversion more or less summed up by the fact that—in those days—British Guiana had by far the weakest cricket team in the West Indies. It was never a place I had had any particular desire to visit.

In the late fifties and early sixties this sense of separateness, of a peculiar destiny to be molded (I derive this last phrase from the title of a book by Forbes Burnham, the Guyanese Prime Minister), was underlined when the country remained aloof from the short-lived West Indian Federation. With the turbulence of Guyanese racial warfare echoing in my ears, I sailed for England in 1964. By then, the sickly Caribbean Federation had died and Trinidad (like Jamaica) had become an independent state. In Guyana, Forbes Burnham, his political fortunes assiduously fomented by the CIA and the British Colonial Office, was waiting for the downfall of the Marxist Cheddi Jagan—a drama that was to reach its climax at the end of the year.

In the years that followed I had only fitful news of Guyana. Almost all of it was alarming. Independence eventually came in 1966 with the suitably right-wing Forbes Burnham as Prime Minister. In 1968, by determined rigging of the general election held that year, he was returned to power with an increased majority. The director of the Opinion Research Center in London was moved to remark on a television program that the doctoring of the overseas vote (an important element in Mr. Burnham's electoral success) was unprecedented for a Commonwealth country. It was, he said, a pretty awful and disgraceful episode.

When I returned to Trinidad in 1970 to spend a few months, Guyana was being converted into something called a Cooperative Socialist Republic. At the time no one could say for certain what that was supposed to be. Nor can anyone today. The only concrete effect seems to have been in the field of letter writing: ministers and civil servants sign their communications "Yours cooperatively . . ."

The news got steadily worse after 1970. Burnham, whose moderation and "coolie"-baiting politics had so appealed to his American and British sponsors, now began to discard his moderation —but not his racism—and pose as a Third World militant. Photographs started to appear of the Comrade Leader—as he now liked to be called—dressed in Chinese-influenced tunics and dashikis. (The dashiki is a colorful smock worn by radical-minded politicians in the Caribbean.) At some point he had himself created a general—necessitating a further addition to his growing wardrobe. I noticed that he attended a conference of nonaligned states in Lusaka, Zambia; offered Guyana as a home away from home for African freedom fighters and handed over a check for fifty thousand dollars to assist the liberation struggle.

In 1973 the rigging of the general election reached new heights. In fact, it could hardly be called rigging anymore: the Army simply seized ballot boxes and did with them as they wished. The Comrade Leader embarked on a policy of extensive nationalization. He began to hint that he was a Marxist-Leninist. It was around this time that he proclaimed the birth of New Guyana Man.

In 1976 I read that a Cuban aircraft had been blown up and that Mr. Burnham blamed the incident on the CIA The Americans, in turn, called him a bold-faced liar. They stopped assistance to the shattered economy. An old friendship was on the rocks.

Finally, in 1978, the Guyanese Government announced that it would be holding a referendum. Mr. Burnham told a European journalist, "It's very simple: it gives us an opportunity to rewrite our Constitution which in our circumstances has become irrelevant." The rewritten Constitution was designed to give the Comrade Leader sweeping powers and, in effect, to make it unnecessary to hold any more elections. They were becoming a nuisance. One was inured; it hardly seemed to matter.

As a result, I was not particularly surprised when, one morning, I heard on a BBC Radio news program that an American Congressman, who had gone to Guyana to investigate an agricultural commune inhabited by hundreds of fellow Americans and run by a socialist preacher from California, had been shot and killed in an ambush at a remote jungle airstrip. Such an event, I felt, was entirely in keeping with the atmosphere of the Cooperative Socialist Republic.

Journalists, I was aware, were not generally welcome in Guyana. Not long before, at a conference in Jamaica, the Guyanese Minister of Information had insisted that Guyana, by its lights, had a free press. But not, she added, in the Western sense. The Government-controlled press would publish only those speeches of the Opposition which it regarded as conducive to development. I understood this to mean that Guyana did not have a free press. Nor was travel about the country untrammeled: Guyana, by its lights, had freedom of movement—but not, of course, in a Western sense. Foreigners as well as citizens required special permits to visit extensive tracts of the interior. After the massacre at Jonestown the country had been invaded by the world's press, an influx it could not credibly frustrate. (Guyanese, however, were not told of the disaster for some days.) Now, however, the crush was over and one could expect a reassertion of control. Further news about Jonestown, one had to assume, would not be regarded as conducive to development.

The journalists accompanying Congressman Ryan had had a tough time on arrival at the airport. One had been detained for fifteen hours on a vague currency charge; the others had had their five-day permits unaccountably revoked and reduced to one day. I was given reluctant permission to stay for two weeks. A photograph of the Comrade Leader looked down on me with staid benignity. The toilets were waterless. A carefully painted sign apologized for the inconvenience. It had clearly been there a long time: the paint was yellowed with age and stained. On my way out, I met the more sedate of my two traveling companions. He offered me a lift into town.

"My chauffeur," he said, "should be bringing the car round any minute now."

Chauffeur. I was impressed, taken aback, to learn that such grandeur survived in Guyana. The beggar boys congregated at the front of the terminal building restored me to reality. They volunteered to find taxis, to carry bags, to guard bags. When their offers of help were refused, they cringed and asked for money. I was reminded of Bombay, where one of the first sights to greet the arriving traveler is the tiers of urgent brown faces pressed against the walls of plate glass. All the same, this was not Bombay. This was Guyana, a country the size of the United Kingdom, with a population of less than one million. Two English soldiers were sauntering nearby. I wondered what English soldiers might be doing in this anti-imperialist haven.

A big black car stopped in front of us. It was a dated model of some English make, but the paintwork gleamed. The Indian chauffeur got out, saluted smilingly and stowed away our bags.

"This is faithful Ramesh," my companion said.

The car creaked and groaned and rattled. Faithful Ramesh drove gingerly, not exceeding twenty miles an hour. In ponderous state we headed toward Georgetown—some twenty-five miles away.

"It's next to impossible to get spare parts," my host said apologetically. "And not only for cars. . . ." He pulled a Ronson cigarette lighter out of his pocket. "I had to go all the way to England before I could get this repaired."

The road followed a near-continuous ribbon of settlement. Wooden houses on stilts—much of coastal Guyana is below sea level and subject to flooding—reared awkwardly out of the untidy bush. On dark verandas, families cooled themselves. Rum-soaked merriment oozed from bright, congested bars. Odors of mud and swamp thickened the humid air. Somewhere nearby flowed the Demerara River, a presence I could sense but not see. The dusty roadside was lively with pedestrians. They waved and shouted at us, hoping for a ride into town. We did not stop.

"You can't be too careful," my friend said.

"These people won't think twice about choke and rob," Ramesh put in.

Choke and rob: it was the Guyanese equivalent of mugging; and it was rampant. The elemental description had an unnerving precision. Mugging suggested a variety of possibilities. Choke and rob was hopelessly final. We passed sugar and rum refineries, a stock-feed storehouse; the Demerara glinted. The streets of the city were dark and empty. A curfew silence reigned. In George-town, only the brave or the foolhardy walked abroad at night.

I was let off at the Pegasus Hotel, a multistoried polygonal structure facing the sea.

CHAPTER
2

UNTIL RECENT years, I had not been accustomed to thinking of the English-speaking Caribbean (and I include Guyana) as part of the Third World. To begin with, the concept did not exist when I was growing up in Trinidad. I still remember my sense of shock when, in 1955 or 1956, I saw a group of black women parading with placards that proclaimed Dr. Eric Williams—our future Prime Minister—the Messiah appointed to lead his people out of bondage. It was my introduction to the idea that the language of religion could be transformed into the language of politics. It was the first symptom of the cultural and intellectual regression that is now widespread in the region. Becoming part of the Third World is, to some degree, a psychological process; a quasi-religious conversion. It is, at bottom, a mode of being, a state of mind. That state of mind spreads like an infection and begins, after a while, to create its own political, social and personal realities, stimulated by the vocabulary of resentment and racial self-assertion.

That Trinidad (to take the example closest to me) was tiny—we knew; that we were unimportant in the scheme of things—we knew; that we were relatively simple people—we half-suspected.

What went on beyond our island borders was not wholly credible. Just next door was Venezuela. In Venezuela there were coups, revolutions, dictators. We certainly had no solid conceptions of these phenomena. It would never have seriously occurred to any of us that one day we too might have our coups, our revolutions and our would-be dictators. Such things simply did not happen in Trinidad. The result was a happy innocence: we laughed at the whooping, barbarically painted Africans in Tarzan films; we loved cowboys. Those days have gone. Consciously, brutally, we have set about remaking ourselves in the Third World image.

As imperial ties and restraints dissolved, one reality, one self, was lost. Something snapped. Wild dreams rushed in to fill the vacuum. "Call me Atta Kujifi!" says a big headline in a Trinidad newspaper. The article is about a lawyer who is described as a top Port of Spain barrister. He had decided to change his name from Arthur Fleming Lawrence to Atta Khufu Obafemi Kujifi. "You see," he explained to the interviewer, "once you start thinking African then a name like Arthur Fleming Lawrence is a plain embarrassment. . . ." It was Africa which had given the world law, philosophy, medicine, religion, astronomy, music, magic and science; it was Africa which had civilized Europe, and not the other way around, as the white man had been misleadingly teaching the world.

Atta Kujifi certainly did not exist twenty years ago. Inevitably, there is an element of play, of masquerade, in the barrister's change of name. Some carnival fantasy is involved, the sort of fantasy that briefly led a steel band to adopt the swastika as its symbol and call itself Gestapo. That, I suppose, we can smile at and let pass. For those involved, the Gestapo would have meant little more than a rather attractive uniform. But we cannot smile at Kujifi without a tremor of anxiety. We have to exercise caution; we have to look about us warily.

After a six-year absence, I returned to Trinidad in 1970, just in time to witness student-led unrest. I saw the riffraff of Port of Spain saluting with clenched fists and shouting, "Power! Power!" Later, there were small-scale riots, broken shopwindows, burning buildings. Later still, a section of the Army, under the leadership of an officer who tried to look and dress like Fidel Castro, mutinied and attempted to march on Port of Spain. The mutineers were stopped by the timely intervention of one Coast Guard vessel. Farce and revolution: both walked hand in hand, confused beyond separation. A State of Emergency was declared; a curfew was enforced. Jeeps full of loyal soldiery in combat fatigues patrolled the empty streets of the city. It could have been an elaborate carnival tableau. Only the city's silence warned that this was no masquerade; that this, however obscurely, however fantastically, was for real.

Army mutiny! Curfew! It was not easy for me to accept that these things were happening in Trinidad. I was distantly acquainted with one or two of the faces and voices that figured prominently in the marches and rallies. I had been to school with some of those people. Obviously, it was no longer the island I had known. Times had changed, and so had the people with whom I had grown up. The masquerade could now be deadly. New gods, imported from the Rastafarian cult of Jamaica, had made their appearance among us. Young, marijuana-doped blacks with matted hair stalked the streets. They symbolized the regression, the primitivist impulses seething through the lower reaches of the society. When I returned to Trinidad eight years later, their numbers had multiplied. Their market-type stalls crowded the pavements of Port of Spain's central shopping district. By then, they had become something of a political force. Intellectual respectability was being conferred on them. A Catholic priest saw these matted-hair illiterates as being in possession of a "critique of bourgeois society which has much in common with that of the genuinely revolutionary political forces." He was convinced that there must be a union of Rasta with other radical tendencies, that Rasta had an important part to play in the overcoming of the old system and the establishment of the new order that was waiting to be born.

Incredulity had to be stilled. I had, after all, only to look across the water to Grenada, whose Prime Minister (since overthrown by

a left-wing coup; and, incidentally, once assiduously courted by
Pastor Jim Jones) had built a giant cross on a hill overlooking the
capital, St. George's, who flirted with Rosicrucianism, who composed long prayers to the Almighty and who had once lectured
the U.N. General Assembly on UFOs. A street-corner eccentric, a
mystical maniac, had become a Prime Minister. He ran a secret
police recruited from the jails; he maimed and occasionally killed
his enemies. The masquerade was no laughing matter. Anything
was possible.

One day I visited a showpiece school modeled on a blueprint
developed by the World Bank. The brand-new two-storied buildings spread over many acres were an impressive sight. Tennis
courts emphasized the grandeur of the concept. The school had
sixteen hundred pupils of secondary-education age. Both vocational and conventional academic training were offered. I was
shown kitchens equipped with gas and electric cookers and big
refrigerators; the machine-tool shed; the welding shop; the de-
partments specializing in plumbing, masonry, carpentry, electronics, garment manufacture, cooling systems, engine assembly
and repair. Girls learning secretarial skills sat behind ranks of
typewriters. Everywhere I looked I saw shining new machines.

My incipient elation did not survive a conversation I had with
one of the teachers in the machine-tool section. The idea, he said,
was not merely to teach the students how to mind the machines.
It was necessary to instill in them a knowledge of theoretical principles. This kind of technical education required more than a
passing acquaintance with addition and subtraction. The students
needed to have a grasp of mechanics, additional mathematics,
trigonometry and so on.

"It requires," he said with some passion, "as much brainpower
to handle one of these machines as it does to understand Shake-
speare."

A proper technical education presupposed a sound academic
foundation. If a student could not even read English properly,
how was he to understand the most elementary manual of instruc-
tion? The prevailing attitude made nonsense of these shining

machines. It was the unacademic students, the dunces, who were being shunted toward these vocational courses. He had talked to the Ministry of Education about it, but they had paid him little attention. Increasingly, his thoughts turned toward Canada and exile.

All the omens were bad. In the school at large, only ten percent had passed English at Ordinary Level. Fewer still had passed the mathematics examination. None had passed Spanish. None had managed to scrape together five passes. After those results, the morale of the staff had plunged. The machines were a standing invitation to theft. They had hired a security staff to deal with the problem—but it was becoming clear that the security people themselves had been involved in some of the thefts.

I dropped in on the agriculture section. Each student here, one of the teachers explained, was supposed to be in charge of his own little plot. I could see nothing growing on any of the plots— nothing, that is, except for a shriveled, blackened clump of herbage in a far corner of the field.

"What's that?"

The teacher squinted in the direction I indicated, shielding his eyes from the glare. "That's a cucumber plant. At least, it used to be a cucumber plant. The foolish boy put so much spray on the damn thing that he kill it dead."

"But what about the rest of the plots? Why is there nothing planted?"

"We letting the land lie fallow," he said. I thought he looked shifty.

My gaze fell on a muddy tractor, parked not far from the dead cucumber bush.

He guessed my thoughts. "It break down last week," he said, "and we still waiting to get it fixed." The hard soil, he expanded, was bad for it. "Come," he said suddenly, "let me show you the chickens."

As we made our way to the chicken coop I asked him if he enjoyed his job.

"No," he replied.

"Why not?"

"I feel like an old-time estate overseer when I'm telling my students to plant this and plant that. It make me and them think of slavery."

I had heard few more elaborate excuses for dereliction of duty. The chickens did not look well. One was lying on its side.

"What's the matter with that chicken?"

"It's just having a little rest," he said.

"Are you sure? It looks sick to me."

He went into the coop. He tickled the chicken. It remained motionless. He brought it out of the coop. Its head lolled. It turned out that the chicken—all the chickens—were starving. The agriculture section had not been able to buy enough feed because the firm from which they normally obtained their supplies was no longer prepared to extend credit: the Ministry of Education took far too long to honor their claims.

I looked at the broken tractor, the burned-out cucumber bush, the "fallow" field, the dying chicken; I thought of all those misunderstood shining machines; I thought of the essays I had been given to read—the broken grammar, the fractured, nebulous prose that almost seemed to hint at a kind of universal mental retardation. The previous day I had visited the remains of another high-minded project—a cooperative farm. Only one man valiantly clung on, trying to grow pineapples. For nearly two hours that hot, rainy afternoon I waded waist-deep in grass over land that was supposed to be blooming with ordered cultivation.

An old friend from school days was dejected and defeated.

"I've gone into internal exile," he said.

We were sitting in a café that tried to do things nicely: it was furnished with bentwood chairs and decorated with Aubrey Beardsley posters. Across the way was the Queen's Park Savannah, a dark, unkempt presence; a hole in the Port of Spain night.

"I think we're all a little mad now," he said.

He wanted to go away, put his thoughts together, maybe write something. But he didn't have the money. He had reached a dead end, and he was afraid for himself. During the last few years he had been politically active. His party, intellectual to a fault and moderate in its message, had had marginal impact. He had been left stranded with his idealism.

I think of another friend, now approaching middle age.

"What is the world?" he asked.

He answered his own question. "It is a mental construction. The world we perceive with our senses is not the only one there is or even the most important one. It's an illusion."

I listened as he talked about the many levels of Being.

"I've experienced Krishna consciousness," he said. "I know what it is to be dead. Death too is an illusion."

His soft mulatto eyes were clear and steady. Once, we used to have long discussions about Marxism, about the revolution that would transform the Caribbean.

"One day," he said, "I was sitting in my garden when something like a nuclear explosion seemed to occur inside my head." There was light everywhere. No one could approach him. It was as if a magnetic force fenced him in, keeping people away. He stood for hours in his garden, bathed in light. Now, his wife gone, he lives alone. His house is gradually falling into ruin. Weeds sprout in the garden. Walls flake and crack. His books collect mold and dust.

"I'm at peace," he said.

Everywhere in the region, society was in disarray and men seemed to be decaying. Third Worldhood had bred regression, and that regression was ending in personal and political catastrophe. "You is a princess," a slum girl was assured again and again in a local play. "You is a princess." Often, our madness finds its support and confirmation abroad among the self-avowed, metropolitan friends of the oppressed. Consider a man named Michael de Freitas, otherwise known as Abdul Malik, otherwise known as Michael X. In London he peddled dope and worked as a strong-arm man for a slum landlord. He became a convert to Islam and Black Power. Eventually, his rabble-rousing led to trouble with the English police. He fled home to Trinidad. In Trinidad, subsidized and encouraged by his rich English patrons, he started an

"agricultural" commune. It climaxed in murder. He was sentenced to death. Sitting in jail, Michael X was succored by Tom
Wicker of *The New York Times, The New Statesman* and other foreign friends of the oppressed. According to the Angela Davis
Defense Committee, Malik's only crime was "his commitment to
the world movement for peace and justice." It was absolutely
necessary, they went on, that he be allowed to continue his work
for peace, justice and progress in behalf of all oppressed people
in the world. (Later, in his time of tribulation, Jim Jones too
would receive messages of support and solidarity from Miss Davis
herself.) Another New York–based group was even less restrained. They asserted that if Trinidad persisted in its determination to hang Michael X, it would be found guilty by the
community of civilized nations and be suitably judged by the Almighty.

Those who ought to know better nourish our crazy dreams of
resurrection and redemption; those safely beyond the borders of
our madness underwrite our lunacies.

It is Guyana's distinction that it has traveled farther along the
Third World road than any of the other Caribbean territories. In
the days before he transformed himself into the Comrade
Leader, Forbes Burnham would often adorn himself in flowing
white robes and refer to himself as the "Kabaka"—the kingly title
of the ruler of Uganda's Baganda tribe. In Guyana, the atavistic
ideal of the Big Black Chief—the archetype so superbly realized
by Idi Amin—has, despite the socialist gloss, been almost fully
achieved. Although Indians form the majority of the population,
black supremacy reigns unchecked.

The Burnham who governs Guyana today was foretold—somewhat eccentrically, it is true—by his late sister Jessie in a pamphlet
(titled "Beware My Brother Forbes") published on the eve of Independence. "Often," she wrote, "especially as he grew older I
would catch Mother watching Forbes with a worried eye." The
Burnhams were staid, respectable and poor. It was on the bright

young Forbes that the family settled its hopes. He was a small boy for his age and was almost daily set upon at school. One can only speculate on the effect these frequent beatings must have had on him. One day she overheard him listing his varied ambitions to their father. He wanted to be Mayor of Georgetown, Chief Justice, the first Prime Minister of the West Indies or, failing that, the first Prime Minister of an independent Guyana. " 'Boy, you're mad or what?' asked my father. 'Be sensible and start as a magistrate and work up to be Chief Justice.' 'Magistrate?' retorted Forbes scornfully, 'there're always exceptions and why can't I be one?' " Forbes, his sister says, is a schemer, a plotter, a slick talker, who had steeped himself in Machiavelli's *The Prince*. For him, the end would always justify the means. He ran his Party much as King Christophe had once governed Haiti; and if he got hold of the country he would treat it in the same way. "I fear for my country and for my people should my brother Forbes become Premier or Prime Minister." Guyana under his rule was doomed to torment. Nothing that has transpired since has disproved her fears.

Forbes Burnham has been undisputed king, paramount chief, of Guyana since 1964. But it was only from 1970 on—that was the year in which the country was transformed into a Cooperative Socialist Republic—that he began to show symptoms of radicalism, to thrash around for the left-wing credentials he so conspicuously lacked. The reasons behind his frantic search are not hard to find. Since the middle sixties, the mood of blacks in the Caribbean had been getting steadily worse. Under the influence of the Black Power philosophies imported from the United States, they were becoming increasingly restless, increasingly demanding.

"Massa day done!" Eric Williams had proclaimed to enthusiastic Trinidadian audiences in 1956. The slogan had been satisfying and, for a while, it had done its job. But, after a decade of freedom, Caribbean blacks were beginning to suspect that Massa's day was not quite done; that their leaders were only outwardly black. Black dignity, black consciousness, required something more. Outward blackness was no longer good enough. You had to be inwardly black as well. Nothing less than a black soul would do. Thus arose the then novel—and to many, bewildering—phenomenon of the black masses rising up in open revolt against their black governments. Those politicians sensitive to the change immediately began to discard their suits and ties and to appear before their mutinous populace in bush shirts and dashikis. In Trinidad, however, Eric Williams stubbornly refused to conform; and it was also in Trinidad—but this may be mere coincidence—that the government came closest to being forcibly overthrown.

The people, it was clear, wanted to remake themselves; to be recast into an image more recognizably Third World, more self-assertively "black." They demanded that their governments reflect this new idea of themselves. Burnham, in 1970, had a long way to go. The bloody simplicity of racial politics which had served him so well in the past could no longer guarantee his survival. It would go on being useful, but it would no longer be sufficient. Somehow, it would have to be supplemented. Nineteen seventy found Forbes Burnham without a single left-wing credential. His unsavory political lineage had to be reckoned with at the outset. It was an open secret that he had been installed in power by the CIA and the British Colonial Office. If there was any political party in Guyana with viable revolutionary credentials, that party was certainly not Burnham's People's National Congress. Cheddi Jagan's People's Progressive Party alone could claim that honor. Until 1970, Burnham had caused his patrons in London and Washington few headaches. Guyanese bauxite and sugar remained under the control of American, Canadian and British interests. Guyana did not recognize Cuba—the darling of Caribbean intellectuals. It did not recognize China. It did not even recognize the Soviet Union. The only controversial state with which it had diplomatic relations was Israel. Guyana in 1970 was a model of neocolonial obedience. As if to put his loyalty beyond doubt, Burnham had imposed a tax of ten percent on all goods from Communist countries; doctors trained in those countries were virtually debarred from practicing in Guyana. At home, his rule had become illegitimate, based with increasing nakedness on force and fraud. In election after rigged election those thousands of ethereal entities known as overseas voters continued to show exemplary political consciousness by voting, almost to a man, for the People's National Congress.

Badly in need of a new image, Burnham set off for the 1970 Conference of Nonaligned Nations being held in Lusaka, the Zambian capital. Lusaka was the stage set against which he would make his international debut as a Third World militant. On his way there he announced that he would be establishing diplomatic relations with the Soviet Union. At the conference he spoke impassionedly about the People's Republic of China. Nor did he forget Cuba. He hinted that the Cooperative Socialist Republic might bravely acknowledge the existence of both these pariah states. But the high point was the check for fifty thousand dollars which he handed over to President Nyerere of Tanzania—Guyana's contribution to the freedom fighters of Africa. Forbes Burnham, it could be said, had been born again. Dressed in the new revolutionary style, he cut an uncompromising figure. To lend credence to his new role, he offered Guyana as a refuge to African freedom fighters. In Guyana, he promised, they would find a safe haven, solace and support.

There was calculation in Burnham's radicalism. Yet it is undeniable that he began to enjoy the role he had selected for himself; even to half-believe in it. Nothing could have better suited his Kabaka aspect. He had always relished being the Big Black Chief, and now that chieftainship could be played out in an international setting. He could not fail to be charmed by the prospects it must have opened out before him. The effect must have been aphrodisiacal—it must have been like finding out that you could become a Chief Justice without ever having been a magistrate; it was a leap into transcendence. He had always been attuned to blackness, peculiarly vulnerable to its burdens and fantasies. He did not have to be schooled in the sensibilities and lusts that raged in the hearts of the *lumpen* hordes who had taken to the streets in Trinidad, Jamaica and elsewhere. Their cries of "Power! Power!" would have been easily understood. The lines he had to say—

enhanced by his considerable oratorical gifts—would come naturally to him. Cynicism, calculation, genuine conviction, downright
lies: all would be hopelessly confounded. Together, they would
create a typical—and deadly—Third World potion.

There was action to back up the words. Third World militancy,
once embarked upon, has a logic that cannot easily be thwarted.
Burnham's Guyana was swept away on that tide. In 1971 the
Canadian-owned bauxite mines and installations were nationalized. In 1972, at great expense, Guyana staged a Caribbean Arts
Festival. Fleets of limousines were bought for the occasion. Many
of the cars were wrecked and abandoned even before the end of
the Festival. That year saw another display of Guyana's newfound
grandeur when Burnham played host to the Nonaligned Foreign
Ministers' Conference. For this, fleets of police motorcycles were
flown in from Japan. In 1973, diplomatic and other relations
were established with Cuba. In 1974, relations were severed with
Israel. In 1975, the American-owned bauxite mines and installations were nationalized. The following year the British-owned
sugar estates and sugar refineries were nationalized. Socialism—
Kabakahood—had come to Guyana with a vengeance.

New Guyana Man had been born. Every citizen was now officially a soldier in the cause of liberation and cooperative socialism.
Militarism was no mere metaphorical effusion. Guyana was overrun by organizations that could be classed as either military or
paramilitary.

There was the People's Army, otherwise more prosaically
known as the Guyana Defense Force, which had sworn its "unconditional loyalty" not to the State but to the Comrade Leader himself, because of its profound appreciation of his cooperative
socialist philosophy. They were to be hunters, fishermen and
farmers as well as soldiers.

There was the People's Police. They too had taken their oath
of loyalty not to the Guyanese State, but to the Comrade Leader
and his philosophy of cooperative socialism. Their specific task
was to unearth "detractors" and "enemies of the socialist revolution": that is, detractors and enemies of Forbes Burnham, since

he, the State and cooperative socialism were one and the same. They, strange to say, were also expected to be hunters, farmers and fishermen. It was hoped that, at the very least, they would establish agricultural gardens around their station houses. As one by no means unfriendly, by no means ironic commentator remarked, the lack of significant social unrest must be taken as a tribute to their vigilance and zeal. But this had had its drawbacks: they had not been able to do too much hunting, farming or fishing, "being too busy with the day-to-day administration of law and order and buttressing the regime . . ." (According to the same writer, the People's Army has suffered from a similar complaint. "Its role at present . . . is one of defending the regime and very little effort is now being given to the other tasks with which it has been optimistically commissioned.")

There was the Guyana National Service. This was designed to be the womb out of which New Guyana Man would spring. Among its tasks were the development and population of the interior and national defense. Its declared aim was to "socialize" —or "resocialize"—Guyanese. From the age of eight they were to be instilled with a correct sense of national consciousness, a socialist outlook and unswerving loyalty to their Comrade Leader.

While on paper membership in the National Service is not compulsory, in practice it has been made so. Admission to the University of Guyana—the country's sole institution of higher education —cannot be had without it. Nor is it possible to find any but the most menial of jobs if one has not served in its ranks. Life in its hinterland camps is, by all accounts, an unpleasant business. Unpleasant and secretive. I tried in vain to get permission to visit one. Like the People's Army and the People's Police, the Guyana National Service, despite the large amounts of money siphoned into it, continues to fall short of its stated ideals—in particular, its agricultural ones. There is still no sign of the cotton or black-eyed peas it is supposed to be growing in vast quantities. Even our indulgent commentator, who approves of the militaristic "paradigm" of development, is gloomy about its achievements. It is, he says, a rigidly authoritarian institution "where functional superiors demand compulsive obedience and inflict punishment . . .

its role in nation building is primarily one of buttressing the regime. . . ."

The People's Army cannot perform its developmental role because it is buttressing the regime. The People's Police cannot do any hunting, farming and fishing because it is buttressing the regime. The Guyana National Service cannot raise consciousness because it is buttressing the regime. But the list is not ended. There are the Young Socialist Movement and the Women's Revolutionary Socialist Movement—this last presided over by Viola Burnham, the wife of the Comrade Leader. Both are armed; both have sworn fealty to Forbes Burnham; both openly exist to buttress the regime. Crowning it all, there is the People's Militia with its motto "Every Citizen a Soldier." Its tasks are to support the People's Army and the People's Police and to engage in agricultural work. "Its role in nation building," confesses our commentator, "is primarily one of buttressing the regime. . . ." Guyana, on the eve of the Jonestown massacre, was spending one-sixth of its budget on its military and paramilitary organizations—four times as much as it was spending on health.

In a very real sense, there is no such institutional abstraction as the Government or the State left in Guyana. This is made explicit in the theoretical fount of Burnhamite cooperative socialism, the *Declaration of Sophia,* a speech delivered in 1974 to mark ten years of his party's rule. It had been decided, the Comrade Leader announced, "that the Party should assume unapologetically its paramountcy over the Government, which is merely one of its executive arms." The People's National Congress had become "the major national institution."

Over all of Guyana, after that speech, there fell, with unmediated harshness, the shadow of the Big Black Chief. In the Caribbean, only Haiti could furnish parallels to this almost complete subversion of the very idea of government. King Christophe had been reborn.

The Government, unafraid of precise commitment, had said that it would "feed, clothe and house" all the people by 1976—a program with which the People's Temple had closely identified itself from its very first days in Guyana. It had provided one of its major justifications for being present in what it called "this progressive South American country." Sixty-five thousand new housing units had been promised by the end of 1976. Only seven thousand had actually been built. The shops had bare shelves. In Guyana it was not easy to find meat, milk, fish, flour, potatoes, rice, cooking oil, sugar. Malnutrition was prevalent. Hungry children and adults combed the refuse dumps. The Mayor of Georgetown showed some concern in one of her radio broadcasts. She said she had received complaints that people had been rummaging through the garbage dump near Roxanne Burnham Gardens (named for a daughter of Forbes Burnham). This, she warned, not only was injurious to their health but interfered with the work of the sanitary department. Hospitals had no drugs to treat their patients. No wonder that Jonestown with (as we know now) its overflowing pharmacopoeia could boast of the medical miracles it was performing in the northwestern corner of the country; no wonder invalids flew from Georgetown to receive treatment they were denied in their People's Hospitals.

The queues of visa seekers outside the embassies of the United States, Canada and the United Kingdom were growing longer and longer. Emigration was turning into a stampede. Twenty-eight thousand had departed during the previous four years. Altogether, over fifty thousand people (and this, let it be remembered, out of a total population of eight hundred thousand) had left the country since 1965. Strikers were being beaten up and jailed. The streets of Georgetown were lawless. The last traces of freedom had been taken away by the fraudulent referendum on the Constitution. Such was the country in which the People's Temple made its home.

Eusi Kwayana was formerly General Secretary of the People's National Congress. Born Sydney King, he changed his name to Eusi Kwayana (it means "black man of Guyana") in the late fifties when he became a convert to negritude. In 1971 Kwayana defected from the PNC. The issue was corruption. (Forbes Burn-

ham is reckoned among the ten richest black men in the world.)
Kwayana says that the idea of calling Guyana a "cooperative republic" was originally his. No doubt the cooperative model he had
in mind was that of the idealized African village popularized by
the theorists of African socialism—President Nyerere of Tanzania chief among them. Burnham appropriated it and presented
it as his own. It was no more than a gimmick, an empty tag used
to add luster to Guyana's conversion to republican status. Plagia-
rism aside, it was unlikely that a cooperative republic—with its
implied diffusion of power and authority—could ever have had
any real meaning in a Guyana governed by Forbes Burnham, a
power hoarder by instinct. Given the personality of the leader,
the idea, from its inception, would have been ludicrous.

Kwayana, chasing after corruption, demanding codes of conduct, watched from the sidelines as the Cooperative Republic
lurched between farce and tragedy. A cooperative venture with
which he had been involved was starved of funds by the Cooperative Bank and eventually had to go out of business.

"Farmers, carpenters—the *small* men Burnham is always talking about in his speeches—had given up their jobs in the city to
go to the interior," Kwayana says. "They were all ruined. The
Government said we were training guerrillas there. Nonsense.
Complete nonsense."

There might have been another reason for the expulsion.
Rumor had it, Kwayana says, that the site had gold. Burnham, it
is well known, is fascinated by gems and precious metals. In the
days before he became a Marxist-Leninist he had been connected
with the diamond business. He was certainly not unaware of the
extra-agricultural attractions of the interior. "Let it not be felt,"
he had said some years before in a speech delivered to a group of
Amerindians, "that as Prime Minister I do not know what happens in some parts of this country—about those who come with
the Bible and leave with the diamonds."

Like every other institution, the cooperatives had been transformed into mere instruments of personal whim and lust. One
group had been drafted to build—without pay—a Minister's

house. The same Minister had also commandeered materials and vehicles to assist in this project. I saw the house, palatial by Guyanese standards, opulent by any other, with its split levels, cleverly pitched roofs, verandas, patios, spacious grounds and solid fence. Another cooperative was honored with the attention of no less a person than the Comrade Leader himself. "He had their people working up at *his* house," Kwayana laughs. With the help of the Cooperative Bank, a bill of two hundred thousand dollars was run up on this development project. By some mysterious process of compound dis-interest this debt shrank first to eighty thousand dollars and then to thirty-six thousand dollars. Finally, the cooperative went into liquidation. Kwayana tells of the government-appointed architect who refused to inflate his estimates for a building. He was summoned to Burnham's presence.

"You are a *stupid* black man," the enraged Comrade Leader is reported to have stormed at him.

"The point is," Kwayana says, "that Burnham and the people who surround him actually believe that black people have a *right* to steal and cheat and rob in order to get rich."

It was the nearest I had yet come to the dark heart of Burnhamite ideology.

Chasing corruption, cataloguing the examples, is a dangerous pastime in Guyana. The man who does so automatically becomes a detractor, an enemy of the socialist revolution; and, by the terms of their commission, the legitimate quarry of the People's Police.

Kwayana soon discovered that his life was (and is) at risk. "An order went out that I was to be eliminated. I have proof of that."

He was not being melodramatic. I met one of the victims of governmental revenge, a dissident academic, who was badly wounded by an assassin. Kwayana knows about the officially sanctioned murder squads that lurk in the shadows of Guyanese political life. Burnham, he says, is not able to trust anyone completely. He surrounds himself with private armies, little bodies of armed supporters dependent on him and him alone. His Party had subverted the State and he had subverted his Party. The latter, it could be said, had become merely one of his executive arms. He, not it, was Guyana's major national institution.

But to the outside world, defying all reality, Guyana could paint quite another picture of itself—and, it seems, be believed. "Africans, Indians, Portuguese, Chinese, Amerindians, Europeans come face to face with each other as Guyanese," says a brightly illustrated publication supplied to all foreign journalists by the Ministry of Information. Guyanese culture, inexhaustibly rich, was a magical blend that fascinated the world. All of the country's eight hundred thousand citizens were working heart and soul to build an egalitarian society. The Comrade Leader, defying the forces of reaction, was steering the country with unwavering determination toward its socialist objectives. He had introduced sweeping changes that had brought considerable social and economic benefits. The Guyana National Service had been praised by Tanzania, Zambia, India, Liberia, Venezuela, the German Democratic Republic, Sweden and Cuba. One hundred and fifty varieties of fruit grew on its fertile soil. Agricultural production had increased "manifold." For the first time in four hundred years the Amerindians were content. There are photographs of industriously smoking sugar refineries; of powerful machines at work in wavy seas of rice; of sleek cattle; of a street market, each stall a cornucopia; of the Comrade Leader being mobbed by many-colored throngs of grateful people—his rainbow family. Blessed, bountiful land. The happiness of the people, a European journalist told his readers, had just been made complete by the introduction of a new Constitution. It was going to provide equality for women. It was going to ensure that land went to the tiller. It was going to give the right of a free education from nursery to university. Even the Comrade Leader seemed to tire somewhat of enumerating the virtues of the new Constitution. He did, however, warn of the tendency to interpret human rights too narrowly, in terms of purely European or North American experience. That was an imposition he would not tolerate. That was cultural imperialism. Human rights had to be understood in other than a Western sense. "They hold elections; right, we hold elections. But the more important rights are the rights to a full life. . . . There is a right to be looked after in old age. . . . Those rights are important. . . ." It was his way, I suppose, of saying that Guyana was going to sacrifice the lesser right of holding elections.

The lies fall like a steady rain. Around the time those words were being spoken, a document, the work of several anonymous hands, appeared in Guyana. It could be described as an affidavit of despair, of utter hopelessness. Its subject was the referendum, but it looked behind and beyond that event. The writers cursed both the People's National Congress and the People's Progressive Party. They cursed racialism. They cursed socialism. They lamented the thousands who had fled—who, taking their skills and, even more important, their intelligence, had defected from the Guyanese nightmare. The country had been—and was being—denuded. Intelligence had been driven out, replaced by empty slogans. ("Power! Power!") Rational debate, they said, was no longer possible in the prevailing atmosphere of threat and violence. The struggle for survival was all that was left. They could not penetrate the gloom; they could see no solution. Could this situation have been avoided? Or had Guyana always been doomed? They did not know. One suspects they are almost afraid to know. Maybe, they suggested, to come to any kind of understanding of this near-total breakdown of human relations, of human decency, one would have to go right back to the colonial and slave roots of the society. Even so, they wonder if any answers will ever be found. Could a country like Guyana have any genuine existence of its own? Or, on its own, given the burden of its history, was it inevitably doomed to suffering and decay?

Bewildered, they fall silent.

CHAPTER

3

IT WAS raining. From the tiny balcony of my room I watched the Atlantic roll its waves toward the dune-lined shore. A concrete pier jutted out into the gray-brown sea. It was a desolate scene, belonging to the North, rather than the equatorial tropics: a far cry that morning from the fairy-tale land of perpetually balmy blue skies and gentle trade winds Jim Jones had evoked for the benefit of his ghetto-bred followers.

Breakfast was being served on a sheltered patio overlooking the pool terrace. A lone guinea fowl wandered disconsolately about a bright green lawn. Beyond the lawn the dunes began, separated from the cultivated grounds of the hotel by a fence. A guard, draped in a cape of black plastic, patrolled the dripping garden. There were some five or six Americans on the patio when I arrived. I assumed they must be either leftover journalists or agents of some kind. These men had a businesslike, preoccupied air, their conversation, for the most part, conducted in whispers. They exuded privilege and terrifying competence. The Guyanese waiters and waitresses were a little overawed. So, for that matter, was I.

I had come to Guyana with no definite plans, no clear idea of how I was going to set about my task. Already some of the journalists who had accompanied Congressman Ryan on his mission to Jonestown were on the point of publishing accounts. The sight of these men with well-weathered briefcases aggravated my uncertainty.

I turned to the *Guyana Chronicle* for relief. Its lead item was an official rebuttal of a story put out by the Associated Press asserting that the Guyanese Minister of Home Affairs, Vibert Mingo, had, among other things, put pressure on the police to abandon an investigation into conditions at Jonestown earlier in the year (1978), that he had intervened in behalf of Jim Jones in a child-custody case and deliberately obstructed due legal process, and that he had been actively involved in arranging for thousands of Temple members to illegally vote in the constitutional referendum.

This Associated Press report was based on documents picked up at Jonestown after the massacre. Mr. Mingo, the Government statement said, had done none of these things. His behavior—and that of the Government—had on no occasion ever strayed beyond the bounds of the strictest propriety. Suggestions of illegality were even more outrageous. If the People's Temple had been welcomed in Guyana, that was only because the group had come equipped with the most outstanding credentials. Even after the commune had been established, they had been flooded with literally hundreds of testimonials from the United States.

(I knew those testimonials. One of the first acts of the Guyanese Government after the disaster was to release scores of them. Just one will suffice to illustrate the prevailing tone of these mass-produced flyers which, if we believe the official claims, exercised such a great influence on the attitudes of the Guyanese authorities. This particular specimen comes from the pastor of a Baptist church in Oakland, California. It is addressed to the Prime Minister.

> I consider it an honor and a privilege to write to you on behalf
> of Rev. Jim Jones, whom I esteem as the foremost spokesman

for Christian socialism in the United States today. The depth of
his character and his dedication to human kind are measured
each and every day in the practical help he extends to all people:
homes for the homeless; food for the hungry; education for
countless youths; medical, dental, and legal assistance for the
poor . . . The list goes on and on. In People's Temple the most
essential teachings of the early church are revived. Love of one's
brother and sister, equal justice and equal opportunity, and the
sharing of one's earthly possessions for the common benefit of
all—these are the elements of radical faith which Rev. Jones
and his congregation have translated into actions. Their success
has inspired and has challenged church and community leaders
throughout California and the United States; they have shown
conclusively that Christian socialism is a viable alternative to the
rapidly deteriorating fabric of our highly competitive, acquisi-
tive society. Rev. Jones has consistently praised the progressive,
humanitarian philosophy of the government of the Cooperative
Republic of Guyana. On many occasions he has spoken publicly
of the courage you and other government leaders have shown
in the struggle for a just society and the right to self-determination for your country. Such devotion and character as he has
described in you is rare among public leaders. I believe the
cooperation between your government and your people with
the members and leader of People's Temple is highly propitious
and will have a profound, long-lasting effect on all of us who
are committed with you, in the struggle for a better world.

The date of the letter—August 2, 1977—is interesting. Just a few
days before, Jones had fled from San Francisco to Guyana to
escape the repercussions of an article published on August 1 in
the California magazine *New West.*)

The Government of Guyana, the statement went on, had dealt
with the People's Temple in exactly the same way it dealt with all
other foreign organizations in the country—a no doubt uninten-
tionally ambiguous counterclaim. Nor had Minister Mingo been
lax in the performance of his duties. He had been a vigilant and
faithful watchdog of the state's interest: Jonestown had been constantly visited by officers and senior officials of the Guyanese

Government. As was only to be expected, the Comrade Minister had had many contacts with representatives of the People's Temple; but these contacts had come about solely in the course of legitimate duty, arising from the portfolio he held as Minister of Home Affairs.

As for Jonestown residents' voting in the referendum, that was a patently ridiculous assertion. The application of a little logic was enough to disprove that charge. American citizens had no voting rights in Guyana. The residents of Jonestown were American citizens. Therefore, the residents of Jonestown could not have voted in a Guyanese referendum.

Nor had the Minister intervened to frustrate due legal process in the child-custody case. How could he? For him to have done so would have been illegal. Therefore, he could not have done it.

With regard to the documents said to have been found at Jonestown, it was indeed regrettably true that the first correspondents to get there had shamelessly taken advantage of the situation and removed various papers and records. But what did that prove? Any sensible person could see that if the Government and Comrade Minister Mingo had had anything to hide—which they did not—scrupulous care would have been taken at the outset to eradicate all incriminating evidence of their complicity. The fact that this had not been done was sufficient proof (if proof was needed—which it was not) of their innocence. All that the Government of Guyana could now do was speculate on the motives of the Associated Press in publishing these unfounded allegations. In fact, they were speculating about the whole Jonestown episode. Minister Mingo and the Government were as puzzled as everyone else. They could not—as the Minister of Information had already informed the world—find words to describe their reaction to the terrible thing that had happened in Guyana. It was an unfathomable mystery.

In the annals of the People's Temple, the Pegasus Hotel has its own modest part to play. It is one of the newest and most modern buildings in Georgetown; the nearest the Guyanese capital comes to having a five-star hotel. In most other cities, it would draw little attention. But in Georgetown the Pegasus stands in a class by itself. For Guyana is not a country to which tourists come. There really is no reason for them to do so. (Jonestown may have changed all that. There are reports that the Guyanese Government is thinking of preserving the settlement as a tourist attraction.) Lacking rivals, the Pegasus has succeeded in establishing itself as one of the major centers of Georgetown's social life. It is the sort of place where the local Lions Club will meet for lunches and conferences; where the well-to-do will hire rooms for cocktail parties and wedding receptions. On Saturday afternoons, a steel band plays on the patio overlooking the swimming pool and the silted ocean. You can drink rum punches and watch the hotel's guinea fowl saunter decoratively about the well-kept lawns. Later in the evening you can dine and dance to a live band in the ballroom—the Jonestown ensemble was rousingly received when it performed there—and let your gaze dwell on the brightly dressed groups of whores.

Naturally enough, it was to the Pegasus that the Ryan delegation had come. But the Pegasus had played a role several months before during the visit of a free-lance journalist, Kathy Hunter, from Ukiah, a small town in the wine country north of San Francisco. Ukiah is not far from Redwood Valley, the sylvan enclave Jones had made the headquarters of the People's Temple when, in 1965, together with about one hundred and fifty of his most devoted disciples, he had migrated West from his home base in Indianapolis, allegedly seeking a safe retreat from the nuclear holocaust he had predicted. It was here that he and Kathy Hunter had first become acquainted. She had written a number of generally favorable articles about the Temple and its good works. In May 1978, with the Temple now surrounded by scandal, she came out to Guyana to seek Jones in his final retreat. She booked into the Pegasus. Fires started to break out. There were bomb threats. She was harassed by Temple members and allowed neither to see Jones nor to travel to Jonestown. Finally, she was called to the

Ministry of Home Affairs, where, she says, she was treated in a "most insulting and contemptuous manner" and informed that her visa had been withdrawn because she was a disturbance to the peace. She was deported from Guyana the following day. The fires and bomb threats that had haunted the Pegasus during her stay suddenly ceased.

The Ryan delegation, accompanied by an anti-Temple group calling itself Concerned Relatives, arrived in Georgetown toward the middle of November 1978 to find that the bookings they had made at the Pegasus had been mysteriously cancelled. All of the Pegasus' 109 rooms were occupied—the desk clerk said there happened to be three conferences going on simultaneously. Some managed to find another hotel; most, however, spent their first night in the lobby. The omens had never been good. Eight days before he had left for Guyana, Ryan, who had written to Jones telling him of his plans, had received in reply a strange letter from Mark Lane (he and Charles Garry were the Temple's chief lawyers) raising difficulties about the visit. Jonestown, Lane pointed out, was a private community. In that remote area there were neither hotels nor restaurants. Ryan and his staff would therefore be entirely dependent on the hospitality of the commune. Jonestown was willing to do all that normal courtesy required—but they needed time to prepare.

Logistics, however, was only part of the problem. Various agencies of the U.S. Government had for a long time, Lane said, been oppressing the People's Temple, which was a religious organization. If some of its members had left the United States and come to settle in Guyana, that was only because they had been denied their constitutional rights at home. Two countries, "neither one of which has entirely friendly relations with the U.S.," had already offered asylum to the much-persecuted residents of Jonestown. A continued witch-hunt might compel them to take up one or other of these offers. Ryan was invited to reflect on the embarrassment such a migration would cause the United States. The Congressman declared himself puzzled and disappointed. He was asking no more, he felt, than any parent might "whose son or

daughter is away at school." As for threats of foreign entangle-
ment, he was not in the least impressed or intimidated by them.
He was going to Guyana.

Ever since Jones had fled from San Francisco, there had been
intensifying talks of plots and conspiracies directed against the
People's Temple. Charles Garry, the Temple's other lawyer and
a prominent California radical, was also a vocal proponent of that
idea. According to him, the People's Temple had been plotted
against for the last seven years; government denials were meaningless. While its lawyers crusaded, the Temple busied itself after
its own fashion.

In March 1978, they appealed to the U.S. Congress and Senate.
It was a chameleonic performance, slithering elusively between
patriotism, blackmail, threats and sentimentality. They said they
were tired of being harassed, that their patience was almost ex-
hausted. Radical Trotskyite elements were accused of orchestrat-
ing a campaign of hate against them because they, the People's
Temple, had refused to countenance their programs of violence.
The Federal Communications Commission was attacked for dis-
rupting their radio transmissions. This was particularly vicious
because through the use of radio they had saved many lives and
spread tremendous goodwill. They invariably extolled the United
States over the air and voiced support for its policies not only in
the Caribbean but around the world. Their agricultural project in
Guyana had been applauded by everyone who had seen it. The
commune was imparting a new image of the United States. It had
been praised by the World Council of Churches and a Russian
magazine—even though the Temple had expressed staunch support for the Russian Jews in their plight. They were constantly
receiving letters from Russians. Indeed, they were constantly receiving letters from people all over the world. Everyone was heap-
ing praise on them for the good work they were doing in the
Guyanese jungle. "In fact," the Temple's letter said, "several overtures have been made from Russia which sees our current harassment as a form of political persecution." But they did not want to
become an international issue. They had no political aspirations.

Their only desire, they said, was to be let alone. Consider their achievements. They had brightened up the image of the United States in a left-leaning corner of the world. They had saved American taxpayers millions of dollars by removing from the scene thousands who would otherwise be burdening the welfare rolls. To be persecuted for doing so much good was something they were not prepared to tolerate. "I can say without hesitation that we are devoted to a decision that it is better even to die than to be constantly harassed from one continent to the next."

The following month another statement was issued. It was read in Charles Garry's San Francisco office. The radical Trotskyite elements had disappeared. Their place had been taken by the Concerned Relatives. They accused the latter of recruiting mercenaries to invade Guyana and kidnap people living in the commune. Their response had been to alert the President, the State Department and the Government of Guyana. The use of mercenary force, they observed, was not unknown to them. Not long before, agents had entered Guyana and tried to assassinate Jim Jones. They hoped that the public would come alive to the "cruelty and evil" underlying the "base, nasty motives" of the Concerned Relatives. Their community was "a dramatic expression of our deep desire to build a meaningful future for mankind through cooperation and sharing and eradication of class division." The by now ritualistic quota of testimonials was supplied: the chairman of the Guyana Livestock Corporation had visited them and been overwhelmed; they had been visited unannounced by a party of thirty-five teachers who had been extremely "impressed"; representatives of "one of the world's largest news agencies" had spent several days at the commune, as had representatives of other news agencies—they had all recorded their admiration. More visitors were expected during the next week, including some parents who had children in the commune. All this went to show that they had no objection to being scrutinized. On the contrary—they welcomed inspection. But they would have nothing to do with the so-called Concerned Relatives whose sole aim was to sow discord.

In Jonestown, they reminded their listeners, people were finding new lives. They had thrown aside the shackles of inner-city
life. The People's Temple, they repeated, was saving taxpaying
America hundreds of thousands of dollars by looking after those
for whom the society had no use. Jim Jones had undertaken to
build a community for those "who have been hurt, angered, alienated and victimized by adverse conditions that prevail in the de-
clining inner cities of advanced Western society." Others not
affected by these conditions had joined in the undertaking because of their idealism, the peace and beauty of life in the Guyanese jungle, the wonderful weather. They referred to their
previous statement in which they had announced their willingness
to die. That declaration, seized on by liars and slanderers, was
now being used as a weapon against them. But people possessed
of bravery and integrity would have no difficulty in understanding their position. Martin Luther King had said that it was necessary to have the kind of courage that enabled one to die for a
cause. Well, they had a cause and they were ready to put their
lives on the line in its service and defense. It was not their wish to
die. They believed passionately in life; their deepest desire was to
celebrate it, not stifle it. Nevertheless, they had no intention of
marching like sheep into the gas ovens. Theirs was the spirit of
those who had fought and died in the Warsaw Ghetto. Jim Jones
had never been one of those who cursed the darkness: he had
always preferred to light candles. But, under attack, they knew
what had to be done; and they saw no reason to apologize to
anyone for their decision to die if that became necessary.

In May they elaborated further in a lengthy statement that was
vituperative to the point of unreason and, in a curious way, introspective. One feels that according to the terms they had laid
down for their own existences, they had begun, in a very real way,
to fight for their lives; that, however dimly, however rhetorically,
they had begun to stare at their own deaths and were struggling
to come to terms with and ready themselves for the doom they
sensed was coming down. This was something more than another
exercise in political bombast and personal invective. They had
begun to write their obituaries.

Again, they began by referring to the "preposterous attacks" instigated by the Concerned Relatives. People's Temple was only one of a number of progressive groups marked down for destruction because they were bringing together the poor and the working-class and defying racial barriers. The fact that they had highlighted the failure of the free-enterprise system; the fact that they had been able to create successful survival programs providing food, medical care, jobs and vocational training; the fact that they had demonstrated the corporate power and solidarity of the dispossessed—a corporate power and solidarity that racist forces seemed to regard as their unique birthright; the fact that they had been able to generate wealth from a "cooperative life-style" rather than from the dog-eat-dog ethic of capitalism; the fact that they had distributed a free newspaper attacking all manifestations of injustice . . . these were the real reasons behind their persecution.

The Concerned Relatives were a sordid crew. Their crimes were many and various. Some were blackmailers. Some were terrorists who liked to advocate ridiculous and mad schemes of violence in order to advance their fraudulent revolutionary aims. All were *agents provocateurs.* Worse than that. In their ranks they harbored child molesters. Some had even sexually assaulted their own children. One Temple member (Maria Katsaris—she was one of Jim Jones's mistresses) had only just publicly exposed her father. They had operated credit-card rackets, embezzled Temple funds, forged checks, cheated on their income-tax returns. The racists among them had been known to treat young blacks like house slaves. Nearly all of them had unstable personalities. Several were sexual sadists. They were conspirators and collaborators. They were liars. They were so vindictive, so callous, that they had tried to starve old people in Guyana into submission by agitating for the severance of their pensions. These were documented facts. Such were the would-be saboteurs of their beautiful agricultural project, a model of cooperation, which had had heaped upon it the world's praises. Shamelessly, their criminal enemies prattled on about human rights, wearing masks of "outraged, antiquated morality."

The Concerned Relatives were led by a man (Stephen Katsaris —Maria's father) who was simply unable to accept the fact that his twenty-four-year-old daughter had finally asserted her independence and rejected his emotional tyranny. "This individual is also a clergyman of sorts [Katsaris had been a priest in the Greek Orthodox Church] and once instructed her to 'worship me as an icon unto God.'" At bottom, his concern—like the concern of those who were following his lead—was spurious. What could these people possibly mean when they accused Jim Jones of being power-hungry? What kind of power were they talking about? Power of the kind they meant could not possibly exist in the cooperative, socialist atmosphere of Jonestown. The opposite was true. It was they, the Concerned Relatives, who were power-hungry, who did not wish to relinquish control over those who had ceased to care for them and their ways. Those who had decided to devote themselves to a cause, to an ideal, who had rejected narrow self-interest, would always unnerve people like the Concerned Relatives. They did not have it in them to "relate" to such commitment. It was beyond their capacity to comprehend anyone devoted to a larger-than-self cause like the pursuit of human justice and human liberation. Such dedication bewildered and threatened people who did not have that commitment; whose lives, moving on a superficial moral plane, were circumscribed by a thousand fears. They had to compensate somehow for the dim realization that their own lives were empty and meaningless and devoid of principle.

Power hunger was always ascribed to leaders like Jim Jones who were trying to raise humanity to a higher road. Inevitably, those who chose to follow such a leader would desert their "biological relatives," not simply as an act of rejection but because of the conviction of conscience which ultimately transcended mere biology and genetics. Those left behind, those still trapped in the grip of emotional sickness, could not understand these others who had moved beyond their reach and were dancing to the beat of a different drummer. They would become enmeshed in hopeless contradiction: they would see the validity of the new road but be unprepared to follow where it led. Their pain could be eradicated only by trampling on, vilifying, sabotaging and crucifying the standard-bearers of the higher vision. In ancient Athens parents had also complained about a teacher who was supposed to be corrupting the minds of children. Thus had it been since the beginning of the world and thus would it always be.

That was the perspective within which the Concerned Relatives must be looked at. They were adorning their infamy with high-sounding words, but no one should be fooled. Jonestown repudiated once and for all the group and its accusations. The Temple's project in Guyana was an open book. They had been inspected by hundreds of people. It was a community of joy, beauty, industry and accomplishment in which racism had been abolished. Countless individuals had testified to that. They repeated that they had notified the President, the State Department and the Government of Guyana that terrorist plots were being hatched against them. "We state without equivocation or reserve that we will never back down, whatever heinous actions are attempted against us." No matter what was threatened or done, they would never abandon the beliefs and practices which had built the most humane community on the face of the earth.

The lawyers kept up the pressure. In early October, Mark Lane held a press conference in San Francisco. He had returned not long before from Jonestown, where he had been accompanied by the writer Donald Freed, a colleague of his on the Citizens Commission of Inquiry—an association dedicated to disputing the official versions of the John Kennedy and Martin Luther King assassinations. Lane, like Charles Garry, had concluded that there was indeed a well-organized conspiracy to destroy the People's Temple, Jim Jones and Jonestown. He was in a mood of high emotion at the press conference. "I have been deeply impressed with what I have seen there [Jonestown]. . . . It makes me almost weep to see such an incredible experiment, with such vast potential for the human spirit and the soul of this country, be cruelly assaulted by the intelligence organizations. . . ." Donald Freed, addressing the Temple congregation, added his encomium. "Martin Luther King, I think, if he could see Jonestown, would recognize it as the next step in his agenda, and he would say, 'One, two, three, many more Jonestowns.' . . ."

On November 13, the day before the Ryan delegation was due to arrive in Guyana, the Temple restated its position. The Concerned Relatives—now more precisely defined as a front organization specifically formed to spearhead activities against them—had recruited, they said, a California Congressman to lend prestige to their year-long campaign of lies and harassment. Leo Ryan called himself a liberal. Yet, they pointed out, he had voted in favor of military aid for the Pinochet regime in Chile, he had voted against reopening the investigation into the assassination of Martin Luther King and, as if his voting record were not bad enough, the constituency he represented was all white and well-to-do. His planned visit was nothing more than a contrived media event; one more provocative tactic. To them, it was clear that their enemies were hoping for some kind of incident. Consequently, they had asked the Guyanese Government for police protection.

They would consent to see Ryan only if three conditions were met. (1) Bearing in mind the all-white, affluent nature of his constituency, Ryan must be accompanied by other "Congresspersons" more representative of Third World concerns. (2) Mark Lane—who had all along been insisting that he would be otherwise engaged at the time of the projected Ryan visit—must be present. (3) Under no circumstances was Ryan to bring in his train of journalists not previously approved by them—or, it hardly needed saying, any of the Concerned Relatives. Jonestown, they repeated, had nothing to hide. Hundreds had lauded their accomplishments. The commune had been called a society of the future, a first-rate example of community life, a model of cooperation. But they would, they insisted, have nothing to do with the liars and slanderers who made up the Concerned Relatives and whose single, overriding purpose was to bring about their destruction.

All the portents were bad when Ryan's camp followers arrived in the small hours of the morning at the Pegasus to discover there was no room for them. Stephen Katsaris was making his third visit to Guyana that year. He was accompanied by his son, Anthony. Anthony would be wounded when the shooting started at the Kaituma airstrip. Maria, in whose behalf they had come, would soon be dead. Prominent too were Timothy and Grace Stoen, Temple defectors, whose five-year-old son, John, Jim Jones claimed as his own and whom he kept out of reach at Jonestown. For more than a year the Guyanese courts had been stalling on the custody suit his parents had brought. The boy would soon be dead. Sherwin Harris, former husband of Linda Amos, the woman who ran the Temple's Georgetown headquarters, had come to find his daughter Liane. Liane too would soon be dead. So would be Linda Amos and two more of her children by another marriage—they would be found in the Temple's Georgetown house, their throats crudely slit with a knife. Harris, when he heard the news, would go into a state of shock. Howard and Beverly Oliver had come for their two teen-age sons, Bill and Bruce. Bill and Bruce would soon be dead. Howard Oliver would suffer a stroke. Three of the press corps would soon be dead. Leo Ryan would be dead. Jim Jones would be dead. Jonestown, a model of cooperation, the society of the future, would be dead. But Charles Garry and Mark Lane, after an uncomfortable night in the jungle, would be alive; and Shirley Field Ridley, the Guyanese Minister of Information, would say, "I really can't find words to describe our reaction to this terrible thing that has happened in Guyana." In strict accordance with her non-Western conception of press freedom, all news of the event would be suppressed in Guyana for some days. Forbes Burnham was also unable to find words. He would remain a model of un-cooperative silence.

When I arrived two weeks later at the Pegasus, the lobby was quiet and sedate. In the twilit restaurant, candles glowed peaceably under perforated clay domes. Most of the captains and kings of press and television had already departed. There were no conferences. The desk clerk was affable and offered me a choice of rooms.

It was on Christmas Day 1974 that the following advertisement appeared in Guyana's *Daily Chronicle:* "The Blind See! The Deaf Hear! The Crippled Walk!"

The Greatest Healing Ministry Through Christ on Earth Today had arrived in town.

This modern-day Apostolic ministry, readers of the *Chronicle* were told, was in the process of establishing an agricultural mission in Guyana. It was their intention to assist the Government in its feeding, clothing and housing of the Guyanese people. One Eugene Chaikin, described as a wealthy California attorney, asserted that Pastor Jones was the most loving, Christ-like human being he had ever met. After this testimonial, there was a curious little digression: the People's Temple, the advertisement said, was well known for its support of local governments. But the text soon reverted to the matter at hand. Pastor Jones, it continued, possessed all nine gifts of the Holy Spirit. He had been able to cure thousands of "every kind of affliction!!!" It gave as an example a young woman whose X-rays had revealed holes in the bone as large as twenty-five-cent pieces. Pastor Jones had assured her that she would be all right, and, after his laying on of hands, the pain—which no sedative had been able to ease—had vanished. This was typical of the miraculous Power of Christ which channeled itself through Pastor Jones. The public was invited to attend a healing service where they would see with their own eyes the restorations performed by the wonderful powers with which Pastor Jones had been invested. This performance would take place at the Sacred Heart Church on December 29. The Catholics were praised for the ecumenical spirit they had shown in allowing one of their churches to be the venue of this supernatural display.

Dutifully, the *Chronicle* supplied an account of the service on December 30. It had been a great success. "Long before the service started, Guyanese from all walks of life, many of them old and infirm, deaf, blind, paralysed . . . filled the pews and aisles of the church. Scores of others . . . crowded the doors and the churchyard to witness the ceremony." Miracle after miracle was performed that afternoon in Georgetown. Pastor Jones chose at random people he said were sick. One woman was told that she was suffering from a pain in the head and had a cancerous growth. The woman agreed that he had diagnosed correctly and was told to go to the bathroom. She reappeared a few minutes later, loudly proclaiming that she had cast off the growth and that the pain in her head was gone. A man suffering from knee pains jumped for joy after Pastor Jones had prayed for him; a woman's stomachache disappeared; another announced that her high blood pressure had been cured. The Catholics, who, days before, had been congratulated for their ecumenical spirit, were suddenly upset. Nothing, however, could now be done about that.

A Jesuit priest, Father Morrison, recalled the day in late 1974 when a group of "very presentable" young Americans had come to see him. They told him of the pioneering work they were engaged on up in the northwest; they had come to Guyana, they said, because they wanted to help the developing countries of the world. It all sounded so very good, so wonderfully Christian. Here were all these young people showing their love not only by word but by deed. Practical Christianity—that was what he thought the People's Temple stood for. The presentable, courteous Americans had a favor to ask of him. Would it be possible for them to use the Sacred Heart Church for one of their services? From its pulpit they would announce the good news of their ministry. He discussed their request with the parish council. The chairman liked the idea. So did Father Morrison. Guyana was in bad shape physically and spiritually. It needed all the help it could get. He felt that given a chance, those young men and women could light some candles in the Guyanese darkness. Permission was granted for the service.

Father Morrison was not prepared for the advertisement that followed. Not once had they hinted to him that it was to be a "healing" service, a platform for the self-display of their Pastor.

"I was horrified. It was so terrible, so disgusting, what they had gone and done."

He argued for its cancellation—without success. The Charismatics would not hear of it. They were extremely curious and wanted to see what the healing would be like. Others argued that cancellation would be contrary to the ecumenical spirit. The show went on as scheduled.

The Temple representatives wept when Father Morrison accused them of having deceived him.

"Wept?"

"Weeping was one of their favorite tactics. They would use tears as propaganda. They were most adept at projecting hurt feelings."

They had no idea how the misunderstanding could have come about. They thought they had made themselves clear. They had never intended to deceive him. Oh, dear! Oh, dear! So they wept before him and wrung their hands.

But the damage had been done.

(The Temple's use of tears as a weapon was mentioned to me by someone else. On this occasion, it involved an attempted real-estate transaction in Georgetown. The owner did not want to sell at the price that was offered, but the Temple's representatives were persistent. They would telephone and call upon her at all hours of the day and night. On one of these visits, a Temple female started to cry. "If only you knew what would happen to me if I don't get you to agree! Do you love me? Do you care about me? Does the fate of another human being not matter to you? If you really loved me and cared for me as a human being you would sell your house." The owner was flabbergasted. She argued with them. How could she buy another house with the money they would give her? They replied that she need not buy another house. She could go to Jonestown. There she would not need money; there all her needs would be met and she would experience perfect fulfillment and happiness. She was spared, however, when the Temple became interested in another property and swiftly discarded her.)

Thus did Jim Jones and the People's Temple come to socialist Guyana—with tears, deception and voodoo.

It is hardly a cause for astonishment, given the history, beliefs and practices of the People's Temple as we now know them to have been, that Jim Jones should have been drawn to Guyana; and it is equally unastonishing that the Guyana of Forbes Burnham, given its history, beliefs and practices, should have accepted him. Guyana, over recent years, has shown a predilection for welcoming, assisting and sheltering strange people, a weakness springing from a peculiar sort of gangsterism that can contain within itself both corrupt cynicism of the highest order and ideological motivation. "You're a stupid black man," Burnham is reported to have said to the architect who refused to inflate his estimates. That outburst reveals the complex nature of Burnhamite gangsterism. It is about being Black and Third World as well as about being rich; it is a point of view. Within that point of view, criminality, nationalism, corruption, altruism of a kind, can all coexist. What holds them together is the personality of the Big Black Chief who operates, so to speak, by institutionalizing his manias, lusts and fantasies. This makes him and his country— which is no more than a projection of his caprice—vulnerable to appropriate calls from the wild.

For instance, in 1971 a dope dealer from Bermuda came to Guyana to drum up support for a so-called Black Peoples Congress. The Government obliged with a handout. However, the Black Peoples Congress is yet to take place. Then there was the man who claimed to be an Angolan freedom fighter. He was honored with Guyanese citizenship. It turned out that he was an American black in flight from the police. Like the Bermudan, he was also involved in the dope trade.

These were not isolated pieces of bad luck. The Bermudan and the pseudo Angolan belong to a common pattern of vaguely ideological misadventure. After he had committed murder on his Trinidad commune, it was to Guyana that Michael X had fled. There he was met at the airport by a Minister of the Government and given the red-carpet treatment. (Admittedly, at that stage, the murders had not yet come to light; but the less than salubrious past of the man now calling himself Michael X was well known.) The state-owned *Chronicle* published a photograph of the Minister and his guest gazing deep into each other's eyes. Beneath the photograph was the caption "When Two Revolutionaries Meet."

Less controversial, perhaps, but equally revealing of the mood of Guyanese hospitality, was the visit of the American Black Power activist and theorist Stokely Carmichael. He had originally been invited to Guyana by a dissident group of academics and students. But they quickly dissociated themselves from him when they heard the sort of things he was saying. "All the talk was of bloodshed and fighting," a member of the group said to me. "He said Black Power meant African power. He said we had to learn how to kill. It was the wrong message for a place like Guyana. We had had enough of racial killing by then." Carmichael was not left either embarrassed or marooned by their hasty desertion: he was quickly picked up by the People's National Congress and, like Michael X, given the red-carpet treatment by the Guyanese Government.

Toward the end of 1978, *The New York Times,* reporting from Georgetown, stated that there were at least four Americans wanted back at home for an assortment of crimes—rape, murder, armed robbery, blackmail—who were living in Guyana under Government protection. One of these had been made a senior training official in the National Service. "This is a position of considerable responsibility," a "Soviet-bloc source" was quoted as saying. "The Government wouldn't give him the job if it didn't have faith in him."

But the most notorious of Burnham's criminal courtiers is a black preacher from Tennessee calling himself Rabbi Washington. Back home, where he is known as David Hill, he is wanted by the police on charges of blackmail and violence. But in Guyana, where he surfaced in 1972, he is a figure of consequence. He has created around himself a religious sect—the House of Israel— which espouses a messianic doctrine of black redemption. His Guyanese followers adorn themselves in the colors of the ruling

party, which also happen to be the national colors. They arrive by
the busload to take part in Government-sponsored rallies and
parades; they help to break up Opposition meetings. In a sugar
strike called by a union unfriendly to the Government, they
played the part of scab labor. The Rabbi lives in considerable
style. His benefactors have, in addition, provided his organization
with two farms. The House of Israel calls itself "Burnham's
Church." It has even included him in its theology: the Comrade
Leader is Moses; the Rabbi is Aaron.

There was nothing extraordinary, therefore, in the warm welcome extended by the Guyanese Government to Jim Jones and
his People's Temple. Agricultural communes staffed by the disciples of various (largely black) American sects and cults were
springing up all over the Guyanese interior. (The agricultural
vogue, though, does not benefit the Indian population of Guyana
—the country's traditional farmers. Most of them have their requests for land refused. Occasionally, what they do have is actually taken away from them. The most recent case concerned a
livestock cooperative whose lands were seized at gunpoint and
turned over to supporters of the People's National Congress. I
have a photograph arising out of that incident. It shows a smiling
Parliamentary Secretary, wearing a dashiki, standing in a field
and looking on as a couple of the new owners ride about on a
tractor. Beside him are posted armed guards, presumably on the
lookout for any of the dispossessed who might be thinking of
making some trouble.) When Jim Jones described Guyana to his
flock as "paradise," he knew what he was talking about. He was
an ideal applicant: he had money, he had hundreds of devoted
disciples, he had good contacts in California, he knew what politics was about. Guyana had the land, the protective privacy and
the ideological cloak of feeding, housing and clothing the people.
It was a marriage made in heaven.

The People's Temple was not the only agricultural commune
in the northwest. Max Krebs, United States Ambassador to Guyana from 1974 to 1976, stated in the memorandum he submitted
to the Congressional committee investigating the circumstances
of the massacre that there was a similar agricultural project get-

ting under way in 1974 not far from the nascent Jonestown. This other project, also staffed by Americans, was called Shalom. It was having financial problems and had made little progress in clearing and cultivating its tract. Shalom's residents, the Ambassador remarked, seemed to be composed mainly of remnants from the hippie movement of the 1960s. He noted as well that there was some suspicion that its promoters "were really (or hoped to be) engaged in the cultivation of marijuana." When one recalls the Guyanese Government's penchant for becoming involved with dope traffickers, this little detail could hardly be considered unusual.

There was more purposeful activity going on at the better-financed People's Temple Agricultural Project, as the enterprise was officially designated. Ambassador Krebs, on his brief tour of inspection, observed that the main occupation of the Jonestown pioneers was clearing the jungle. Only about twenty-five acres had actually been brought under cultivation. The track leading to the heart of the settlement was a mire, impassable even by four-wheel-drive vehicles. He saw a muddy group of twenty to twenty-five Guyanese laborers hard at work planting a cleared tract. While the Guyanese labored in the mud, the American pioneers operated bulldozers. The buildings were primitive—except, that is, for "the comparatively sumptuous roofed cage in which was housed a chimpanzee (or some other kind of primate), reportedly rescued from an unkind fate with a circus or zoo in California and brought to Guyana." The apostolic ministry did not limit its compassion to injured humanity. Ambassador Krebs, like so many of those who were to follow in his footsteps, did not see the failures and the misery. Only much later would some of the pioneers whom he had seen that day tell how tormented they were by the snakes, the mosquitoes, the rain; how they were made to work from sunrise to sunset; how those who incurred displeasure, even in these early days of the settlement, were deprived of food, had their heads shaved and were beaten; how rain washed away the exposed topsoil; how the Amerindians pilfered without mercy; how a fifteen-thousand-dollar sawmill came with the wrong blades and was swiftly ruined; how a six-thousand-dollar

diesel generator burned out because the pioneers had misunderstood the wiring instructions.

By the middle of 1975, the Shalom commune was out of business. But the People's Temple Agricultural Project was prosper-
ing. Gradually, the Temple insinuated itself into Guyana's
political fabric. Linda Amos, who was in charge of the Temple's
Georgetown office, was a member of Viola Burnham's Women's
Revolutionary Socialist Movement. In August 1978 a WRSM delegation had spent three days in Jonestown. The People's Temple
marched in behalf of the People's National Congress, flaunting
their banners. They were part of the May Day celebration committee; they mounted agricultural exhibitions; they played basketball matches against police and Army teams; their pop-music
band gave concerts and became a conspicuous element in the
cultural life of the capital. Jim Jones and the Guyana of Forbes
Burnham appeared to have a thorough understanding of each
other's needs.

Ambassador Krebs, in his memorandum, says that in the early
days of the Temple's involvement in Guyana—around 1975—the
organization was active in the Protestant Guyana Council of
Churches; activities whose chief purpose appeared to be the
building of public support and confidence. This took the form of
being liberal with their money. They donated two thousand dollars to the Council itself, another two thousand to assist in the
setting up of a seminary and an undisclosed sum to further the
restoration of the Episcopal Cathedral.

Their eagerness was short-lived. A palpable decline in their
interest occurred soon after Jones took up permanent residence
in Guyana sometime in July 1977. During the Council's difficult
deliberations on the issue of the constitutional referendum, Temple participation in its affairs ceased completely. This apathy may
not have been unconnected with the fact that the Council openly
opposed the Government's desire to "rewrite" the Constitution
and turn it into a tool of dictatorship.

Jones showed himself ready to accommodate the sensibilities of
his hosts in other little ways. Among the incriminating "confessions" of wrongdoing Jones thought it worth his while to extract

from his followers (these confessions, designed to ensure silence in the event of defection, had become standard Temple practice) was this one mentioned by Yolanda Crawford in her affidavit of April 1978: ". . . Jim Jones ordered me to sign a number of self-incriminating papers, including a statement that I was against the Government of Guyana . . . that I was part of the PPP [People's Progressive Party] . . . and that I had come to Guyana to help the PPP." That this should be thought a criminal act demonstrates Jones's masterly comprehension of his hosts. Just how accessible top members of the Government were to the People's Temple in times of need is shown by an incident that happened near the start of Leo Ryan's mission. A reporter from the *San Francisco Chronicle* descended unannounced on the Georgetown house of the Temple. On his return to the Pegasus he was told that the American Embassy had called. The Guyanese Foreign Minister had been in touch with them, accusing the reporter of jumping over a fence and forcing his way into the house. The speed of communication was—to use a favorite Jonestown word—impressive.

Discordant noises—the stir created by the revelations about everyday life in the People's Temple published in *New West* in August 1977; the sudden self-imposed exile of Jim Jones from San Francisco; the insistent accusations of the Concerned Relatives; the enigmatic and halting career of the Stoen child-custody case in the Guyanese courts; the strange adventures in Georgetown of free-lance journalist Kathy Hunter; the growing number of sworn affidavits released by defectors from the organization; the furor in the San Francisco press—these and other discordant noises were making an increasing clamor. But they seemed to go unheard. The marriage between Jim Jones and the Cooperative Socialist Republic of Guyana rode out the facts and rumors and proceeded on its untroubled course. That marriage, made in heaven, between Jim Jones and the Government of Forbes Burnham lasted until that moment when a dump truck full of armed men appeared at the far end of the Kaituma airstrip—and the killing began.

CHAPTER

4

REPORTS COMING out of Jonestown suggested that the earthly paradise was at hand. A glossy brochure titled "Jonestown—A Model of Cooperation" described the miracles that were being enacted in the Guyanese bush. The brochure heralded itself with an outline of the map of Guyana superimposed on a portentous sky. In Guyana the settlers had ". . . found themselves in a land of spectacular beauty, graceful trees and beautiful, friendly people of many races." Only in Guyana were they able to put into practice their cherished principles of racial and economic equality, human service and cooperative living. They wanted to pay homage to the unique and important role of Guyana and her Government in the leadership of the developing nations of the world. That Government's goal of feeding, housing and clothing the people was identical with the human-service ideal that had come to fruition in the person of Bishop Jim Jones. Streams of visitors were coming to see the transfiguration of Man and Environment that had occurred in Jonestown. The guest book oozed with commendation. "Your socialism will win through!" "Most fascinating and laudable experiment." "Wonderful." "Beautiful CooBeration." Many of these guests, the brochure said, were from various Ministries of the Guyanese Government.

The jungly mire, the sodden Guyanese laborers, the primitive shelters had all vanished, giving way to the sweetest pastoral. It was indeed a wondrous transformation. Crops of all kinds—cassava, sweet potatoes, cabbage, cutlass beans, bananas, sugar cane, breadfruit, avocados—were flourishing on the hundreds of acres that had been cleared and planted. The jungle had receded. It now distantly framed gently rolling pastures, croplands and orchards. On those rolling pastures grazed plump cattle. Horses frolicked in the rich meadows. Pigs grew fat and content. Chickens laid an abundance of eggs. Guyanese experts and the local Amerindians gave freely and generously of their ancient and modern wisdoms. Those who were not working "productive season after productive season" on the fruitful land were occupied in cottage industry. From their hands flowed exquisite and many-hued baskets, rugs, toys and clothes. Each artifact reflected the loving work of skilled hands in the peaceful and creative environment that had been brought about by cooperative living. The laughter of children rang through the Jonestown air. (Their education must have been somewhat unconventional if a confessional letter written to "Father" by one of the teachers is anything to go by: ". . . Sometimes I'm overhard on the children I teach which Im sure studds their groth . . .") So impressed were the Guyanese authorities by the quality of the education being imparted that it was rumored they were planning to open a school run along the same lines.

"The warm gentle trade winds have come up," Jim Jones wrote, "and the glow of evening is subsiding quickly into the star-filled night. There is such peace here. There can't be anything so fulfilling anywhere as living this communal life. We watered the garden today. . . . We sang and joked the whole time, and in the spirit of joy in our accomplishment, urged each other on to a faster pace. . . . I love to work. I was at the beginning of the line, bringing spring water up out of the well that brims full no matter how much we take from it." He worked in the fields whenever he could; whenever—because even this idyll is shadowed with the threat of corruption—he was not engaged in coordinating the defense against the attacks directed against them from the United States. He was saddened when he thought of all the people at home daily oppressed and ground under by the regimentation and pressures inherent in a technological society. The fruit of that was hypertension, strokes, physical diseases of all kinds, endemic mental stress. Alas, it was always the fate of those who sought to break with that madness to be persecuted. Yet how secure and creative his people were! They enjoyed every type of organized sport and recreation. Musical talents and arts were flourishing. They shared every joy and every need. Their lives were secure and rich with variety and growth and expanding knowledge.

Money could not buy the happiness that existed in Jonestown. Look at Howard Hughes, money-rich beyond the dreams of ordinary mortals, and, in the end, dying alone, a man unloved, uncared for, unwashed. Look at J. Paul Getty, so obsessed with the preservation of his fortune that he would not pay the ransom demanded for his kidnapped grandson. The wealthy lived such brutish existences. Jones had heard from a member of his church who had devoted many years of her life to the care of very wealthy and elderly people that sometimes even before they were properly dead, their families descended and stripped their houses of everything that was valuable. In Jonestown it all was so different. They had liberated themselves from those lusts. Not long before, someone had needed cosmetic surgery. They had paid for it to be done—despite the fact that, strictly, the money could have been more usefully expended on other things. Why had they done that? They had done it because her full psychological development was being retarded. Human values must always take precedence over material ones. People without such ideals lived solitary lives and died surrounded by rejection.

In Jonestown the residents lived according to their ideals, and there was contentment. The old people—the "seniors"—had at last been freed from "loneliness and the agony of racism." Children no longer had bad dreams. They no longer wet their beds. Collectivism had endowed young and old with a new life. In

Jonestown, they were no longer ensnared by the opiate of religion. They had discarded the tyrannical narcissism that expressed itself in the desire for eternal youth. Even so, they were being invested with immortality of a kind. Warmed by the "balmy" tropical sun and fanned by the gentle trades, they were shedding the physical afflictions of the dog-eat-dog world they had left behind. Diseases like arthritis, diabetes, kidney ailments, hypertension had been all but vanquished. "There are high relationships here, ones that do not come just out of sex, but by sharing and living the highest ideals. We have passed beyond alienation and have found a way of living that nurtures trust—one that could speak to a society grown cynical and cold."

Jim Jones portrays an earthly paradise; one of his mistresses, Maria Katsaris, in a letter to her father writes, for the most part, as if she were having an earnest but, at the same time, highly enjoyable holiday in an exotic summer camp. But, then, Maria was young—she was still in her twenties. Sailing down the Kaituma River, she told her father, was one of her favorite pastimes. It was impossible for her to describe the beauty of the river; it was impossible for her to convey its peacefulness. She liked to sit out on deck and watch all the scenery. The animals and birds enthralled her, as did all the exotic tropical plants. When the boat passed close to a village, Amerindian children would run out to the bank and wave at her.

At Jonestown she lived in an exceedingly pleasant wooden cottage. Not everyone did. Some of the other "cottages" were made from "a kind of plant, sort of like palm leaves, but not really." She explained how it was done. The Amerindians went into the bush, cut down the trees and brought back the leaves. These were dried and woven on to a pole frame. "It is absolutely waterproof," she wrote reassuringly, "and looks very nice." Her life was busy and full of variety. She "sort of" helped to coordinate—what exactly she sort of helped to coordinate remained obscure—and also spent a great deal of time in the medical clinic and school. As though sensing the misunderstanding that could arise from this catalogue of somewhat cloistered and aristocratic occupations, she was quick to point out that in addition, she took full part in the democratic joys of Jonestown's outdoor life. She loved being out in the open. She loved working in the fields. She loved helping to tend the plants. Why, she had even started taking classes in elementary carpentry! Working with one's hands was such a great joy. She could honestly report that she had never been healthier or happier. Maybe the climate—that balmy tropic sun! those gentle breezes at dawn and dusk!—had something to do with her sense of well-being. But no . . . it was not only the climate. It arose as well from being able to do work, real work, in an atmosphere that had been rid of the tensions and pressures of city life. She was convinced that her father would love it in Guyana because she knew how much he enjoyed "working outside and stuff."

She mentioned the pigs, the goats, the cattle—these last had not yet arrived but already, in the mind's eye, they were dotted over those lush pastures. "I don't know if you have ever heard of cassava which is a plant grown here. It is kind of like a potatoe. It can be made into bread or fixed like any kind of potatoe." She seemed to have paid close attention to the cassava and its uses and properties: she did not spare her father the details. He was informed that a syrup called casareep could be obtained from it. It was "sort of like soy sauce is to Chinese food." But casareep was thicker than soy and did not taste the same. The leaves were used for animal food. All these conversion processes were carried out in their cassava mill. But fond and knowledgeable as she was, she was reluctant to leave her father with the impression that cassava was the only thing they grew. There were "acres and acres of crops." Unfortunately, she did not know what they all were.

The Project was industriously investigating and developing new kinds of food. For example, they had discovered that the cutlass bean had an extremely high protein content, and so they were experimenting with different ways of putting it to use. In one of their preparations it was made to look and taste like sausage patties. They could, as well, concoct some semblance of a meat loaf out of it. That had been dubbed a cutlass loaf. Cutlass loaf was delicious. "It is one of my favorite things and I wouldn't care if I never ate meat again if I had my cutlass patties. . . ." The Government was so impressed with their endeavors that they had called the Project the best model of agriculture in the nation. She promised in the next letter to tell him more about the sawmill, carpentry shop, medical clinic and school. "I guess I am really rambling on but I just want to share my enthusiasm with you for what is going on here. I know you would love it like I said. It is hard to describe all the beauty of the jungle and all that is going on at the Project too."

A short time before, they had staged an exhibition in Georgetown for the benefit of Government officials and Parliamentary representatives. It was held in a large room. Jonestown showed off its achievements and breakthroughs in agriculture, education, recreation, the arts, medical care and so on. One table was arrayed with the various foods they had "developed." Papaya fried pies. Plantain chips. Bean burgers ("which I also love"). A breakfast cereal made from plantain. And, "lots of other stuff." The event had been a big hit.

Lured by the commune's spreading fame, a constant stream of visitors descended on them. (Jonestown's remoteness—of which so much was to be heard and made later on—seems to have presented no barrier at all to sight-seers during those palmy days.) That very day no fewer than sixty-three teachers had come through. They had much admired the way the school was set up and intended to incorporate some of the same ideas in a school the Government was building nearby. The day before that, the Guyanese Ambassador to the U.N. had turned up with his wife. They had brought with them a four-year-old Venezuelan boy suffering from malnutrition—an affliction from which, Maria told her father, all his brothers and sisters had previously died. The boy, who was "really cute," was going to be adopted by the mission. She mentioned, in passing, that many local children had taken up residence with them. "One thing that has been done by the medical clinic is that gastroentronitis (if that's how you spell it —which I'm sure it's not) has been virtually wiped out in this area." She did not explain, however, how this remarkable feat was carried out. If the starving Venezuelan child was cute, no less so were the three baby armadillos, threatened with abandonment by their mother, which she had rescued. She was feeding them with an eyedropper and hoped they would respond to her tender nursing: "It would be neat to have little armadillos running around."

A shadow suddenly darkened the jungle paradise. "One last thing—please, please, please do not get disturbed by the bad publicity the church has gotten. I am more convinced than ever of conspiratorial and political set-ups." It was truly incredible, she wrote, that the press was allowed to publish such a filthy bunch of lies. Strange words to flow from the pen of a girl who, until that moment, was kind of like . . . sort of, you know, enthusiastically innocent. A little reflection showed her, nevertheless, that there was no need for astonishment. Any organization advocating racial and economic equality was not likely to be tolerated by a society founded on economic inequality and classism. Lies, though, would not succeed. People's Temple had done far too much good and helped far too many people for that to be allowed to happen. The trouble was that most people tended to believe everything they read in the newspapers. They were "unobjective." She appealed to her father to talk to her mother, to tell her that there was nothing at all to be worried about. The Project was, in any case, only one aspect of their work. What the other aspects of their work were she did not vouchsafe.

The foot soldiers of the cause, old and young, added their voices, confirming and elaborating the paradisal message. "Man," gushed a youthful black from San Francisco, "the Fillmore has seen the last of me!" A seventy-one-year-old woman thanked Jim Jones for allowing her to be a member of his beautiful socialist family. She praised him for practicing "the highest principles of Socialism-Communism." This he managed to do better than anyone else in the entire Universe. Another woman—eighty-four years old—tempered her gratitude with a timid hint of personal discomfort. "I am so glad to be in Jonestown. This is the happy time of my life. . . . I have something to die for now and something to live for. I love the little chilrens, see them grow here, them crying, see them smiling. . . . I brought four blankets here. Have not got one now, someone else have them. I love to have one nice blanket. Thank you. . . ."

People were so free in Jonestown, said nineteen-year-old Roseann Ruggiero. They looked different. That freedom caused their eyes to glow. "No more drugs," she exulted, "no more racism, no more rapes, no more prisons or jails." To his father, who wished to rescue him and his brother from the commune, Bill Oliver wrote, "I'm doing fine here its very very beautiful here. The wheather nice and the people here are very friendly. Always willing to help you. The only sorrow I have is that you guys are not here with me. . . ." He hoped his mother would join him soon and share in his happiness. All the pressures and tensions of city life, he added, disappeared in Jonestown. Bill Oliver was nineteen years old. His brother, Bruce, one year younger, was equally ecstatic. ". . . I'm here in Jonestown and all I got to say is that you have to see it to believe it. . . ." This was the place where he wanted to spend the rest of his life. It was the most beautiful place he had ever seen. ". . . I often think of things you taught me about being a man, you were right since I been here I feel like I'm grown a lot. . . ."

Donna Ponts, fifteen years old, told her grandmother that most of her time was spent at school and she was getting good grades and making a multitude of friends. There were a few different foods she had never heard of before—like the soursop. Although the soursop was difficult to describe, it was delicious. Like Maria Katsaris, she too went into some detail. The soursop, her grandmother was apprised, could be eaten both frozen and fresh; when it was frozen, it tasted like sherbet. Another novelty was the granadilla, the pulp of which could be used to make cobbler. Granadilla cobbler was very like peach cobbler but tasted much better. Abruptly, after all this nutritional information, a shadow fell. "I am sorry to hear that you called the radio station but since you did I will not be writing to you any more. I don't know what you

think—all I know is that I *love* it in *Guyana* and I *truly* am *happy!*"
The childish scrawl ended.

The pilgrims continued to come; the guest book continued to
be filled with their adulation. For the chairman of the Guyana
Livestock Corporation, it was the purest egalitarian society he had
ever seen. A Guyanese dentist was dazzled by the sight of so many
races working side by side in such harmony. It was a dream come
true for a Dr. Balwant Singh. Nicolai Pedorovsky, a physician
with the Russian Embassy, was slightly more restrained. He
thanked his hosts for their attention and hospitality and asked to
be counted among their friends. One of the most noteworthy of
these pilgrims was the Temple lawyer Charles Garry. He visited
Jonestown in late 1977. On his return to the United States, Garry,
famed in California for his radicalism, publicized his findings.

He had been, he said, to Paradise.

"I saw it. It's there for anybody to see." What, precisely, had
Mr. Garry seen? He had seen, in the first place, a community in
which racism had ceased to exist. He had seen, in the second
place, a community in which there was no "sexism." He could
think of no other human grouping in the world that had been
able to solve the problem of male sexual supremacy as had Jonestown. He had seen, in the third place, a community in which
there was no "ageism." In Jonestown young, middle-aged and
old, black, brown, yellow, red and white, male and female had all
succeeded in making a common spiritual life. Everyone mixed
with everyone else; everyone shared with everyone else. He had
never before been surrounded by so many happy faces. "I want
that captured [he was hoping a documentary film would be made,
recording the marvel for posterity] . . . I want that captured so
that skeptical America will know what it is when you live without
fear of the rent being due, and all the other problems we're surrounded by."

Only in Switzerland had he come across better sanitation facilities. Jonestown was so clean that you could eat off the ground.
Medical care, especially as it was lavished on the aged, was unsur-
passed. Every morning a member of the medical team visited all

the senior citizens in their cottages. He would ask if they had had any problems during the night. Garry was convinced that there was much that could be learned by the medical schools at home —and by the American Medical Association. To that end, he had urged the Jonestown doctor to write up his daily experiences. In the United States, the aged were condemned to a life of pauperism and beggary; in Jonestown, they flourished in a cocoon of security and compassion. Animals were treated better in Jonestown than human beings were in the United States. The commune's pigpens resembled palaces. Many homes he had seen in America could not measure up to the sanitation, the cleanliness, the spaciousness, of a Jonestown pigpen. The chickens he had eaten were luscious in flavor. Food, generally, was delicate and nourishing. The Jonestown diet automatically lowered the blood pressure; it caused diabetes to disappear; it stripped off layers of bourgeois fat.

He praised the school, whose teachers were drawn from a pool of at least fifty people who had advanced degrees. The only school in America that he could compare it to—which, presumably, did not studd the groth of its charges—was the Oakland Community School run by the Black Panthers. Nor was Jonestown, so tender to its old people, so devoted to the educational needs of its young, so sound in its food habits, so triumphant over race, sex, age and disease, so generous to its pigs, deficient in entertainment and fun. For three and a half hours Garry had been regaled in the commune's auditorium—a large, open-sided shed. Poetry gushed from the mouths of six- and seven-year-olds. Jonestown had provided him with the most exquisite entertainment in the world. He had never, he said, been exposed to such a display of talent in his entire life. (Garry is in his late sixties.)

How to account for this remarkable efflorescence in the middle of the Guyanese jungle? Such astounding achievements were possible in Jonestown because the people there were learning a new social order; they were learning the answers to a better life. What was happening at Jonestown was a credit to humanity. He emphasized that he was not peddling propaganda. "I'm not a propagandist. I'm a hard-hitting, factual analysis lawyer. I saw this with my own eyes. I felt it."

Jones never ran short of influential friends. The Reverend John Moore, a Methodist minister, two of whose daughters had become members of the People's Temple, visited the commune in May 1978, six months before the crash and just under a year after Jones had fled from San Francisco. His account of what he found and felt there is more down-to-earth than that left us by Charles Garry; but despite the pedestrian and factual style, his response to Jonestown was no less enthusiastic than Garry's had been some months before.

As with so many of the rest, the first word that came to his lips was "impressive." On entering the compound, he saw the senior citizens engaged in calisthenic exercises and little children being busily cared for. He was introduced to the doctor, who showed him slides and the new portable X-ray machine Jonestown had acquired. He met the nursing staff—one of his daughters was in charge of medical supplies. The clinic, he reported, did not confine its services to commune members but reached out to the local population. Amateur radio operators helped to keep Jonestown in touch with a network of physicians. By this means the doctor had carried out a successful cesarean delivery of twins. The president of a medical association (unspecified) had given the clinic his imprimatur. When two Guyanese dentists visited the settlement they could find only two cavities among all the scores of children. He attributed this to the wholesome diet.

The school, recognized by the Guyanese Department of Education, was making rapid progress. Soon it would be offering a high school curriculum. He was struck by the enthusiasm of the teachers, who, liberated from constricting convention, were free to experiment with novel techniques and ideas. (Regrettably, we are not told what these were.) Residents of all ages attended classes, since Jonestown re-educated as well as educated.

Jonestown's isolation from the world was only geographical. A public-address system kept everyone in touch with current affairs. Films of all types were shown in the evenings. One night he saw a double feature—*The Heart Is a Lonely Hunter* and a documentary on the status of women in the Soviet Union.

Like Garry, he too was swept off his feet by the cultural life of Jonestown. He listened to the band playing jazz, "soul" and rock music. The audience response left nothing to be desired. A seventy-five-year-old woman got up and did a Moms Mabley routine, and a preacher roughly the same age sang and danced. (The audience participation that exhilarated Rev Moore was viewed with a tinge of distaste and alarm by Congressman Ryan when he was entertained in similar fashion by the commune on the night before the massacre. "Strange," Ryan said to Charles Krause of *The Washington Post:* "the teen-agers might get off on soul music but middle-aged men and seventy-year-old women?" Krause himself, incidentally, was not immune to the charms of Jonestown. "The truth was," he wrote, "that I rather admired Jim Jones's goals. . . . It seemed to me that the People's Temple had a legitimate purpose, a noble purpose, and was more or less succeeding.")

Rev Moore admired the living arrangements. Single people shared dormitories. Families were given houses. The authorities were receptive to the point of indulgence: when one older woman expressed the desire to have a house of her own, a small cabin was constructed for her. (But the inquisitive Charles Krause stumbled upon a dormitory containing at least one hundred elderly and mainly black women.) The buildings were simple but adequate, with wooden walls and metal roofs; and because there was running water in the guesthouse, he "presumed" there must be running water in the houses and dormitories. Cooking was done in a central kitchen on wood-burning stoves. He marveled at the organization that must have been needed to prepare three meals a day for more than a thousand people, and exclaimed over the quantity and quality of the food he was served. Nearly all of it, he was told (and he believed; he believed everything), was grown and processed by the commune. Their agricultural efforts were diverse and bold in concept. They were experimenting with the dry farming of rice. Starting with only twelve seeds of the protein-saturated winged bean, they hoped to plant ten or twelve acres by the fall. Amerindians "share their wisdom with the people about food and medicinal herbs." He was shown the machine shop, an underground chamber they were excavating for storage purposes, a windmill they were erecting. Homage was paid to the pigs and chickens. Jonestown had "some cows" and soon would have modern dairy equipment.

But it was the treatment of the old people, the "senior citizens," to which he harked back. Nowhere had he ever seen them in such a flourishing state. They worked and contributed to the community as they were able. He watched one woman assiduously hoeing her garden. Others had neat picket fences around their cabins. At the sight of the old woman hoeing her plot, Micah's words came back to him: ". . . they shall sit everyone under his vine and under his fig tree, and none shall make them afraid. . . ." The fears that were a normal part of city life had gone from these people.

In Jonestown everyone ate and slept in the same way. Everyone was expected to work—the workers were out in the fields from early in the morning—and to do so without any hope of special reward beyond the joy of labor itself. Young people who had never had a chance to acquire any skills were doing so now. Morale was high. Individuals were breaking out of old ruts, crossing boundaries and extending themselves. A lawyer was in charge of the citrus and the winged-bean experiments. Delinquent city youths were learning the gentle art of agriculture.

The sense of common ownership, of a shared life, of loyalties larger than those dictated by self-interest went deep. They were not robots: suggestions and criticisms were encouraged. "I was asked by a reporter if I had asked people if they were happy. As I thought about that question later, it seemed like asking people celebrating at a party if they were happy, or coming down out of the stands and asking members of the team who were moving the ball towards a touchdown if they were happy." He dismissed charges of brainwashing and mind control. The members of the commune were not being held there against their will. People's

Temple, he was firmly persuaded, would prefer to expend energy
assisting those who were unhappy to leave; it was not to anyone's
advantage to restrain those who wanted to depart and return to
old ways. Everyone who was there was a volunteer. They were
there because they wanted to be there. "I had a feeling that everybody was somebody. I thought of Israel's understanding of herself, and later, the Church's self-understanding: 'We who were
nobody are now God's people.' "

CHAPTER
5

BREAKFAST SERVICE on the patio was slow. The guinea fowl ambled among the tables, pecking at crumbs. A solitary American stared blankly at the line of dunes.

For want of anything better to do, I asked a hovering waitress what she made of the Jonestown affair.

"It's a strange thing," she answered readily enough, "but not many Guyanese ever hear of that place till they went and kill themselves."

"That's odd. I thought Jonestown was supposed to be a model of cooperative agriculture. You would think everybody would have been told about it."

"Well, they didn't tell me." She laughed sourly, kicking away the probing guinea fowl.

Guyanese man-in-the-street ignorance of the commune and its stirring deeds in the interior was confirmed by everyone I spoke to. Some dimly remembered the healing service that had taken place in the Sacred Heart Cathedral some four years before—a performance the Temple did not repeat; quite a few knew of the band; one or two were aware that there was a basketball team. But about Jonestown as such, New Guyana Man, for whom it was supposed to be blazing a new trail, had known next to nothing. As I was subsequently to discover, its miracles were more widely publicized in California than in Guyana. One could only assume that news about it had been adjudged unconducive to development.

I turned my attention to that day's editorial in the *Guyana Chronicle*. The subject was strikes in the nationalized industries—which control eighty percent of the Guyanese economy. It strongly disapproved. The editorial quoted the Comrade Leader as having recently lamented the fact that while the ruling party was thoroughly Socialist in outlook and policy, Guyana itself was not yet Socialist. This lag was causing considerable trouble and misunderstanding. Guyanese still betrayed far too many colonialist-derived tendencies in their behavior. Most conspicuous among these was their tendency to go on strike. This baffled the writer. He conceded that in colonial days striking was a legitimate weapon (the Comrade Leader himself had shown the way, exploiting worker unrest to bring down the Socialist regime of Cheddi Jagan in the early 1960s—but at that time, of course, the country was still a colonial dependency) because colonialists were, by definition, exploiters. But under Forbes Burnham, Guyana had banished its exploiters. The Small Man—the Small Man is a variant of New Guyana Man: the relationship between the two is a little obscure —was himself the boss. He was indisputably the master of the means of production. Hence those who chose to go on strike were, in effect, striking against themselves. Which was absurd. The editorial called for a campaign that would educate the workers into understanding that whenever they thought in terms of industrial action they were thinking in colonial fashion.

(The *Chronicle* was to become really indignant a few days afterward over an incident that occurred at a ceremony to honor Cuffy, the Guyanese national hero who led a bloody slave rebellion in the eighteenth century. In imitation of a well-known statue of the hero, a private in the People's Militia mounted a forty-five-gallon oil drum and there struck an appropriately warriorlike pose. The *Chronicle* tells it best: ". . . as his comrades were about to dismantle the 'monument' and proceed with the rest of the afternoon's programme, Private Blaize seems to have been so inspired by the part he was portraying that he had to be 'awakened.' The whole performance sparked a sorry reaction from the big crowd of onlookers. They laughed! While it's true that there's hardly a serious event which doesn't have its lighter side, blatant, unthinking laughter could be heinous. The portrayal . . . was a very serious thing . . . the blatant, unthinking laughter that accompanied it was heinous." Nothing, I suppose, could have better illustrated the lingering colonial mentality of the Guyanese.)

Elsewhere in the paper was a report of a speech by the Comrade Minister of Education, Social Development and Culture (subsequently murdered by a gunman in October 1979) commemorating the thirtieth anniversary of the Universal Declaration of Human Rights. There was a promise from the Ministry of Trade to keep a close watch on the garlic shortage. It was announced that on the following Sunday, the Deputy Prime Minister, Comrade Ptolemy Reid, would be heading a Government delegation to the Second Biennial Conference of the Guyana United Apostolic Mystical Council. Founded in 1974, this body sought, somewhat enigmatically, to protect the freedom and traditions of the Faith without regard to color or race. It seemed that the Congress was going to be an instructive affair: the United Apostolic Mystical Council was planning to hold an exhibition of its craft work—and to show off the results of its cooperative agricultural endeavors.

"Hello! Freedom House. Can we help you?" The voice at the other end of the line was surprisingly cheerful; surprisingly friendly.

I had telephoned on the off chance, trying to locate Cheddi Jagan, the leader of the Opposition. Mr. Jagan was out of the country. Nevertheless, I thought I would drop by.

The ramshackle two-story building in downtown Georgetown looked more like the sort of premises usually occupied by old-fashioned Chinese restaurants than the national headquarters of a major political party. Directly opposite was a tawdry cinema—the Metropole—its billboards scaly with peeling posters advertising forthcoming kung-fu films. The Metropole could, in a modest way, be regarded as one of Guyana's historical monuments. It was at a congress held there in 1954 that the original People's Progressive Party had split into its Burnham (black) and Jagan (Indian) factions, the former eventually turning itself into the People's National Congress.

Two Indian youths, sitting at a stained and chipped wooden table, guarded the grilled entrance. A sign warned that all bags and parcels would have to be searched. I climbed a long flight of wooden stairs. On the wall facing the landing was displayed a Russian-supplied poster of Lenin—for both of Guyana's main political parties claim to be bearers of the authentic socialist message. It is the official view of the People's Progressive Party that the People's National Congress is "reformist" and "opportunist" —in short, it is pseudo socialist. It is the official view of the People's National Congress that the People's Progressive Party is a "phrase-mongering, soi-disant leftist party"—in short, that it is pseudo socialist. Ideologically, both groups avoid the race issue, the one abiding reality of Guyanese politics. Practically, both parties owe their existence to it. Socialism in Guyana is carried on the back of racial fears and loyalties.

This contradiction, I believe, causes genuine concern among the leaders of the PPP—which does take its socialism seriously. In 1975, Mr. Burnham, his newfound radicalism getting out of hand, had all but alienated his American patrons. There was talk in Guyana of military invasion from right-wing Brazil, from Venezuela. The Socialist Revolution, beleaguered by imperialist enemies, threatened by CIA subterfuge, was in danger! The PPP, which had been boycotting the National Assembly after the frauds and murders accompanying the 1973 general election (the election in which the People's Army had intervened and seized ballot boxes), changed its policy. Declaring that his party did not have a monopoly on socialism—and believing, no doubt, that a little bit of pseudo socialism was better than no socialism at all—Dr. Jagan announced a policy of "critical support" for the Government. For the first time in many years, Cheddi Jagan and Forbes Burnham shared the same platform, avowing a common purpose in defending the country against the encircling imperialist forces. There were some within the PPP who thought that the policy of critical support did not go far enough. One of the party's leading theoreticians ("That man *knows* his Marxism," a former comrade of his said to me) suggested that they give the Government "unconditional support." He went even further than that: he advocated to the PPP that it liquidate itself. The party did not laugh. It actually debated the proposition that it commit collective suicide—or maybe I should say revolutionary suicide.

In the end, the PPP demurred. The man who knew his Marxism defected to the Comrade Leader, saying that the PPP were Mensheviks and the PNC were Bolsheviks. He was rewarded with the directorship of the Cuffy Ideological Institute, the powerhouse of cooperative socialist doctrine. (It is strange how left-wing intellectuals, who never cease vilifying the imposition of metropolitan standards and prejudices on colonized peoples—cultural imperialism—are able, without the slightest embarrassment, to apply equally alien ideograms in their attempts to describe local conditions. There are no Bolsheviks and Mensheviks in Guyana. There are transported Indians and Africans locked into poverty, resentment, ignorance and delusion.)

The qualified rapprochement between the two parties did not last long, foundering on the controversy generated by the then newly created People's Militia: it had soon become clear that it was to be composed almost exclusively of the PNC's black supporters. Dr. Jagan withdrew his policy of critical support. It was all such a shameful waste. The Cubans, who were providing the arms and the training for this "popular" body of mass defense, had (so, at any rate, I was told by a mournful PPP man) gone so far as to produce blown-up photographs of both the leaders—as necessary a prerequisite for this sort of activity as arms and training. Such are the pitfalls of socialist politics in Guyana.

In retrospect, it seems amazing that Forbes Burnham and Cheddi Jagan could ever have worked together. As it was, their alliance had begun to crumble at the first temptation of power—immediately after the 1953 general election. Burnham had instantly thrown the victorious party into turmoil by demanding the leadership. There is another interesting incident connected with the 1953 election. When the newly elected PPP legislators marched from their headquarters to the opening session of the Legislature, they made quite a splash in their white sharkskin suits. "The decision on attire," Cheddi Jagan wrote afterward, "had been made by Burnham while I was [away] . . . If it had been left to me, I would have selected a simpler and less conspicuous outfit." Those sharkskin suits were as telling an omen as Burnham's earlier bid for the leadership. Guyana had, in a sense, started on its long and ostentatious march to tragedy.

Janet Jagan—Dr. Jagan's American-born wife—greeted me in her small office. I remembered her formidable reputation. A Marxist of many years' standing, she had held a number of important posts in the troubled administrations formed by the PPP between 1953 and 1964. In the 1950s she had featured prominently in the political demonology of the British Caribbean, her adversaries painting her in the starkest colors they could mix. She was held to be an almost Mephistophelean force, forever urging her husband on to new acts of extremism. She was the dark power behind his Communist throne, the hardest of hard-line ideologues, a creature in thrall to the Kremlin.

Her fame spread to England. In 1953, the London *Daily Mirror,* commenting on the events leading to the suspension of the British Guiana constitution in that year, branded her thus in a headline story: "Janet Britain-Hater—Hatred of Britain is Mainspring that makes Mrs. Jagan tick." It was all very heady stuff, and she suffered the consequences. She was subjected to a banning order restricting her movements. Later, she was imprisoned, sentenced to three months at hard labor. On the eve of Dr. Jagan's removal from office in 1964, a rumor was spread that she had stabbed to death a party colleague in Freedom House.

Janet Jagan in the flesh bore no resemblance to her once blood-curdling image. She was a small, frail-looking woman, unassuming and low-key in manner. She explained that she was busy working out the details of a rally the party was organizing. We agreed that we would meet for dinner at the Pegasus the following evening.

The atmosphere in Freedom House was austere. In that ramshackle, Chinese-restaurant ambience (I half-expected to see fly-blown paper lanterns hung with tassels), the mysteries of the revolutionary process, of the revolutionary consciousness forging itself, became palpable. I was surrounded by believers, by men and women possessed of and possessed by a faith, who saw the world very differently from me. It impressed on me afresh the power of ideas to remake men, to turn them into different kinds of creatures.

I was introduced to a man who had been to Cuba on a prolonged visit. I asked him what he had been doing there.

"I was attending some seminars."

"What were the seminars about?"

He looked at me with cold irony. "They were about all different sorts of things."

"What sorts of things?"

He smiled hieratically, not answering. It was as if he had been initiated into rites that could not be communicated to the profane. His Cuban experience was sacrosanct. He would divulge nothing of what had transpired there. I observed that his colleagues treated him with respect, that with them too his behavior was ponderously hieratic. After a while, I gave up my attempts to make conversation with him.

There was a pretty young girl who had just returned from Lumumba University in the Soviet Union.

"Are you a Communist?" I asked.

"Not yet."

"What do you mean by that?"

"I mean that my consciousness isn't fully developed. Being a Communist isn't just a matter of saying so. It takes time and effort. I still have a long way to go."

She frightened me.

Despite the warnings of the guards downstairs, I decided I would walk back to the hotel. It was the middle of the afternoon, and it was hot. Georgetown and its inhabitants looked derelict. The shuttered shops were uninviting, starved of goods. Sullen black faces stared out of the doorways of rum shops and cafés. Others, gathered in small groups in patches of shade, watched me without friendliness. There was little traffic about. I was (rather foolishly) wearing a jacket and carrying a briefcase, two items that clearly marked me out for attention. That—as well as the heat and humidity of the afternoon—made me regret my decision to walk. But there was not a taxi in sight.

Wracks of refuse floated in stagnant gutters. Smells of decay hung in the still air. Solitary beggars slept in the shadows of peeling buildings. I began to feel that the city itself was rotting away slowly in the suffocating heat. Walls were covered with faded referendum posters and scrawled graffiti.

"Vote Yes! End Exploitation Now!"

"Burnham Is King!"

"We Have Burnham Fever!"

"Every Nigger Is Born a Star!"

Away from the center of the city, I came to quieter, cleaner streets. Elegant, white-painted wooden houses stood silent in bushy gardens. These colonial houses are the glory of Georgetown. Looking at them, I could see why it was once reputed a beautiful city. But now their elegance was faded (many had been converted into offices of one kind or another) and their beauty was sad and elegiac, serving only to emphasize the sense of disintegration. The air freshened as I approached the sea. Families and courting couples strolled along the esplanade or sat on benches embedded in the concrete, facing into the salty wind and gazing at the mud-laden breakers.

On the terrace of the Pegasus a steel band was playing. The hotel's clients were relaxing—drinking rum punches, sunbathing, splashing in the pool. It was a convivial weekend scene. I made my way to the little bar at the far end of the pool.

"Hi! How're you doing?" An American leaning against the counter winked at me. He wore a straw hat, dark glasses, denim shorts with frayed edges. His shirt was unbuttoned, exposing a hairy, sunburned chest. He seemed to have walked straight out of an advertisement for Bacardi rum.

I said I was doing fine.

"You from Guyana?" He eyed a shapely mulatto girl sitting on the rim of the pool, dangling her legs in the water.

I stated my business gingerly.

He laughed. "Another one!" He touched my arm. "You see that guy over there?" He pointed at a bearded fellow American sprawled on a deck chair. "He's writing a book. You see the guy behind him? He's writing a book. You see that fat guy? He's writing a book. I'm writing a book. You're writing a book. In fact, there's hardly a single person around this pool who isn't writing a book. But mine's going to be different."

"How so?"

Again he touched my arm. "Sex."

"Sex?"

"Sure . . . sex. Race. Suicide. Murder. Corruption. A hot Third World country. That's a classic mix. Pure Graham Greene. Can't miss if it's handled right."

He nudged me. A white woman and a black girl about seven or eight years old had appeared on the terrace. The woman had an arm curled protectively about the girl's shoulder. Heads turned to watch their progress. They were pursued by a knot of writers.

"Look at the black girl's neck."

I looked and saw a ring of scar tissue circling the upper part of the girl's throat.

"They nearly had her too that night in the Georgetown house."

I had had my first Jonestown sighting.

Janet Jagan, the receptionist said, was waiting for me in the lobby. When I arrived, she was in conversation with an impeccably dressed black man. We were introduced. The man excused himself briefly while he greeted another acquaintance. Mrs. Jagan told me that he was formerly a stalwart of the PNC and an old enemy of hers. He had occupied a reasonably influential position in the PNC hierarchy and had often behaved with particular viciousness toward her. But now (I was not told why) he was out of favor and jobless. She had just happened to run into him in the lobby while waiting for me. Sooner or later, everyone, even old enemies, will meet in the Pegasus. The man returned. I invited him to join us for a drink.

"You can't imagine what it's like looking for a job in Guyana," Mrs. Jagan said as we walked toward the bar. She gazed with what seemed to be genuine sympathy at her now-fallen enemy.

When we were seated, the talk turned to some strange American black, with the rank of lieutenant-colonel, who always seemed to surface in Guyana at election times, playing an undefined and, it was therefore assumed, sinister role.

"I'm pretty sure he's connected with the CIA," Mrs. Jagan said.

The man was less sure. "I believe he works here on some sort of commission basis. Giving advice on this and that. They say he's very bright."

"But what exactly does he do to earn his commission? Help to rig elections?"

The man looked suave and kept silent: he might have fallen out of favor, but he was not going to betray every secret to his onetime adversary.

"He's not the only one, either," Mrs. Jagan said. There were many odd characters stalking about the Guyanese political jungle.

There had been, I knew, a recent addition to that flock—an American public relations expert (white) had been hired by the Government to mediate between it and the foreign press corps in the aftermath of Jonestown. It seemed, on the face of it, a peculiar assignment; but Guyana was a peculiar country. I had seen this individual bustling about the Pegasus, but to date I had had no dealings with him.

The conversation, as it always tended to in Guyana, drifted around to Mr. Burnham. All roads, in due course, led back to him. Did he really believe in anything at all? I wondered aloud.

"He believes in one thing," the man said. "Himself. That's the only ideology he has. I have to laugh when he calls himself a socialist."

"Not *socialist*," Mrs. Jagan corrected with a smile. "*Marxist-Leninist*."

"He doesn't know the first thing about Marxism-Leninism."

"Of course," Mrs. Jagan said. "But he claims to be one; therefore we must call him one."

"Okay. Marxist-Leninist. A Marxist-Leninist who drinks only Chivas Regal. Meanwhile, the people starve." Burnham, he went on, loved power for power's sake. And if there was one thing that rivaled his love of power, it was his love of money and luxury. His greed was boundless. He had accumulated more wealth than either he or his children or even his grandchildren would ever need. Yet he ceaselessly looked for more.

"When did you see the light?" Mrs. Jagan asked drily.

The man looked suave. Finishing his drink, he took his leave.

I asked Mrs. Jagan what she thought of Burnham.

"A slick cynic." Only very rarely did they meet socially. When she rose to speak in the National Assembly, he would shout, "Sit down, you stupid American!" He said that again and again.

Did she ever despair of the PPP's returning to power?

"No!" But naturally, after fifteen years in the wilderness, it was impossible not to feel twinges of hopelessness now and again.

What messages did Jonestown have for her?

"Beats me how so many people could fall for that. I think there were a lot of social misfits involved."

Was that all?

She laughed apologetically. "I'm sorry. I'm so completely wrapped up in day-to-day politics I haven't had the time to think properly about it. I suppose there are deeper meanings to the whole business. . . ." She shook her head wearily. "We tried to raise the issue in the National Assembly—to have a debate, you know. But the Speaker wouldn't allow it. He more or less said it wasn't worth a debate."

Why not make a fuss? Why not a stage a walkout or something like that?

"We have walked out too many times." She laughed again. "It's ceased to have any effect."

Even the massacre of a thousand people could be absorbed without disturbance into Guyanese political realities. The PPP attitude seemed to be largely confined to muttering and theorizing about CIA plots to discredit socialism.

Our conversation reverted to the PPP's chances of coming back to power. The year 1978, leaving aside the Jonestown debacle, had been a particularly bad one for Burnham. His popular appeal had all but vanished. New levies were biting hard into pay envelopes. The Trades Union Congress had actually proposed a general strike, though nothing had as yet been done about it. Agriculture was in a terrible state—before coming to meet me she had been subjected to hours of complaint by rice farmers. Burnham had gone for quick industrialization, but it had not worked. The PPP line was that the country must build from a strong agricultural base. The party was calling for a "Patriotic Front of National Unity."

I listened. How often over the past fifteen years, I wondered, had its leaders scanned their Marxist charts and, discovering all the forces of historical inevitability to be in perfect alignment, predicted that the end of the regime was in sight? that the "contradictions" could no longer be sustained? that the long years of

waiting were nearly done and the construction of the New Jeru-
salem (patterned on Cuba) was at last to begin?

They had, I was saddened to see, become part of the Guyanese
futility, prisoners locked up beyond hope of rescue in the cages
wrought by their Marxist ideology. Fifteen years of useless battle
had taught them nothing, leading only to staleness and stagna-
tion, to the interminable repetition of bankrupt formulas. They
had nothing to offer but their sincerity; they inhabited a make-
believe world, a sort of Marxist dollhouse, populated by Mensheviks and Bolsheviks. Why is the idea of cooperative socialism as
such (I do not refer to its Burnhamite parody) condemned as
"revisionist" and "downright reactionary"? What purpose does it
serve to describe the PNC as petit bourgeois, bureaucratic bourgeois, et cetera, et cetera? Whence the "changed correlation of
class forces" that allows Guyana the possibility of becoming a second Cuba? The parroting of textbook abuse and textbook hope
was worse than pointless. It was worse than pointless because it
created false pictures; because the words described nothing that
existed and could only lead Guyana further and further away
from any understanding of its condition.

A child could understand that the PNC was a black-supremacist
party of the worst kind, a projection into public life of savage
instincts and gangster ideology. But not, it appeared, the PPP.
The racial question was reduced to a footnote, an inconvenient
warp in the rigid theorems of their Marxist geometry. Guyana,
Janet Jagan had written, "is not in reality a stratified, racially
divided nation." Well, what was Guyana if it was not a racially
divided nation? Mr. Burnham would, quite justifiably, laugh. For
fifteen years he had lived off the spoils of racial division. He, at
least, understood the situation. In the PPP scheme, racism is
scaled down to a "malpractice." It was a distortion introduced by
the British colonialists and, later on, exploited by CIA intrigue.
Race was an artificially created antagonism. Once that was understood and appropriate action was taken to counteract its baleful
influence, the antagonism would disappear of its own accord.
Indians and blacks would then join hands and walk bravely into

their predestined socialist future. Such touching misapprehensions can have no other effect than to compound the Guyanese tragedy.

That morning's editorial in the *Guyana Chronicle* announced a "rainbow of peace and reconstruction." Its topic was the much-heralded People's Congress, advertised as a dialogue between the Party and the Masses, a dramatic manifestation—if manifestation was needed—of the Comrade Leader's profound commitment to consultation and the democratic process. The editorial referred to a national crisis, but the nature of that crisis was not spelled out. "We are conceding in the spirit of self-criticism that the Party has made errors in the process of reconstructing the society." Nevertheless, given the magnitude of the task the Party had set itself, it was inevitable that a few errors should have been made here and there. Still, ". . . seen in its proper perspective, the progress which Guyana has made from the Crisis Years to the new Socialist Constitution is epic and unprecedented." What that perspective was they did not say. I put the newspaper aside and watched the guinea fowl maunder about the hotel lawn. For a change, it was not raining. The Americans rose in a group and left the patio together. I hurried out after them, assuming that most of them were headed for the Georgetown Magistrates Court. For on this sunny morning of peace and reconstruction, Charles Beikman would be making an appearance there: he was the Temple member held in connection with the knife killings of Linda Amos and her children in the sect's Georgetown sanctuary.

A crowd was gathered around the gates of the courthouse, a modest and fusty relic of Empire. A television camera, swaying above the heads, lent an air of importance to the scene. Beikman, the star of the show, had not yet arrived. I went up to the first-floor balcony overlooking the street. The American journalists were gathered here. My Graham Greene friend was not, however, among them. They had formed themselves into a laager, unapproachable and impenetrable. I was beginning to discover that Jonestown was a closed journalistic world, cultic in its self-protection and secrecy. Intruders like myself were barely tolerated.

A young white man, his arm in a cast, his shirt undone, appeared in the courtyard below. His appearance raised a flutter of excitement. Some of the Americans raced down the stairs and surrounded him.

"Who's he?" I asked.

"Beikman's son," a Guyanese journalist said.

The young man appeared on the balcony, his escorts scribbling.

"How did you break your arm?"

"Have you seen your father? Have you spoken to him? How's he bearing up?"

"Do you have any idea what his defense is going to be?"

Beikman's son mumbled his replies. I gathered he was not being excessively forthcoming.

In due course Beikman himself arrived. We crowded into the courtroom. The Americans engulfed the Guyanese lawyers. Beikman sat quietly in the dock, apparently oblivious to the surrounding confusion. He was a well-built man of middle age, an ex-Marine. Rumor had it that for all practical purposes, he was illiterate—and fanatically devoted to Jim Jones. He sat there, absolutely still, staring straight ahead of him.

Silence was requested: the court was in session.

It soon became obvious that nothing of substance was going to happen, that this was to be a sparring session between the defense lawyers and the Court. Traffic noises poured through the open windows. It was difficult to catch the drift of even what little was going on. The head of the defense team was doing most of the talking. Beikman, he was saying, had not been given adequate time and facilities to prepare his defense. Witnesses who might have been able to testify in behalf of his client had been allowed to leave Guyana. The police had been holding other potential witnesses, keeping them incommunicado. How, he wanted to know, could the accused be said to have a fair hearing under these circumstances?

The magistrate asked how many witnesses he would like to call upon.

"How can I say that until I have interviewed them?" There were at least two he could think of . . . but how was it possible to be certain at this stage? If the police felt there was a danger that the witnesses might be suborned, it was their duty to take action against the suborners; but it was not their duty to keep witnesses away from him and his client. "Police have no property in a witness. This is an absolute abuse of the Constitution. There could be no greater abuse, really. . . ."

Fat leather-bound books were consulted, judgments read out. It was all very tedious. Most of the Americans, I noticed, had ceased taking notes, I listened to the traffic noises, catching occasional words, occasional phrases.

A Guyanese journalist provided me with a whispered commentary on the dramatis personae. (He worked for the *Mirror,* the PPP newspaper. The *Mirror* had a hard time of it. It was not infrequently reduced to a single, barely legible sheet. Censorship was indirect. Newsprint was rigidly controlled by the Government, doled out in the most niggardly quantities to any who opposed it. But lack of newsprint was not the sole problem faced by the *Mirror.* The paper was produced on an antediluvian press because the more modern machinery they had acquired several years before lay rusting on the docks: they had been refused an import license. The *Mirror,* incidentally, had, on a couple of occasions before the disaster, requested that one of its correspondents be allowed to visit Jonestown. Permission had not been given.) The magistrate, I was informed, had once been Attorney General of Grenada. He was tipped to become a judge. The spokesman for the defense team was closely associated with the PNC. His Indian assistant was a big landlord. He had been with the PPP until 1955, when he defected to the PNC—or, rather, to the faction that was to become the PNC. A third member of the defense team was an adviser to the Government on constitutional issues and a well-known radio propagandist in its behalf—Guyana does not have television.

"Everybody you see here is a Burnham man. I want to find out why they're acting for Beikman. I also want to find out where the money for the defense is coming from, who is paying and why."

The *Mirror* journalist's lively eyes danced about the room; his nostrils twitched.

I looked at Beikman. He remained still and expressionless. He could not, I was sure, hear much of the transactions. Now and then he would blink. It was the only sign of life he showed. It was as if what was going on in that courtroom had nothing to do with him. He had lived for so long in a unique world with its specialized codes, loyalties and visions, its own peculiar sights and sounds, that, more than likely, none of this made a great deal of sense to him. Trickles of sweat shone down the defense spokesman's cheeks and the sides of his neck. His Indian assistant fought off with a start a fly that had settled on his nose. Traffic noise filled the brown room. Beikman somnambulistically shifted his position. The movement caught the magistrate's attention. He interrupted the defense spokesman's flow.

"The accused might trip over, injure himself and sue the Government of Guyana for damages . . ."

The court laughed. Beikman responded with the suggestion of a smile. Straightening himself, he leaned forward and whispered in the ear of the Indian assistant.

It was the morning's most dramatic event.

I went out to the balcony. The crowd had gone from the gate and the city was sunk in midmorning torpor. Guyanese justice had already played a fatal part in the Jonestown drama. It had been through a full-dress rehearsal in the Stoen child-custody battle. Its performance left no room for hope.

> I, Timothy Oliver Stoen, hereby acknowledge that in April 1971 I entreated my beloved Pastor, James W. Jones, to sire a child by my wife, Grace Lucy (Grech) Stoen, who had previously, at my insistence, reluctantly but graciously consented thereto. James W. Jones agreed to do so reluctantly after I explained that I very much wished to raise a child, but was unable, after

extensive attempts, to sire any myself. My reason for requesting James W. Jones to do this is that I wanted my child to be fathered, if not by me, by the most compassionate, honest and courageous human being the world contains. The child, John Victor Stoen, was born on January 25th 1972. I am privileged beyond words to have the responsibility for caring for him, and I undertake this task humbly with the steadfast hope that said child will become a devoted follower of Jesus Christ and be instrumental in beginning God's kingdom on earth, as has been his wonderful natural father. I declare under penalty of perjury that the foregoing is true and correct.

This curious document bore Timothy Stoen's signature and was witnessed by Marceline Jones, Jim Jones's wife. In a letter to one of his Guyanese ministerial friends, written some time in late 1977, Jones gave his own version of the affair:

Some years ago one of the District Attorneys of California who was a member of our church . . . asked me to respond to his wife's many sexual overtures to me, because he feared that she was capable of the most insidious treason to both the organization and the socialist cause, if she met with further rebuff. I cannot describe how much I was repulsed by the idea, but after consultation with my wife of nearly thirty years, and the church's central committee . . . it was collectively agreed that because of this woman's powerful, reactionary family connections, this project be undertaken. She herself appeared to idolize me, but the fickleness of self-centered love is such that any rebuff from me was met with utter hostility—not simply to myself, that would have been of no consequence—but to the collective as well. Out of this unholy union came a beautiful son . . . she had resisted all suggestions of abortion, and went so far as to threaten subversion against socialism unless she were allowed to keep the child. It was a nightmare. The boy is undoubtedly my child; the resemblance is absolutely convincing. That is why she gave me no difficulty when I requested that he go to Guyana. She signed legal authorization for him to come to this country. Her husband also signed such authorization. In addition, he stated . . . that he had asked me to sire a child for him, thinking that if the document ever had to be revealed, it might be more easily understood by non-socialists in that light. Now my counselors, among them Mr. Charles Garry, advise me that unless I stay here in Guyana with my son I shall lose him. I would rather die than see this child sent to wither in the environment this woman now lives in, with a white, southern bigot, and her avowedly racist parents. I would rather die than accept a demand for the return of the child. I pledge to you that myself and all my people will die protecting your borders—we would far rather die defending this socialist nation than return to the sadistic fascist land we have left. . . .

It was in 1970, immediately after she had married, that Grace Stoen, at the insistence of her husband, Timothy, had joined the People's Temple. Timothy, a bright, energetic lawyer, was in his early thirties; Grace had not yet turned twenty. Timothy rose rapidly through the ranks of the church. Jones could say with truth that he did nothing either with respect to the church or with respect to his own personal legal affairs without first consulting Timothy Stoen. Grace also rose to a position of importance in the hierarchy, becoming head bookkeeper. It was in 1976, her marriage in difficulties, that she decided she had had enough.

"I will never forget the night Grace Stoen left the church as long as I live," a Temple member (who remained a loyalist after the catastrophe) has written. ". . . Jim looked like life and breath had been stolen from him. . . ."

Toward the end of the year, John Victor was shipped out to Guyana. Grace Stoen, meanwhile, was suing for divorce and custody of her child. Some months later the Temple had an even greater shock when Timothy Stoen too defected; a shock compounded when he joined his estranged wife in her battle for John Victor. In August 1977 a San Francisco judge awarded custody to Grace Stoen, ordering Jones to produce the child and appear in court.

Grace Stoen's lawyer flew out to Guyana in September. His arrival in Georgetown precipitated a major crisis. The radio mes-

sages from Guyana to Temple headquarters in San Francisco be-
came "frenzied and hysterical." An ultimatum went out to the
Government of Guyana: unless judicial proceedings over John
Victor were in some way halted by the Guyanese courts, the com-
munity at Jonestown would "extinguish" itself in a mass suicide.
The case immediately went into limbo.

It is interesting to trace the passage of these and related events
in the year or so preceding the suicides/murders. This is perhaps
best done in the form of a log.

August 30, 1977: The State Department told the American Embassy in Guyana that Jeffrey Haas, the lawyer retained by the
Stoens, was coming to Guyana with a California court order for
the release from Jonestown of John Victor Stoen.

September 8, 1977: The embassy reported an unsuccessful attempt by Haas to serve the court order on Jones. It had been his
hope that Guyanese officials would respect the California order
and enforce it. That was not to be. The case, it turned out, would
have to be fought all the way through the Guyanese courts. Haas
chartered an aircraft to Jonestown. Maria Katsaris told him that
Jones had been absent for two days. That was a lie.

September 9, 1977: The embassy reported a second futile attempt by Haas to serve the order at Jonestown. On this occasion,
the communards behaved with extreme hostility, tearing down
the notices he tried to pin up.

September 19, 1977: The embassy told the State Department that
the Stoen case had entered "the political arena." This was ob-
structing its progress. The embassy had raised the matter with
the Foreign Minister and the Prime Minister.

September 22, 1977: The Government of Guyana said it would
act on court orders issued on September 10 "in response to the
Embassy's note requesting due process."

September 23, 1977: The Stoen hearings were being held *in
camera.* Embassy representatives were refused permission to attend.

October 12, 1977: A Guyanese judge ruled against a motion
submitted by the Stoens' local lawyers on October 6.

December 8, 1977: Congressman Ryan expressed his concern about the Stoen case.

January 3, 1978: The Stoens arrived in Guyana.

January 5, 1978: The State Department asked the embassy if it could arrange for an observer to be present at another hearing arranged for January 7.

January 9, 1978: The embassy told the State Department that the consul was not allowed to be at the hearing.

January 11, 1978: The Stoens had their visas reduced from one month to two weeks.

January 14, 1978: The embassy sent two diplomatic notes to the Government of Guyana complaining of the "pressure" being put on the Stoens to shorten their stay and of "the apparent intervention of the Government of Guyana into the judicial process in the Stoen case." On that same day the Stoens were ordered to leave Guyana within twenty-four hours. No reasons were given. The Government, however, relented after a direct appeal by the embassy to the Foreign Minister.

January 18, 1978: The Stoens left Guyana, their efforts having got them nowhere. At the airport they were harassed by Temple members and their lives were threatened.

February 7, 1978: Timothy Stoen visited the State Department.

February 14, 1978: The State Department asked the embassy to find out when a decision could be expected in the Stoen case.

February 15, 1978: The embassy replied that delays were not "unusual."

February 17, 1978: The State Department announced that Marceline Jones (Jim Jones's wife) had advised the American Government to stay out of the Stoen case.

May 12, 1978: Timothy Stoen petitioned the Prime Minister of Guyana. He asked him to do whatever he could to prevent the abuse of human rights at Jonestown.

May 30, 1978: The free-lance journalist Kathy Hunter was deported from Guyana.

June 6, 1978: The embassy expressed its anxiety "that Jonestown is beyond the effective jurisdiction of Guyanese authorities."

June 15, 1978: A defector's affidavit outlining the terrors of Jonestown and the plans that existed for a mass suicide was sent to the State Department.

June 20, 1978: Two American journalists employed by the *National Enquirer,* sent out to Guyana to do a story on Jonestown, had their visas cancelled by the Guyanese. The State Department advised the embassy to exercise caution over Jonestown. They fear that its activities might be construed as "interference with the privacy and religious freedom of American citizens."

August 10, 1978: The Guyanese judge handling the Stoen case decided to drop it and return it to the discretion of the Chief Justice. He complained of "persistent efforts of an extra-legal or opprobrious nature . . . intended to influence the outcome of the proceedings."

September 8, 1978: The State Department urged the embassy to impress—informally—on the Guyanese the need to act with due process in the Stoen case.

September 23, 1978: At a press conference in Georgetown, Mark Lane asserted that there was a conspiracy directed by the American Government to destroy the People's Temple.

October 3, 1978: Timothy Stoen told the State Department that he was prepared to rescue his son by force if necessary.

October 10, 1978: The Stoen case was assigned to another judge. It was now more than a year since it had first entered the Guyanese courts.

November 14, 1978: The Ryan delegation arrived in Guyana.

November 18, 1978: Along with more than nine hundred other people, John Victor Stoen died at Jonestown. The case was finally closed.

In this log we have an X-ray of the Jonestown tragedy in its Guyanese aspect. The infected areas stand out clearly; the diagnosis is self-evident.

It was Sunday morning. Only a handful of the hotel's patrons were out on the patio. A front-page photograph in the *Chronicle*

showed a group of black girls dressed in military uniform, shoul-
dering rifles. They were being addressed by their Comrade
Leader, who was also in military uniform. He was talking to them
about Human Rights, trying to clear up certain misconceptions
they might be harboring on the subject.

At about eleven o'clock I set off with a newly made acquaintance for a golf tournament to which he had invited me. I did not
care for my companion: I was a little wary of the attentions he
had been paying me during the past few days—offering to take
me everywhere; obsequiously placing himself at my disposal.
What he wanted in return was not yet clear. I had grown to dislike
his narrow, shiny face, his pinched lips, his spiky, yellowing teeth.
He was a "businessman" of some sort, entangled in a number of
small-scale ventures all of which, I suspected, were shady. His
voice was simultaneously rasping and wheedling. Publicly, he was
a vocal supporter of the Government; privately, he railed at it.
"Man," he had said to me the first time we met, "you have to have
the ability to get on with all kinds. You scratch my back and I
scratch yours. That's the only way. You understand me?" He
jabbed me in the ribs. "We all got to get our hands dirty, eh? You
can't be a saint and get on in this Guyana of ours."

I was having my first glimpse of the Georgetown suburbs. For
mile upon mile the seawall was daubed with referendum slogans.
Indeed, slogans and posters seemed to cover every available surface—even, I noticed, cowsheds and the tops of water towers.
One stood out: "WE WILL DIE FOR BURNHAM." That, I gathered,
was the handiwork of dissident students who, in the dead of
night, had been dragged out of their dormitories at gunpoint and
brought to the seawall. The entire countryside had been defaced
and disfigured. It defied comprehension. Each splash of blood-
red paint seemed designed to obliterate a little more reason, a
little more intelligence. Day and night, for weeks on end, some
savage instinct had been at work. This vandalized landscape was
its monument. I stared at flooded, wasted fields; at ragged boys
tending ragged cattle; at broken-down houses and huts. To our
left, the brown ocean, held at bay by the seawall, glinted and
gleamed.

"You're paying the hotel in foreign currency, not so?"

I looked at the narrow, bony face; at the spiky teeth bared in an obsequious half-smile.

"Why give all that good money to the Government of Guyana, eh? It doesn't make sense."

He jabbed me in the ribs.

"I should have thought of it before. But it's only this morning it hit me. I thought, 'Poor bastard. How they must be ripping him off at the hotel!' You understand me?"

"I understand."

He glanced at me out of the corner of his eye, a caricature of petty crookedness. Reaching into his jacket pocket, he took out a fat roll of Guyanese dollar bills tied with a rubber band. He tossed it into my lap.

I returned the money to him. "I had to sign a currency declaration form when I came in."

"Sure . . . sure. But you didn't tell them the whole amount, I bet." He winked at me.

"I did."

"That won't make problems for you. If they try anything, just grease their palms a little." He laughed.

How calmly he treated the prospect of my getting into difficulties.

He tried again to give me the roll of bills; again I gave it back.

"Think about it."

"No."

He replaced the money in his pocket, setting his face away from me.

What upset me was not that he wanted my foreign currency: that was a natural-enough desire in a country like Guyana. It was the completeness of his corruption, his degeneracy. He was an exhalation of the moral decay I could sense all around me. The society had robbed him of his humanity. It allowed virtually no one to be fully human. I remembered the passengers on the aircraft who had plundered the toilets. He mirrored his country.

We left the coast road, turning inland. Soon we were surrounded by sugar-cane fields. Irrigation canals reflected the sky.

The asphalt was crumbling and potholed. After about a mile or so, the paved road turned into an uneven dirt track. This was an Indian area and therefore neglected. (In Guyana, lines of neat brick houses and properly paved roads invariably signal a colony of Government supporters.) Half-naked children played in muddy ditches. Many of them would attend school irregularly, economic assets too valuable to squander. Old men reclined in hammocks slung under the houses. Women squatted in muddy yards, scrubbing pots and pans. We moved slowly, gingerly negotiating the road's treacheries. Mangy dogs yapped in our wake.

The golf course, a relic of the displaced planter regime, was set amidst the cane fields. Before the sugar estates were nationalized, the road leading to it had been well maintained. Since then, nature had been given a free hand (Mr. Burnham does not play golf), and its deterioration had been swift. Golf and those who played it had no place in a society that was moving inexorably toward socialism. It seemed to be only a matter of time before the golf course, marooned in what had become a rural slum, followed the Georgetown Turf Club into extinction. The clubhouse was a modest wooden pavilion. Gathered here with their aging cars and their children (nearly all the children were infants: most of the older ones were safely abroad) were the remnants of the Guyanese middle class. Ruined people in a ruined setting, seeking after pleasures which could no longer be found, pretending to enjoy themselves.

The shaded veranda on the upper floor of the pavilion was cooled by a wind blowing over the cane fields. The wind carried with it the languorous smell of cow dung. Card tables had been set out on the veranda. Inside, matrons doled out lunch on paper plates. A little rum and beer were offered. Conversation was light and drifting. The golf went largely unnoticed. Time passed slowly. The tedium of a tropical Sunday hung heavily in the warm air.

"You should visit the interior," someone said to me. "It's really quite beautiful. Rivers, waterfalls, mountains, savannas. Few Guyanese know what a beautiful country they live in."

"I suppose it's our Caribbean mentality," someone else said. "The way we crowd together on the coastal strip, we might as well be living on one of the islands."

"I think we're a little afraid of the interior," the first speaker speculated. "We're not a pioneering people. We don't want to make. We want what's already been made, what's to hand. That's one of the sad aspects of this Jonestown catastrophe. I was hoping he could show us what could be done, take the fear out of it. Now it's all darkness again."

She had, I discovered, actually paid a brief visit to Jonestown —the first Guyanese I had met who had done so. She had gone there, she said, with the wife of the regional minister. Her visit had lasted only about two hours, and looking back on it, she was beginning to appreciate how carefully orchestrated it must have been.

"It was clearly a state within a state—all those guards they had posted at the gates and so on. No stranger could just walk in. That disturbed me a little at the time. Also, it was obvious that neither my friend nor her husband, the regional minister, had the faintest idea of what was really going on in there."

All the same, she could not deny that she had been "impressed" —very impressed.

"I wrote 'fantastic' in the guest book, and I think I meant it."

She recalled the long drive (about three miles) from the main gate up to the settlement proper, lined on both sides with flourishing cultivation—mainly cassava plants.

"The cassava was a big thing with them. They said they were doing all kinds of experiments with it." She was given a kind of fudge they had made with it.

She was taken around the hospital nursery.

"It was really well equipped. Better than anything in our hospitals. They had rows of cribs, piles of diapers and sheets and towels. It was a beautiful setup, all ready for babies not yet born."

They told her of their powerful radio communication with the outside world, stressing its medical function: they had, they said, been able to carry out complicated medical procedures by hooking up with specialists in the United States and the United Kingdom. She had observed none of the symbols associated with conventional religion and had questioned Jones about this. He had replied that the commune itself represented no particular orthodoxy, that everyone there was free to worship—or not to worship—as they pleased. Throughout their interview, he had been balanced, cool and articulate.

"He was a very handsome man. Swarthy. With jet-black hair and high cheekbones. I would say there was a definite touch of the tarbrush there." (Jones said that he had Cherokee Indian blood, inherited from his mother's side of the family. This claim has been disputed, usually dismissed as another of the lies he told in order to enhance his "mystique.")

Everyone she had met had struck her as being happy and contented, proud of what they were doing.

"As we were leaving, a woman with a lovely voice was singing 'Amazing Grace.' It was very moving to hear that in the middle of nowhere."

That was not the limit of her contact with People's Temple. Linda Amos had come to her house in Georgetown on at least two occasions. Once she had brought Jim Jones's black adopted son along with her. He had spent most of his time exclaiming over the house and its color scheme. This had puzzled her because, though the house was nice enough, there was nothing specially remarkable about either it or its color scheme. Amos had come to seek the advice of her husband, an expert in jungle lore and agricultural matters.

"I believe she wanted to talk to him about mango trees. They wanted to plant some in Jonestown, and she had come to find out what were the most suitable varieties for the conditions out there. She was quite a thorough lady."

Amos was polite and friendly but, at the same time, curiously impersonal, reticent about anything concerning herself, livening up only when the conversation turned to the commune and what it was trying to do. My informant had not felt entirely comfortable with her. Perhaps as a reward for the advice her husband had given, they were invited to dinner at the Georgetown headquarters.

"That was a rather strange occasion, as I remember—although there was nothing specific you could point to. It was as if . . . as if you had turned up too early for a date and had caught your hosts on the wrong foot, not quite ready to begin entertaining you, but too polite to say so. It's difficult to explain. The atmosphere wasn't sinister. Just out of focus."

The other people present had carefully kept themselves in the background, drifting in and out, their behavior discouraging too much communication. Amos, friendly but impersonal as ever, had done most of the talking. She could not remember what they had talked about. At the time, it was just one more boring social encounter arising out of her husband's work.

"I don't believe the mystery of that place and those people will ever be solved. I *saw* Jonestown with my own eyes. I *talked* to no less a person than Jim Jones. He seemed sane. I was impressed by him and what he was doing with those people nobody else wanted. Was it all really just one big hoax? Is it possible to be fooled so completely?"

The afternoon had become yellower. She gazed out over the cane fields.

"I'm sorry it had to happen here," she said quietly. "I am sorry for Guyana. It makes me feel quite ashamed."

Tony (the man who had brought me) called me over to his card table. He introduced me to his brother and his brother's English wife. Her name was Sharon. I had noticed Sharon earlier, my attention drawn by her sickly, unhappy face and her air of detachment from the noise and laughter surrounding her. She responded inconsequentially to the introduction, turning away to look at her two children who were squabbling nearby. Her scolding having brought them to order, she frowned at her cards, picked one at random and tossed it on the table. It was all done with deliberate carelessness. The play brought a mild rebuke from her husband. He was ivory-colored and plump. His fleshy cheeks were blistered with the scars of pimples. He cupped and

caressed his private parts. Sharon shrugged off the rebuke, blink-
ing dully into the bright, dusty afternoon. Her green sleeveless
dress exposed pale, thin arms that had been ravaged by mosquito
bites. I reckoned her to be in her middle twenties—younger even.

Tony mentioned that I lived in London.

Sharon looked at me with interest. "Which part of London?"

I told her.

She fell silent, staring at her cards. "I used to live in Barnet,"
she said after a while. "Barnet's a lovely place. I used to work
there in a hairdressing salon." She gestured at the landscape.
"This is quite a change from that." She fabricated a small laugh.

I murmured agreement. Her husband, kneading his private
parts, watched her. Sharon picked up a shawl that had fallen on
the floor beside her and draped it across her shoulders.

"What you should tell him," her husband said, "is that I rescued
you from a hairdressing salon." He looked at me. "She used to
wash hair."

She drew the shawl more securely about her shoulders. "I had
no idea it would be like this. None at all. He never told me he was
bringing me out to the jungle."

Her husband reached forward to touch her; she recoiled from
him.

"I didn't know I was coming to a jungle," Sharon repeated.

"We ought to be going home, Sharon," he said. "It's getting
late. The children . . ."

The sky was beginning to cloud over. It looked like rain.

"I don't want to go home. I want to dance, have some fun." She
tapped her feet, shook her shoulders. "Let's go someplace where
we can all dance." She threw down her unplayed cards.

"The children, Sharon. You're a mother now. Remember. . . ."

"I don't want to remember," Sharon said. "I want to forget. I
want to dance."

"Why don't you all come over to my place?" Tony suggested
uneasily.

We drove through the twilight to Georgetown, to Tony's house.
It was drizzling when we arrived. Rum punches were served.

Sharon put on the record player, kicked off her shoes and began to dance by herself in a corner. Her husband had disappeared— presumably to take care of the children. The drizzle turned to heavy rain. Heavy drops slanted past the wide-open windows.

"Dance with me!" Sharon extended her pale, mosquito-ravaged arms toward me. She was a little light-headed from the rum punches.

I told her I did not dance. She came to my chair and led me back to her corner. Her arms encircled my waist. She pressed herself hard against me, whispering into my ear.

"Take me away with you! You must take me away from here!"

I tried to extricate myself from her embrace, but she refused to let me go.

"He lied to me. He told me it was paradise." Her feet continued to beat out the dance rhythms. Her body beneath the green dress felt light and frail. "I will die if I stay here, and I don't want to die in Guyana. I have nightmares about those people dying in the jungle. Every night I dream it's my turn to drink the poison. . . ."

I managed to free myself. She swayed unsteadily, laughing and crying, leaning against the wall for support.

The rain beat steadily on the roof. It was, after all, a little like Graham Greene.

From the *Guyana Chronicle:*

TALKING ABOUT EDUCATION

Today on station GBS Part 1 of the REVOLUTIONARY SPEECH DAY held last Friday at Queen's College with a Star Studded Cast in String Band and Combo—Comrade Avis Joseph, Music Mistress, on Saxophone . . . Tomorrow Part 2 . . . of the Queen's College Revolutionary Speech Day . . . The Comrade Headmaster Clarence Trotz' Annual Report . . . to the large gathering of Comrade Parents, Students and Staff will be presented. The School Orchestra plays "If I Were A Rich Man" from *Fiddler On The Roof* and for SPOKEN WORD—Elocution—there will be extracts from THE BANANA MAN and FREEDOM.

I closed the newspaper and watched the guinea fowl peck at the crumbs that had fallen around my table.

Later that morning, the man at the Ministry of Information exuded charm, goodwill and amiability. He was, he said, at my service; ready to help in any way that he could. It pained him to have kept me waiting and he sincerely hoped that I had not been inconvenienced by the delay. He was well aware what busy men we journalists were. During the last couple of weeks, he had been run off his feet, become a stranger to his bed, his wife, his children. He hoped—ha! ha!—that there would be no more mass suicides in Guyana for some time to come. They gave rise to far too much work. Not nice to be making jokes, he knew. Very serious business. Still, laughter was the best medicine when you got down to it. Laughter alone kept you sane in trying times. Guyanese had a great sense of humor. One of the best. He supposed I must have discovered that by now.

Not all the foreign journalists had appreciated how difficult it was for him—for his Ministry, for Guyana—to cope with their demands. He could tell at a glance that I was not like the rest of them. He had had a really rough time with some of those journalists. They would lose their tempers all the time. Sometimes they would come storming into his office—this very office where I was now—and begin to shout and scream at him. It was terrible the way some of them had carried on. They behaved as if Guyana were at fault for being poor and not having the kind of facilities to which they were accustomed in the United States and Europe. Instead of sympathizing with Guyana in its hour of tribulation, they cursed and ranted. Was it Guyana's fault that nine hundred Americans had come and killed themselves on its territory? They did not understand that the country was doing its modest best in a most unusual and delicate situation. How glad he was to run at last into someone like myself, someone to whom he could unburden himself.

But he was talking far too much . . . I must be a busy man. What could he do for me? How could he be of help? An interview with the Prime Minister? Of course. Of course. He would put my name down on the waiting list straightaway. Naturally, he couldn't absolutely promise anything. It wasn't in his power to do so. The Prime Minister was an extremely busy and overworked man. Just suppose he was not available—would I like to see his deputy, Dr. Reid, instead? I would? Wonderful! My name would be entered on the Reid list straightaway. What else could he do? A look at Jonestown? But of course. My name would go down on the Jonestown waiting list straightaway. What else? A visit to a National Service Camp? But why did I want to go to a National Service Camp? What did that have to do with the People's Temple? He wasn't too sure how that could be arranged. All the same, he would see what he could do. Anything to be of help. What else? Did I have sufficient background material on Guyana? No? That could be remedied instantly. Here were brochures, magazines, pamphlets. Take one. Take two. Take them all! What else? Nothing? Was that all? It had indeed been a rare privilege to deal with me. Yes, sir. A privilege and a pleasure. I could return anytime I wished. He was at my disposal. No, no, he didn't want thanks. Simply doing his job. That was all. I realized that the American public relations consultant hired by the Government had been hard at work.

Out on the sun-struck street a wiry black man, his eyes hidden behind dark glasses, trailed me back to the hotel. At lunch, he occupied the table next to mine on the terrace. When, to test my suspicions, I went inside to have coffee, he followed shamelessly. I smiled at him. He remained inscrutable behind his dark glasses. So, I was being spied on. Had someone put him on to me? Or was he merely working free-lance—a casual informer who had attached himself to me for want of something better to do? Whatever the answer, it was an undeserved honor. I went out into the lobby, dogged at a discreet distance by my spy, who now took the trouble of buying himself a newspaper, which he pretended to read.

Christmas was in the air at the Pegasus. Some young people were hammering together a gingerbread cottage in one corner of the lobby. Tinsel sparkled. The sound of carols was everywhere.

That evening—and all evenings until Christmas—Comrades Angelo and Sebastiani would be entertaining on guitar and piano in the Rum and Raleigh Pub. The Pegasus—"Your Festive Place in Guyana"—was trying its best. That afternoon, the management, in keeping with the spirit of the season, was going to perform its annual rite of charity: they would be feeding and handing out presents to a collection of Guyana's aged destitute. Piles of brightly wrapped and ribboned boxes and parcels were being taken out on wheelbarrows to the terrace.

A hand fell heavily on my shoulder. It belonged to the American public relations consultant. He looked harried. Beads of sweat shone on his forehead.

"You are in luck. You are one of those who have been chosen to interview the Deputy Prime Minister. Meet me on the front steps of the hotel in exactly one hour." He dashed away, disappearing into one of the elevators.

My spy, lurking behind his newspaper, watched interestedly.

At four o'clock I joined the little journalistic delegation gathered on the front steps. Buses were drawing up in the parking lot. Each was disgorging a flock of the lame and the halt: the aged destitute of Guyana were assembling for the festivity to be held in their honor. The PR man checked a sheet of paper with a list of our names. He frowned.

"We've got an extra person," he said, counting us.

"That would be my wife," one of the journalists replied. "She's coming with me."

"She's not down on my list," the PR man said.

"I tell you she's with me. We're working together." The journalist spoke stubbornly, his eyes glazing with truculence.

I had seen this couple several times, but we had never spoken. They were a formidable pair. Rumor had it that they were planning to write the definitive book about Jonestown. The man was lanky, slightly stoop-shouldered and mustachioed. He moved proprietorially about the hotel, radiating intensity and impa-

tience, his small, narrow eyes set hard with self-absorbed pre-
occupation. His wife, short, round and plump, clung to his
presence, always clutching a reporter's notebook. She radiated a
mulish intensity. I had never seen them apart from each other;
nor had I ever seen them talking to anyone but each other. If you
happened to pass too close, they would lower their voices or stop
talking altogether until you were out of earshot. If they happened
to be working on their notes, they would so position their bodies
that the papers would be hidden from view. Their fractiousness
terrorized the hotel staff.

Only the night before I had witnessed a small but embarrassing
scene they had created in one of the hotel's restaurants. They had
arrived to find the table they had reserved occupied by a Guyanese couple. "Intolerable!" the man had told the disconcerted
headwaiter in a voice that carried. "This is absolutely intolerable,
an infringement of my rights. I won't stand for this sort of treatment. I demand you do something about it." The headwaiter,
admitting his fault, apologized profusely for the oversight. If they
would delay their dinner for half an hour, he would have a table
ready for them. The man would not compromise. He had reserved the table. It was his right to have it. The headwaiter, looking quite wretched, went across to the Guyanese couple. He bent
low; he whispered agitatedly. The Guyanese couple departed.
Man and wife sat down, glancing about them contentedly.

"You should have told me there would be two of you," the PR
man was saying. "A list is a list."

"We work as a team," the journalist said. His wife, rocklike in
her silent tenacity, stared at the cover of her reporter's notebook.

I watched the aged destitute toil across the parking lot.

The PR man gave in. We climbed into a van supplied by the
Guyana Broadcasting Service. But our troubles were not over.

"What are we doing in this van?" the journalist asked. "Where
are we being taken?"

"To the studios of the GBS," the PR man replied.

"I protest."

Somebody groaned.

"I was not informed that this interview was going to be broadcast. This is totally unethical, an infringement of my rights. I
demand an explanation."

"Who said anything about the interview being broadcast?" the
PR man asked. He mopped his sweating forehead.

"I demand an explanation. This is outrageous. My employers
specifically forbid this kind of thing. My wife and I demand to
know why we are being taken to the studios of the GBS."

"It's like this," the PR man said, much as if he were about to
start reading a bedtime story. He explained that there was nothing in the least sinister about the press conference's taking place
in the studios of the GBS. It just so happened that after the press
conference—which, incidentally, had only been granted as a
favor by the extremely busy and diligent Deputy Prime Minister
—Dr. Reid was scheduled to record a program that had nothing
to do with Jim Jones or Jonestown. We were meeting at the studios to suit his convenience.

"I worked on Watergate," the journalist said.

"This has nothing to do with Watergate," the PR man said.

"I feel," the journalist said, looking at his wife for confirmation
(which he got), "that we should have a statement of some kind in
writing."

The PR man swore softly.

At the GBS studios, the journalist stalked around the room into which we were ushered. He scrutinized the walls, looked
under the chairs, gazed grimly into the untenanted technicians'
cubicle.

At last, man and wife consented to sit down.

She stiffened suddenly, sniffing the air. "I smell cigarette
smoke." Her voice was faint.

Her husband was on his feet instantly, addressing the room.
"My wife, I would have you gentlemen know, is highly allergic to
cigarette smoke. She has extremely delicate sinuses." His eyes fell
on the culprit. "I demand that you put out that cigarette immediately."

"Could I have that in writing?" the culprit asked.

"This is outrageous. It simply shouldn't be allowed . . ."

The door opened. We all rose to our feet to greet the Deputy Prime Minister of the Cooperative Socialist Republic of Guyana. The cigarette was forgotten. Dr. Reid beamed at us. The PR man beamed at Dr. Reid and at us.

"Gentlemen . . . gentlemen . . ." Dr. Reid said, waving his briefcase, "do sit. . . ."

We sat down. Dr. Reid was dressed in a conservative rather than revolutionary mode—he wore a suit. His lined, chocolate-colored face was adorned with a fringe of gray beard. His avuncular affability foretold the pointlessness of the meeting. It was to be a well-tutored exercise in the art of public relations. Nothing more.

("Testimony from some witnesses," remarked the overcautious and coy U.S. Congressional Report on Jonestown, "suggests that support extended to the People's Temple by Deputy Prime Minister and Minister of Development Ptolemy Reid was born of an ideological compatibility with and endorsement of the Temple's Socialist philosophy. . . . While such support was exploited in the sense that it had the ultimate effect of furthering People's Temple objectives, it did not appear to be generated for illegal reasons." The coy caution, however, came with a caveat. "In reference to these findings regarding the relationship of the Government of Guyana to the People's Temple, the Staff Investigative Group was precluded from confirming or dispelling various allegations by the refusal of the Guyanese Government to meet and talk with the Group.")

Dr. Reid declared himself ready to answer all questions that might be put to him.

What was the Guyanese Government planning to do with Jonestown?

They were, he replied, considering a number of options. They had reached no firm decision as yet.

Had the Jonestown disaster affected the Government's ideas on the agricultural development of the interior? Had it caused any second thoughts?

None at all. Development plans for the interior would continue along the same lines. The Government was not going to be deterred by one setback. Jones's program had been a good one. It had been entirely consistent with the thinking of the Government of Guyana on the subject. Nothing had changed. As far as he was concerned, it was business as usual.

Would the Government continue to import foreigners to assist in the execution of its programs for the Interior?

Naturally it would. Guyana's population was small; the Interior was big. There would always be a need for foreigners. The Guyanese Government had never been afraid of letting people come in—unless there was something very much against them. Even now there were all kinds of groups in the country working peaceably, assisting in its development.

Could he name some of those groups?

Sure. Guyana had imported Jamaicans. (The Comrade Deputy Prime Minister could have been more specific—he could have mentioned that most of these Jamaicans were Rastafarians.) They had also brought in settlers from other Caribbean islands. St. Vincent and St. Lucia came immediately to mind. There was a group of Baptists and another connected with the Assembly of God. He couldn't remember them all on the spur of the moment. But there were many. All were law-abiding, hardworking farmers. Guyana was not afraid of outsiders. Jones and the People's Temple had been allowed in on exactly the same conditions and for exactly the same reasons as these other groups. To do agriculture. To help in the development of the Interior. He had been Minister of Agriculture at the time permission was granted to the Temple. They had been given three thousand acres of raw, undeveloped land. (The amount of land leased to the People's Temple is a matter of dispute. Twenty-three thousand acres is the most commonly quoted figure. This is the figure mentioned by the Temple itself. The confusion may be due to legalistic quibbling, possible future options being lumped together with what was actually granted at the time.) They had produced a plan. An excellent plan. That was why they had been allowed to come in.

Had he ever visited Jonestown to look at the work that was being done there?

He had not.

Wasn't that a little strange considering his enthusiasm for the project?

He did not think so. He was a busy man. In any case, he had been transferred from the Ministry of Agriculture. His direct responsibility for such ventures had thereupon ceased.

Would he say that the Government of Guyana had exercised proper jurisdiction over Jonestown? Or had it been, as some would say, allowed to become a state within the State?

The Government of Guyana had done its best. But there were limits to what it could do. We should all know by now how remote the northwestern region was, how cut off it was from the rest of the country. The Guyanese Government had done all it could with its limited resources. Only those ignorant of the difficulties would suggest that it could have done any more than it did.

Was it true that the regional minister had once been refused entry to the commune?

That was, to his knowledge, a fabrication.

Was there any basis to the allegation that the People's Temple had taken part in extra-agricultural activities?

None. How could they? They had come to do agriculture.

Would he completely deny that they had dabbled in the internal politics of Guyana?

It was not impossible that Jones could have taken part in what could be called political activity. But he personally knew nothing about that.

An American journalist who had come in May 1978 to do a story on the People's Temple had been harassed. Mysterious fires broke out at the Pegasus, where she was staying. There were bomb threats. The Guyanese Government, instead of prosecuting the troublemakers, had deported *her*. How did he explain that?

The Government had become concerned about the image of

the hotel. All those fires and bomb threats were giving it a bad name.

Did he have nothing more to say about that?

Nothing.

Was it true that other foreign-led groups played active roles in Guyanese politics?

Name the outside group or groups.

The House of Israel, for example.

He denied that they played any political role.

Why, then, did the House of Israel dress itself up in the Party colors?

That was a mere coincidence. It did not mean anything.

Wasn't that hard to believe?

Not at all. Those colors were also the national colors. They were part of Guyanese culture. The House of Israel must have chosen them for that reason.

(The PR man glared angrily at me—I had asked this last question. "Don't you know the colors of the Guyanese flag?" he asked.)

Had either Dr. Reid or his Government learned any lessons at all from the Jonestown debacle?

Maybe that even religious groups would have to be looked at somewhat more carefully in the future.

No other lessons?

He could think of none.

The Comrade Deputy Prime Minister beamed at us. He picked up his briefcase; he looked at his watch.

Did the gentlemen of the press, he wanted to know, have any more questions?

The gentlemen of the press shook their heads.

Smiling, swinging his briefcase, the Comrade Deputy Prime Minister of the Cooperative Socialist Republic of Guyana rose, thanked us for taking the trouble to come and see him, and went out.

The PR man was still angry with me.

"Why couldn't you ask sensible questions?"

"Give me an example of a sensible question," I said.

He swore under his breath. "You should know what the colors of the Guyanese flag are by now."

"I also happen to know the colors of the PNC."

I could not understand why he was so upset. Was it tiredness? Frustration? How does one begin to present a government like this in a good light? He had been given an impossible task. Perhaps he was slowly discovering that not even the subtle arts of public relations could turn night into day.

At the hotel, my spy was nowhere in sight. To put my mind at rest, I checked my room. Everything was in order. I went down to the terrace. The aged destitute had finished their feasting. They sat quietly, each with a brightly wrapped present, listening to the tinkling steel band. The light of the setting sun glowed on their childish, sated faces.

Later that evening, the reception clerk handed me a note. It was from the PR man. Early the following morning I was to report to Ogle Airfield. I had, he said, been assigned a place on the next flight to Jonestown.

CHAPTER
6

It began badly.

For some reason, my alarm did not go off, and I overslept. I arrived at the airfield (which is on the outskirts of Georgetown) about a half hour after the appointed time. I was relieved to see the aircraft still safely on the ground. Someone else was late—the Government-appointed administrator of Jonestown, who would be acting as our guide and chaperon. My relief did not last long. The Guyanese in charge of the seating arrangements seemed surprised to see me.

"But, man, the plane is already full up. Your place has been taken."

It was my turn to do a little cursing.

He was sympathetic, clucking his tongue. "Wait here," he said.

He walked across to where the party of American journalists had gathered. My heart sank when I saw him returning with the fractious journalist and his wife. What had happened soon became clear. The journalist, swiftly seizing his opportunity, had persuaded the Guyanese to substitute his wife's name for mine. His vulturism angered me; he, for his part, was not in the least apologetic.

"You weren't here at the appointed time," he said fiercely.

"But I'm here now."

"You weren't here at the time they told us to be here. Therefore, so far as I'm concerned, you forfeited your place."

"Rubbish."

"How dare you speak to me like that!"

His wife, reporter's notebook dangling from her fingers, maintained her usual rocklike imperturbability.

"He's certainly here now," the Guyanese observed mildly. "And he was down on the original list."

"He was late."

"I'll have to check this out with the Ministry," he said. He went off to find a telephone.

He returned after about ten minutes smiling at me. "Sorry, lady. But the Ministry says that this gentleman should be the one to go."

"This is outrageous. I protest." The journalist reddened with rage.

"Sorry, sir," the Guyanese said, scratching out his wife's name and reinserting mine. "The Ministry also pointed out that since he is the only representative from the European press present, he should have the chance to go."

The sole representative of the European press! I quite warmed to the Ministry of Information and its sense of fair play.

The journalist turned on me, waving a fist in my face. "You were late."

"I was late."

He danced about me. "So, you admit it, do you? You actually *admit* you were late?"

"I admit it."

Grabbing his wife, he stalked off.

"Yankees!" The Guyanese spat and laughed.

Eventually, the Jonestown administrator arrived. He introduced himself pleasantly, apologizing for having kept us waiting. Politeness seemed to be reaching epidemic proportions among all ranks of Guyanese officialdom. His name was Emerson Simon, and he wore a wide-brimmed straw hat. Seven of us, including Mr. Simon, would be going on the expedition. I sat next to our courteous, straw-hatted chaperon. As the engines revved, the reporter sitting in front of me produced a pocket-sized cassette recorder and began speaking at it.

"It is now nine thirty-six. Have just boarded the twin-engined plane for the flight to Jonestown. Cloudy morning. Hot and humid. . . ."

We took off, heading out toward the brown ocean. The weather was unsettled. We flew into and out of rain-bearing cloud formations, the little plane shuddering and rattling in the turbulence. Soon we were over the rice-growing islands of the Essequibo estuary, shimmering, waterlogged rectangles of cultivation reflecting the cloudy sky. I recalled that one of those islands was supposed to be as big as Barbados. Mr. Simon pulled down the brim of his straw hat. He fell asleep. We turned back toward the land. Jungle replaced the ocean.

". . . as far as the eye can see there is jungle . . . looks pretty forbidding country . . . what a place for them to have come . . ." The reporter droned on.

Rivers glinted light and dark through the canopy of even green. Scattered wisps of cloud hung like puffs of smoke just above the tree tops. "Coming down the Kaituma River is one of my favorite things. It is hard to describe how beautiful it is. It is so peaceful. I like to sit out on the deck and watch all the scenery. All the animals and birds, plus all the different kinds of tropical plants. The little Amerindian children run out to wave at the boat. . . ." So Maria Katsaris had written to her father. She may not have been lying: she may simply have been describing what she saw; how she felt about what she saw.

In Surinam I had come to know something of the beauty contained in these jungles. Looking at the puffs of smoky cloud, at the shining rivers cutting through the greenery below us, images spawned by that journey—completed just a couple of months before—came back to me. I am in a canoe going upriver. Sunlit forest walls enclose the stream. Birds swoop low, their reflections perfect in the glassy water—water that is blood-warm to the touch. In the distance is a range of blue hills, slopes whitened by drifting mist. Tall, straight-boled palm trees impart a curious architectural symmetry to the tropical profusion of vegetation. I might be looking at a primitive painting. Brown rocks covered with lilac-colored flowers jut out of the water. Sheltered among these rocks are shallow, clear-watered pools and eddies, miniature cascades and falls. The river here is like a water garden. I catch glimpses of villages half-hidden in the forest gloom. Children play on tiny sand beaches. Canoes glide silently along, keeping close to the banks overhung with ferns and creepers. In the early morning, mist obscures the river, shrouding the trees on the far bank. The gray water, striped by bands of light, flows noiselessly. Through the mist, the rising sun glows pink, lighting up the stillness. The jungle can entice. It can allure the romantic; it can charm the ghetto-bred, turning thoughts away from "fascist" evils to visions of primeval innocence and rapture. Given a chance, it could become part of the ideology, part of the commitment to a new life.

After about an hour, a reddish gash appeared below us—the Kaituma airstrip. We landed. At the far end of the runway some boys were playing soccer. A few soldiers of the Guyana Defence Force—the People's Army—leaned idly against a yellow aircraft. They looked bold and tough and dangerous. But when, a couple of weeks earlier, the shooting had started, they had done nothing, running off to shelter. A smell of rain and steamy earth permeated the air. Emerson Simon, wide-awake now, looked round for the truck that was supposed to be there waiting for us. The sun came through a break in the clouds, glaring off the runway. I looked around for a spot of shade, but there was none at hand. Heat waves danced on the corrugated-iron roofs of the Kaituma settlement. I listened to the reporter speaking into his tape recorder.

". . . blistering sun . . . little sign of the violence that occurred here . . . Guyanese soldiers standing nearby, watching us . . ." He stopped. "Hey, Mac," he called out to me, "how's about telling us the names of some of these trees and stuff? How about that one over there with the big leaves?"

"Breadfruit."

"And that one?"

"Mango."

"And that one?"

"Papaya."

"Thanks, Mac." He returned to his tape recorder. "I see all about me papaya, mango and breadfruit trees . . ."

The sun went in behind the clouds. Our transport, an old, battered truck, arrived. Emerson Simon shepherded us onto its roofless bed. As we left the airstrip, it started to rain. Kaituma, I now saw, had a school, a police station, even a "discotheque." This, by the standards of the Guyanese interior, was a small town. I noted tall antennae and what looked like a radar installation. Beside the road ran the railway line that went as far as Matthew's Ridge, about twenty-five miles to the southwest—another center of Guyanese administration. Barges were moored on the black-watered Kaituma River. Kaituma, a bauxite-transshipment center, could be said to have good communications with the outside world, served as it was by rail, air, river and electronics. Its remoteness was distinctly relative. Jonestown, no more than six or seven miles away, connected to it by an unpaved but serviceable road, was unambiguously within its sphere of influence, surveillance and control. After all the talk about "isolation" and "remoteness"—talk which implied that Jonestown had set itself down in a trackless jungle—I was astonished.

But Kaituma had not ruled Jonestown. Jonestown had ruled Kaituma. It was Kaituma that had fallen within Jonestown's sphere of influence, surveillance and control; *it* had become the suburb, receiving and not giving the orders. When the Ryan party had arrived from Georgetown, they were intercepted on the airstrip by the local police, who, with representatives of the People's Temple looking on, had all but refused them permission to proceed farther. The corporal in charge said he had received instructions from his superior that no one was to be allowed to proceed to Jonestown without the express permission of Pastor Jones to do so. Since Ryan and his party did not have such permission, they would have to return to Georgetown. The hitch was sorted out by the Temple's lawyers, Garry and Lane.

The truck went slowly along the uneven, muddy road. Here and there were Amerindian shacks, some surrounded by scratchy vegetable plots—attempts at cultivation barely distinguishable from the bush. Impassive children, many with babies clinging to their hips, watched us go by. The rain had stopped. A ferocious midday sun was beating down again. Insects whirred about our faces. The bush steamed, releasing yeasty vapors. Then we were there. A signboard straddled the entrance to the commune: "People's Temple Agricultural Project."

A green-painted sentry box stood by the gate. The track leading to the heart of the settlement was in terrible condition, deeply rutted and dotted with pools of water. The truck lurched and skidded on the treacherous surface, its engine whining with the strain. Mud rained into our faces. Banana trees, planted three deep, bordered both sides of the track. Beyond the bananas rose the forest wall. The cleared ground bristled with the stumps of felled trees. Jonestown at this point was, in fact, no more than a narrow corridor sliced through the jungle. A fallen signboard— "Welcome: People's Temple Agricultural Project"—lay embedded in the mud. Already, weeds were beginning to choke the cultivation. The banana plants gave way to rows of feathery cassava. Interspersed with the cassava were tiny plots (Jonestown would probably have called them "experimental") of sugar cane, citrus and pineapple.

In a brochure released in 1977 the commune described at length its varied agricultural endeavors. They were harvesting, they said, an average of two thousand pounds of bananas each month. Pineapples too were said to be thriving in the cooperative atmosphere, and they expected, in the near future, to be producing more than they would need. These claims, probably justified for the bananas, become less convincing when applied to the pineapples—judging, that is, by the one token plot of the latter which

I actually saw. (According to figures released subsequently by the Guyanese Government, only 668 acres had been cleared. Less than half of that—301 acres—was under cultivation. After four years, they were using no more than ten percent of their 3,852 acres—to use the more modest version of their lease—to produce food.)

Suddenly, the forest wall receded, opening out to reveal, on either side of the track, a few acres of fenced, rolling pasturage. A signpost bore the inscription "Piggery, Dairy, Chickery, Cassava Mill." In the distance I could see a handful of farm-style buildings. The 1977 brochure had had a great deal to say about the piggery (". . . the pig family has now grown to 130 pigs of all ages . . ."), the chickery ("We have built eight gable-type chicken houses . . . each . . . has a front door made from aluminum and wood framing . . .") and the cassava mill. It was, strangely and untypically, silent about the dairy, although it is known that Jonestown did have some cows: the Guyanese identified twenty-two bovine corpses in their postmassacre census. The brochure betrayed a mania for minute detail, for leaving nothing unsaid that could be said. Take its description of the cassava mill.

> We collect bitter cassava from the field in open 50 gallon drums and wash them in the trailer wagon through the jostling action on the way to the mill. The grater is a heavy table 3′ × 8½′ with a hole 12″ × 14″ in the middle. Two iron pulleys welded together work the grater. The grater blade is made with a small three-cornered file, sharpened to make a small hole at half-inch intervals, with each row offset to the last. We use a 5 HP electric motor to turn the grater . . . Grated cassava comes through the bottom of the mill into a tub lined with a plastic feed bag. This is then lifted to the press, which consists of two heavy truck wheel rims, 21″ in diameter, with a solid bottom, except for a 2″ hole for the juice to escape. Cassava is pressed against the sides of a cylinder which has slits cut about 4″ apart and 6″ in length. In the bottom is a set of five ribs, made of crab wood, 2″ square with spacing to match . . .

And so it goes on. Similarly, we are spared no details about the chickery or piggery. We learn, for instance, the exact dimensions of the chicken coops, the kinds of materials used in their construction and the method of construction; we learn that wood chips—supplied free of charge by Government workshops in Matthew's Ridge—are used for litter and that the composted litter is used for fertilizer; we learn what and how much each chicken consumes during each week of its growth; we are told about the size and shape of the gutters and water tanks and feeding troughs. Each tiny act is ruthlessly magnified. That magnification was necessary: it concealed the paucity and ordinariness of their achievements.

We passed a trailer, loaded with firewood, parked at an angle beside the track. It was a reminder that the life of an entire community had been abruptly arrested; that the summons late in the afternoon must have interrupted the routines of many engaged in what had become everyday tasks—like the hauling of firewood from the forest. Hearing the alert, they would have pulled automatically to the side of the track, jumped off tractor and trailer and hurried up to the pavilion to learn what all the fuss was about. They would probably have guessed that it had to do with the visit of Congressman Ryan. But beyond that, they may have known nothing. The Jonestown aristocracy did not normally share its secrets with the helots who labored in the fields. They must have expected to return before darkness fell, to finish their task. The trailer and its cargo, so casually, so thoughtlessly abandoned, was like a fragment of that afternoon caught and preserved in suspension.

The settlement proper now came into view. I saw a dismal constellation, half-ordered, half-scattered, of wooden structures —open-sided sheds, garages, pavilions, dormitories, cabins—equipped with steep-ridged roofs of corrugated iron. In the distance, on all sides, was the forest. A cloying smell of putrefaction irradiated the lukewarm air. One or two of the Americans covered their noses with handkerchiefs. Smoke billowed from a pit that had been dug near the main pavilion. The Guyanese were

burning mattresses, clothes, shoes, dolls, blankets, sheets. Everything left behind by the communards, Mr. Simon explained,
would eventually be consumed in that pit.

A man in military uniform appeared. He carried himself stiffly,
unsmilingly. Emerson Simon jumped off the truck. The two men
talked for a while. Emerson Simon came back to us. He seemed
embarrassed. A group of armed soldiers came and stood close by.
They watched us sulkily.

"The Major says you are all to keep together as a group," Mr.
Simon said, twirling his straw hat. "He says you are not to wander
off on your own. You are not permitted to touch anything. You're
to go only where you're told to go."

My fractious enemy started to protest.

"I hope that is clearly understood," the Major intervened,
gently beating one of his palms with the baton he was carrying.
The epidemic of courtesy that had spread among his civilian
counterparts had, it was obvious, not touched the Major. "*I* am in
charge here. At all times you must remain within sight of me and
my men. While you're here you're under *my* command. You will
do exactly as *I* say. You go everywhere as a group and only as a
group. Solitary exploration is strictly forbidden." He glared fero-
ciously as he spoke.

Emerson Simon, fanning himself with his straw hat, continued
to look embarrassed. He seemed taken aback by the hard-line
approach of the military occupation force. It was apparent that
he was a victim of a *coup d'état* of sorts. The civilian administrator
of Jonestown was being put in his place. We had reached the end
of the public relations road.

The Major did not hide the fact that he regarded us as intruders who had been foisted on him and that his only desire was to
be rid of us as quickly as possible. It was ironic, this heavy-handed
self-assertion of the Guyanese military; this sudden and unrelent-
ing proclamation of kingship over a domain suffused with the
stench of a thousand deaths. What they had been unable or un-
willing to do while Jonestown lived was now being done with all
the fury of belated vengeance. (Others too seemed to have be-

come afflicted with vengefulness. I think of the Women's Revolutionary Socialist Movement, which had had such a close working relationship with the People's Temple. Jonestown, they had said, should be turned into a prison, a place of permanent incarceration for habitual criminals. Bearing in mind that a delegation of the WRSM had spent three days in the commune and, apparently, had enjoyed themselves, this suggestion hinted at an unbecoming ingratitude.) But the likelihood was that even this late flowering of military concern was a sham; motivated by the same self-interest and duplicity that had once done everything in its power to protect Jonestown. The Government they served, the regime it was their duty to buttress, had already suffered too much from the depredations of earlier correspondents who had pillaged many interesting documents. They were going to take no more chances. What was being protected here was not the abused rights of Guyanese sovereignty, but the lies and corruption of the Government of Guyana which had bartered away that sovereignty—the lies and corruption which had allowed Jonestown to flourish and which, when the time came, had allowed it to take its own life.

Under the watchful eyes of the soldiers, we climbed down from the truck, setting foot for the first time on the soil of Jonestown. The soldiers did not speak, communicating their orders either by pointing their rifles or by clapping their hands if one of us lagged or fell out of formation. Guided by this disturbing pantomime, we picked our way through the mire to the nearest complex of buildings. Nearby was parked a big, mud-spattered open truck. Trailers, wheelbarrows and agricultural implements of one kind or another were scattered about.

The first building we came to was, judging by the look of it, a workshop. Piles of old clothes and shoes were stacked on the floor. Bunches of dried bananas hung on the walls. In one corner I saw a dead bird.

"What did they do in here?" someone asked the Major. "What did they use it for?"

The Major, tapping his baton, did not answer.

"Was this stuff brought here? Or was it found here?"

The Major did not answer. He looked at his watch.

One of the journalists reached up and fingered a blackened banana.

"Don't touch," the Major said. "Nothing is to be touched."

A soldier moved forward, waving his gun.

"Keep moving," the Major said. "I want you all to keep moving."

The soldiers clapped and swung their guns toward the open door.

". . . piles of old clothes . . . shoes . . . bananas . . . the walls seem to be made of some kind of plaited stuff . . . Hey, Mac, can you tell me what this funny stuff is that the walls are made out of?"

"Could be palm leaves," I said. "But I'm not sure."

". . . the walls plaited from what I guess would be some kind of palm leaf they find in the jungle around here . . ."

We went out, following a wooden walkway. It led to a bigger, open-sided shed. A sign said "Launderette," thereby removing any lingering temptation there might have been to elicit information from the Major. Launderette. Why did they not call it a laundry? Surely, one would have a laundry, not a launderette, in the jungle. Here were more piles of clothes, a row of concrete washbasins, crisscrossing drying lines. A kiln, looking for all the world like an abandoned altar, was heaped up with ash. White plastic bottle tops were scattered on the ground. In a corner of the shed was a case of used-up soft-drink containers. Placed on top of it was a cardboard box—"Fla-Vor-Aid Drink Mix." Should revolutionaries have died with the taste of Fla-Vor-Aid on their lips? Why had they not been content with the pure spring water taken from the well "that brims full no matter how much we take from it?"

"Keep moving! Touch nothing!"

The soldiers clapped; they waved their rifles. We went along another walkway, entering what I took to be a generalized cooking area. Firewood was piled up out in the open. Some axe heads were embedded in a tree stump. A film of ash stained the earth. One of the Americans who tried to open the door of a corrugated-iron outhouse was pulled back by a solider.

"Could have been used as a punishment cell . . ."

"Yeah . . ."

"Strange sort of shape . . ."

"Yeah . . ."

We came to a building that advertised itself as the Experimental and Herbal Kitchen. Painted on the door was a colorful jungle scene. Close to the entrance lay a dead kitten. Its stinking, half-decomposed corpse was covered with flies. We were allowed to go in. "One of the first buildings one sees when traveling up the road to Jonestown," says the 1977 brochure, "is the all-purpose kitchen where meals and treats are provided for workers and residents." The kitchen, the brochure tells us, was superbly equipped and met every standard of comfort, cleanliness and efficiency. It had ice-making machines, two stoves (gas and kerosene), a triple-sectioned sink, counters varnished to a high gloss, capacious storage cabinets. Water came from the well that never ran dry all year long. They used a Guyanese-style wood oven to bake their bread —of which, they could not resist pointing out, cassava flour was one of the basic ingredients. Many of the "cutting edges" used in the kitchen had been made in their own metal workshop. One of the walls had been so ingeniously partitioned that the various sections of which it was composed could be raised and lowered, opened and closed at will. This system allowed for the maximum penetration of health-giving sunlight.

Virtually everything they used, they grew or made for themselves; and their food was not only plentiful but lavish. Menus were worked out weeks in advance. This was done so that the medical staff could monitor the Jonestown diet and ensure that it was of maximum nutritional value. The kitchen was a hive of activity twenty-four hours a day as work teams prepared the next day's meals and bagged lunches for those workers whose labors took them far from the main dining area. Meals were always served promptly. Breakfast had three phases. Between 5:40 and

6:30 A.M. the outdoor workers were fed; the senior citizens had their turn between 7 and 7:30, the children between 7:30 and 8. Those who were ill or otherwise indisposed were given their meals in their "residences." The field-workers' bagged lunches were distributed at breakfast. Menus were mouth-watering— "eggs from Jonestown's chickens, cooked cereals, pancakes and homemade syrup and varying fruits seasonally available." In their bagged lunches the field-workers would find cutlass-bean patty, fish patty, peanut butter, egg salad, fried egg, or pork in a variety of forms. The brochure did not say anything about dinner, but if breakfast and lunch were anything to go by, it must have been a spectacular feast.

The kitchen staff and the nursing department were closely co-ordinated. This made it possible to provide special calorie-rich snacks midmorning and midafternoon for the children and for those individuals who were underweight. On the other hand, those who were overweight had at their disposal a variety of delicious low-calorie meals. The cooking staff was under the overall supervision of a registered nurse who at one time had managed an Italian restaurant. Hence spicy savor and sound nutrition were inextricably conjoined. Nor was that the whole story. Because Jonestown was a "rainbow family," a mixture of many races, its food deliberately reflected several cultural and ethnic backgrounds. A special piquancy was added by the ageless herbal lore they had picked up from their Amerindian neighbors. Attention was called to their cleaning-up procedures. "The dishes are cold water rinsed, washed and stacked, then washed in a soapy detergent with bleach and boiling water and put away . . . all surfaces are continually scrubbed and sanitized from ceiling to floor to provide the most healthful environment."

Few traces survived of all this culinary glory. I saw a cardboard box full of rotten oranges, a rack of dusty spice bottles, jars of preserved peppers. Books were scattered about. *How to Feed Your Baby the Natural Way. A Modern Herbal. Drugs and Solutions: A Programmed Introduction.* Brown medicine bottles were gathered in a heap—Rexall Iron Ferrous Sulphate Supplement. Flies buzzed.

The stench of the putrescent cat filled the Experimental and Herbal kitchen.

"Touch nothing! Keep moving!"

The rifles swung lazily; hands clapped.

We went out, pausing at a little shed next door. This must have been the greenhouse. Dying herbs drooped in wooden troughs. We pushed deeper into the settlement, following the network of wooden walkways, going past rows of smaller huts, some with thatched, others with corrugated-iron roofs. Red lilies flourished in enclosed garden plots. Here and there attempts had been made to cultivate lawns. ". . . they shall sit every one under his vine and under his fig tree, and none shall make them afraid. . . ." Already, the neglected gardens had begun to go to seed. We were not allowed to inspect the sealed houses. Close by was a group of shower cubicles.

We came to the medical clinic, a group of wooden buildings like all the rest. A sign said "Jonestown Medical Services. Laurence Schact M.D."

It was Laurence Schact, the doctor whose basic training in Mexico had been paid for by the People's Temple, who had brought his career to its climax when he mixed the cyanide potion. Former acquaintances remembered him as a dedicated person, bent on doing missionary work in South America. Rev Moore had judged him to be not only dedicated but exceptionally bright. Charles Garry had also been dumbfounded by his talents.

That Schact would become the Temple's devoted doctor, the bringer of life and the bringer of mass death, was not wholly predictable. A Temple defector described her first meeting with him in 1971. He was eighteen years old, a nervous and suspicious vagrant, when he turned up at the Temple's Redwood Valley headquarters. Schact would not let his backpack out of his sight for fear it would be lost or stolen. If it disappeared, so would the "treasure" he carried around in it. That treasure was the *I Ching*, the ancient Chinese text of divination. This book had brought him to Redwood Valley. It had given him the message that he should travel north. There he would meet a man possessed of divine truth. Now all was bolted and silent; and the smell of death was everywhere.

"Keep moving! Keep moving!" The Major flourished his baton.

We passed a muddy playground, equipped with all the usual bric-a-brac of swings, climbing frames, slides, ropes and over-looked by a watchtower, a structure whose function in the life of Jonestown remained unclear. Had its main purpose been to keep people out or keep people in? Thick power cables bellied over-head. Smoke billowed out of the incinerator pit.

We were walking on planks laid across the ooze surrounding the main pavilion. The cloying stench became enveloping. It was here most of the bodies had lain, piled three or four deep, burst-ing in the tropical heat, leaking away into the Guyanese soil. De-spite the planks, our feet sank ankle-deep into the ooze. (It was all right, Emerson Simon had reassured us: the entire area had been heavily sprayed and disinfected.) We had reached the heart of the commune.

This main pavilion was really no more than a spacious, open-sided tent. Its centerpiece was the dais and "throne" from which Jim Jones had presided. Here, when there were no visitors to be impressed with the beauties of the cooperative life, Jones had taught and harangued. Here were held the catharsis sessions, those marathons of confession and expiation which could last nearly all night. Here, when the summons was given, they had come to die for socialism and brotherhood.

The pavilion was adorned with quotations and exhortations. "Those Who Cannot Remember the Past Are Condemned to Re-peat It." "Love One Another." "Where the Spirit of God Is There Is Liberty." "All That Believed Were Together and Had All Things in Common."

There were big maps of the world, of the United States and of Guyana. These were no doubt the indispensable props of Jones's geopolitical lessons. Potted plants hung from the roof. A tele-vision set, hi-fi speakers, musical instruments, a sewing machine, soft toys were heaped up on the platform. Bits and pieces of personal property were scattered about on the floor. I saw sun hats, Afro combs, eyeglasses, a set of false teeth, a walking stick, a child's shoe. Recordings of symphonies by Dvořak, Beethoven, Brahms and Tchaikovsky were strewn on a table; and everywhere —books. Jonestown's reading seemed to have been relentlessly political. *Economic Power Failure—the Current American Crisis.* Frantz Fanon's *The Wretched of the Earth.* Lenin's *What Is to Be Done* and *On Marx and Engels. Soviet Democracy. What Is the Komsomol?* Leonid Brezhnev's *The CPSU in the Struggle for Unity of All Revolutionary and Peace Forces.* There were Russian dictionaries and Russian-language primers.

It was a formidable collection, a reminder that, especially toward the end, removal to the Soviet Union had become a well-developed fantasy. As the dictionaries and language primers attested, they had even begun to teach themselves Russian. The most tenuous of threads linked the fantasy to reality. People's Temple emissaries had had discussions with the Soviet Embassy in Georgetown. The commune in turn had been toured by Soviet officials and representatives of Tass. It was probable that the Embassy had supplied most of the books I saw in the pavilion.

"Is it too late for Russia?" a woman's voice is heard asking on the tape recording obligingly made by someone at Jonestown during the suicide ritual. "At this point," Jones replied, "it's too late for Russia. They killed. They started to kill. [The reference was to the Temple assassins at the Kaituma airstrip.] That's why it makes it too late for Russia. Otherwise I'd say yes, sir, you can bet your life."

One can imagine the Russians being curious about Jonestown and its inhabitants. Curious—but also wary. The prospect of a large group of Americans seeking refuge in the Soviet Union would have interested and amused them, particularly so in the wake of Washington's human-rights onslaught against them. They would probably have indulged Jim Jones, listening patiently to his emissaries, sending cartons of books, coming out to visit, speaking vague but encouraging words. But they would have taken care not to commit themselves to anything too specific. They might have sensed that the eccentricities of these self-made socialists led by a faith healer of mercurial temperament and ideology could be more of a potential liability than a potential asset; that the "tremendous Soviet propaganda victory" promised by one of Jones's top lieutenants could all too easily turn into a tremendous propaganda disaster.

There is no evidence that the Russian involvement with Jonestown went much further than I have described. It could, with greater accuracy, be called a flirtation. That flirtation did, however, nourish a cruel fantasy of escape and led to the sad absurdity of eighty-year-old "senior citizens" struggling to master an alien tongue and comprehend Lenin's thoughts on Marx and Engels.

"Keep moving! Keep moving!"

The soldiers clapped and swung their rifles. We left the pavilion, carefully negotiating the planks laid across the ooze, moving away from the smoke billowing out of the incinerator pit. We peeped into the carpentry shop, but were not allowed to linger. Then we were back on the network of wooden walkways. A wheelchair was parked on the veranda of a hut that referred to itself as the Special Care Unit. The ground here was littered with empty pill containers and surgical gloves. Jonestown's pharmacopoeia was breathtaking in both quantity and variety. One of the commune's nursing supervisors claimed that these drugs were used not only for conventional therapeutic purposes but also to keep the more troublesome residents under control. This, he said, was the special task of the Extended Care Unit. On the completion of treatment, would-be defectors no longer evinced any desire to leave.

But if we are to believe the account of Stanley Clayton—one of the handful who managed to escape from Jonestown during the suicide ritual—not *all* would-be defectors were drugged into domesticity and acquiescence. When, a few months previously, the news had got to Jones that he was planning to make a run for it, Clayton was called into the Master's presence. Jones used his usual techniques. "I was made to feel guilty of all sorts of things . . . made to feel ashamed. . . . Then Jim Jones told me there was no point in leaving them at that time. He said I had everything good going for me at Jonestown, that I would get to go to school and move ahead in life and why should I leave and all that. . . ." Clayton stayed. In his case at least, drugs were not used.

I bring this up because it is all too easy and tempting to exaggerate the horrors of Jonestown and, by making it into a freak show, remove it altogether from the province of rational scrutiny. Jonestown may have been no worse than many American prisons. The People's Temple may very well have modeled its therapies on the practices sanctioned by the behaviorist psychologists whose theories seem to dominate these institutions. For the drug advocates, correct attitudes imply correct biochemistry. As some had already said, there was nothing really human inside human beings. If the People's Temple, in its search for socialist solidarity, resorted to Thorazine and other chemical infusions, they were doing no more than following a well-trodden path of rehabilitation. If the criminal was a "sick" man who needed to be cured, it required next to no effort to extend that outlook to the would-be defector from a utopian colony. All is justified in the pursuit of total human happiness.

We approached Jones's bungalow. It was larger than most of the other huts we had seen, but not disproportionately so. Wire netting screened the windows and small veranda, which was furnished with a little cane sofa and an armchair. Boxes of herbal tea —Celestial Seasonings Mellow Mint—were heaped on the armchair. The bungalow was sheltered by a grove and had the secluded air of a retreat. There were breadfruit trees, orange trees in fruit, an almond tree, colorful shrubs.

Jones had shared the three-bedroom house with his female favorites. Maria Katsaris, true to her retiring nature and cloistered habits, had chosen not to die with the hoi polloi in the main pavilion. She had come here, bringing with her a bowl of the potion. Her corpse was found in Jones's bed. In all, a dozen or so bodies had been found strewn on the narrow veranda where we were now standing.

Jones, eschewing the Jonestown diet, had kept his refrigerator well stocked with imported foods. But it was not only food that filled the racks and shelves of the Messiah's refrigerator. Sharing equal space with the canned fruit and bottles of Del Monte ketchup was his personal drug supply.

That Jones was not an altogether healthy man seems reasonably certain. However, that having been said, we are immediately engulfed by obscurity and confusion. Both the nature and the degree of that illness remain mysteries. Was he suffering from cancer? Was it a heart condition? Was it a rare fungal disease that had attacked his lungs? Or was it something quite other? Drug abuse, for example?

About ten days before Ryan arrived at the commune, two American consular officials visited Jonestown, one of a number of visitations made to interview residents whose well-being and freedom of choice had been questioned by relatives. Jones turned up at lunch escorted by two of his disciples who seemed to be physically supporting him. They were told that not long before he had had a heart attack and was running a temperature of 105 degrees. His face was hidden behind a mask of white gauze. His speech was slurred. During the meal, Jones's behavior implied a degree of mental confusion. He tried at one stage to spell out a word he did not want a lurking child to hear but was unable to do so. When lunch was done, he was helped back to his bungalow. The slurring of his speech, his mental disarray, had appeared genuine enough. Nevertheless, the officers also noted that neither his forehead nor his palms were sweating. This was not consistent with the temperature of 105 degrees he was alleged to be running. As with so much else in Jonestown, truth and falsehood, fact and fiction, were so inextricably intertwined that it was virtually impossible to separate them.

To the reporters who came with Ryan he confided his fear that he might be suffering from cancer. He was running high fevers, losing weight—more than thirty pounds, he said, in the last few weeks. ". . . In many ways I feel like I'm dying. I've never felt like this before. Who the hell knows what stress can do to you?"

One of his physicians and staunchest political allies, Dr. Carlton

Goodlett, publisher of San Francisco's major black-read news-paper, asserted at one point that his former patient was suffering from a brain tumor. He told Charles Garry that this tumor was literally burning up his client's brain.

Even darker possibilities, involving the intelligence agencies and mind control, began to be canvassed after the suicides had taken place. According to the Black Panther newspaper, Jones had told a visiting Swedish psychologist that all his thoughts were coming from the CIA. The assertion led the newspaper to ask this question: had Jim Jones been drugged into a hypnotic trance? Had the CIA been feeding him and his followers substances that sabotaged normal mental processes? Thorazine, the Panthers said (Thorazine was found in large quantities at Jonestown), was a well-known ingredient of the mind-control experiments carried out by the CIA. When Jones said that all his thoughts were com-ing from the CIA he might have been speaking literally. Such speculations were to find sympathetic audiences in certain black and white radical circles.

What is beyond dispute is that Jones was swallowing many more pills than was good for him. "His medication intake was high," said Donald Freed, Mark Lane's colleague on the Citizens Com-mission of Inquiry, an admirer of Jones, one of the scores of visitors who had been deeply impressed by what they had seen going on in Jonestown. "He talked," Freed went on, "like a mod-ern-day Moses. Then he would revert to talking about whether an apocalypse was coming. Maybe his own [impending] death triggered him into certain decisions that became mass decisions."

Maybe. But this misses the point about what happened at Jones-town. It does not explain why Jim Jones gained and held the allegiance of so many for so long—long after the evidence against him had begun to accumulate—including the allegiance of Mr. Freed. "Martin Luther King," Mr. Freed had said, ". . . if he could see Jonestown, would recognize it as the next step in his agenda and he would say, 'One, two, three, many more Jones-towns. . . .'"

It was devotion like this which assisted in the transformation of

Jones from a Midwestern faith healer into a Messiah of the socialist gospel, a modern-day Moses. Jonestown was a manifestation
not only of mass suicide but of mass devotion. His medication
intake might have made it easier for Jones to pull the trigger on
the afternoon of November 18, 1978; but it was the admiration
of men like Donald Freed, Charles Garry, Mark Lane, Rev Moore
and dozens like them, men who believed in and promoted his
mission despite all the evidence . . . it was this outrush of admiration and support which helped to create the circumstances
whereby, when Jim Jones did finally pull the trigger, he was able
to pull it not only on himself but on nearly a thousand others.
Excessive medication cannot by itself carry the entire moral burden of the Jonestown catastrophe.

Wind rustled through the grove. Insects flashed and hummed
among the bright flowers. In the distance, beyond the undula-
tions of cleared land, rose the forest wall. The soldiers clapped
and swung their rifles. We moved on.

Emerson Simon and one of the soldiers were having an argu-
ment off to the side.

"This is the *Army*," the soldier was saying. "I want you to remember that this is the Army you're dealing with."

The altercation stopped when they saw us.

"Welcome," said the sign, "to Jonestown Pre-School Nursery."

Ranking nearly equally with its cassava operations, its piggery
and its chickery was Jonestown's educational system. "In Jonestown," said the 1977 brochure, "education is a way of life which
affects all aspects of life. It is our intent to make education rele-
vant to the growth and maturity of the child physically, morally,
socially, intellectually, artistically, and finally with the goal of
guiding the child in the acquisition of habits, attitudes and skills
such as will enable the child to participate in collective thought,
values and activities."

With this in mind, group rather than individual activities were
encouraged. At the preschool level children were taught how to
handle cutlery, the rudiments of hygiene and, of course, the al-
phabet—or, as Jonestown would have it, alphabetic recognition.

In addition, they practiced dance routines with didactic themes. Their learning tools included manipulative toys, puzzles, individual chalkboards and motor and perceptual motor facilities in the playground. These motor and perceptual motor facilities were, I assume, the swings, the seesaws and the slides I had seen.

Elementary education went up to the seventh grade, but there were plans for expansion beyond that level. Classes were organized around ability, not age. Each child was allowed to progress at his own speed. The curriculum, apart from reading, writing and arithmetic, included physical and earth science, political science, social science—"with emphasis on Guyanese history and culture"—arts and crafts and music. Paper and pencil had been replaced by the individualized chalkboard, an innovation that filled them with pride. The chalkboards had become the exciting scenes of structural analysis; syllabication; prefix, root and suffix study. No wonder, with vocabulary such as this ringing in the jungle air, the hordes of Guyanese educators who passed through Jonestown went away deeply affected.

The emphasis throughout was on cooperative rather than competitive values. Fundamental to Jonestown's educational philosophy was the work-study concept. Children, no less than adults, were actively involved in the labors of the commune. They were responsible for the upkeep of their clothing, bedding and "living space"; they looked after lawns and flower beds. Those who became conscientious and productive workers might be given the privilege of participating in special projects. Cooperative child labor, for instance, had helped to build that vital tool of education, the playground.

A timetable, prominently displayed, laid out the schedule of the preschool day, which began at seven in the morning and ended at five in the afternoon. Dolls of many colors and a few children's books were scattered about. The pupils' names were chalked up on a blackboard.

". . . Jay, Will, Lonnie, Jamelia, Yolanda, Tad, Liza . . ." the journalist recited the roll call into his tape recorder.

"For God's sake," someone cried out, "can't you be quiet?"

Lowering his voice, the journalist continued the recital. ". . . Tiffany, Michael, Mark, Angela, Neal, Clarence . . ."

It was a long list.

The Major tapped his baton impatiently; he looked at his watch.

"You have a plane to catch, gentlemen," he said. "The pilot can't fly in the dark. I'm sure you wouldn't want to spend the night here." He seemed to want to smile. "Keep moving."

We were allowed to pause briefly at the fenced-in plot marking the site of the grave of Lynetta Jones, the mother of the Messiah. Jones had brought her out to Jonestown, where she had died. "In commemoration of a true fighter for Justice," ran the text on the memorial tablet, "Who Gave the Ultimate. Who gave up her Son so he could serve the People in the struggle for Justice, for Freedom from Oppression and for the foundation of Socialism."

There was another text. "Asked one day by a religious dogmatist if she believed in the Crucifixion, she replied, "I have witnessed many crucifixions, been crucified many times . . ."'

"Keep moving!"

I can no longer remember the rest of the inscription.

We returned to our starting point. The grand tour was over.

I stared at the smoke coiling up from the incinerator pit, at the dismal assemblage of sheds and dormitories, at the encircling wall of the forest. I breathed in the cloying stench of putrefaction.

For some it had been a paradise. For others it had been a nightmare. There was virtually nothing in common between the descriptions of outsiders (or quasi outsiders) like Charles Garry and Rev Moore and that of an insider like Deborah Blakey, a former financial secretary of the Temple who fled from the commune in April 1978. They might have been talking about two entirely different places.

"The primary emotions I came to experience," Blakey said in her affidavit, "were exhaustion and fear." Every vestige of a personal and private life had been systematically rooted out. "The most loyal were in the worst physical condition. Dark circles under one's eyes or extreme loss of weight were considered signs of loyalty."

The commune lived under a reign of terror. Day and night it was patrolled by armed guards. No one was allowed to leave unless he had a special reason to do so; and even then permission was granted only to the most trusted. Contact with Guyanese was restricted, allowed only when a Temple member was engaged in a "mission."

The Jonestown work schedule was rigorous to the point of cruelty. Most of the people labored eleven hours a day in the fields. (Sundays were better: work stopped at two in the afternoon.) The one hour they were given for lunch was taken up with walking back to the kitchen from the fields and queuing for a miserable handout. (Blakey did not mention the delicious bagged lunches that were supposed to have been distributed at breakfast.) They had rice for breakfast, rice-water soup for lunch, and rice and beans for dinner. On Sundays each person received an egg and a cookie. Vegetables were available two or three times a week. The more debilitated of the senior citizens had an egg every day. However, when Jonestown had visitors—and they were few and far between—the quality of the diet would take a sudden turn for the better. Jones dined separately from the membership, nourishing himself on the choice foods with which his refrigerator was stocked. He shared his privileges with two of his favorite women, Maria Katsaris and Carolyn Layton—the daughter of Rev Moore. John Victor Stoen took pot luck with the rest.

By February 1978, as a result of overwork and semistarvation, conditions had become so bad that half of the commune was stricken with diarrhea and high fevers. She herself had become seriously ill. But no pity was shown. "Like most of the sick people, I was not given any nourishing foods to help recover." Instead, she was fed on water and a tea drink. When she was considered sufficiently recovered, she plunged afresh into the everyday regimen of rice and beans. Nor was that the limit of their tribulations. There were Jones's harangues. He would preach at them over the public-address system for an average of six hours a day, some-times much longer. His voice followed them to the fields and to their beds, plaguing both their hours of work and rest. After the day's work they would have to attend meetings in the main pavil-ion. These would be held, on average, six times a week. The tales of streams of visitors coming to marvel at the wonders of Jones-town were a lie. On those rare occasions when there were visitors they were given detailed instructions on what to say and how to behave. "There was little hope or joy in any of our lives. . . ."

Talk of death was constant, she claimed. They were told that the jungle was swarming with mercenaries, that if the mercenaries caught them they would be tortured and killed. The obsession with death was given ideological shape by the idea of mass suicide for socialism. This became dramatically real during the "White Nights" when the commune rehearsed its procedures for self-extinction. By then she was almost beyond caring. "Life at Jones-town was so miserable and the physical pain of exhaustion was so great that this event was not traumatic for me."

Blakey described the punishments meted out to refractory chil-dren. Sometimes, she said, they were taken into the forest, to a well not far from Jones's bungalow. Two people would already be in the well, swimming around. The child was tossed in. He would be grabbed by the feet and pulled down into the water. All over the commune they would hear the child's terrified screams and pleadings for forgiveness. "I'm sorry, Father . . . I'm sorry, Fa-ther . . ." One wonders—was it the same well that brimmed full no matter how much they took from it? In Jonestown there was not only the well but, it appears, a monster known as Big Foot. Big Foot administered electric shocks. In a Temple publication —*The Rainbow Family Coloring Book*—the ideal Temple child was portrayed as a model of self-effacing obedience: he was consid-erate; he was helpful to old people; he was quiet; he ate up all the food he was given; he picked up trash wherever he happened to find it; but above all else, he was devoted and thankful to Pastor Jim. The Temple's child-management techniques, like so much else, seemed to have become worse with time. In California, children had been subjected to increasingly heavy beatings. After a while was added the refinement of placing a microphone close to the mouth of a beaten child so that his screams would resound all the better.

Deborah Blakey had gone out to Jonestown in December 1977. Yolanda Crawford had arrived there eight months before—at the beginning of April—and left three months later; just before, that is, Jim Jones's final flight from San Francisco. She too issued an affidavit after her defection, but not immediately: it took her nearly a year to do so. Her affidavit, although not as startling as Blakey's, reflected the growing vigor of the campaign being waged by the Concerned Relatives. She mentioned the guards stationed around Jonestown to prevent anyone's leaving. Those attempting to escape, Jones had said, would be killed and their bodies thrown into the jungle. She confirmed that casual contact with Guyanese was discouraged. Mail was censored. Telephone calls were not permitted. They were ordered to spy on each other, to report any act or intention of "treason." Those who broke the rules were severely punished. They were deprived of food and sleep, made to work excessive hours and, sometimes, forced to eat hot peppers.

Toward the end, Stanley Clayton had been working in the kitchen. "All I knew was what went on around us in the kitchen," he said, "and little else of what took place around." Before being assigned to the kitchen, he had been a field hand. He complained about the food—"rice and gravy for breakfast and for most every meal and there was hardly anything more . . . I can't say I had any meal up there that I could call spectacular." Jones's nocturnal harangues were tiresome, but Clayton spoke of them as occurring only occasionally. But he confirmed that there were mass suicide drills and that the residents had little chance of leaving the commune. When he fled from Jonestown on the night of the massacre, he had taken with him an assiduously tutored terror of the Guyanese soldiery: Jones had told them that they would be castrated if they were captured by the People's Army.

Jonestown was ruled by cliques. "Jim Jones was Number One.

Then there were others like Johnny Jones [one of Jones's adopted sons], Carolyn Layton, Maria Katsaris . . . the doctor Larry Schact, Mike Prokes . . . Steve Jones [Jones's natural son]." The commune's basketball team formed another elite. "You had to be liked to get on that team. . . . That basketball team was a gang apart from the others . . . the basketball players didn't associate none with a lot of us back there." The coach, a confidant of Jim Jones, enjoyed throwing his weight around. He behaved, Clayton said, like a punk. (The basketball team, some would have it, also incorporated Jones's "death squad." They escaped the death ritual because they were in Georgetown to play a match against Guyana's national team.) Clayton—and he was not alone in this —did not relish sharing the same Georgetown hotel as the survivors from Jonestown's assorted ruling circles. "Man, I don't like it —we don't feel safe with them around; they were too damned close to Jim Jones and the other top brass; it ain't none too safe."

Armed guards. Sadistic punishments. Semistarvation. Hundreds of cowed and terrorized prisoners—joyless specimens, drugged into submission, overworked, brought to the limits of human endurance, talking only of death. The horror of Jonestown is unrelieved. How is one to bring this extreme picture into alignment with the accounts of Charles Garry, Rev Moore and all the rest who we know (even bearing in mind Blakey's denials of streams of visitors) came to Jonestown, saw with their own eyes and went away with hearts uplifted to announce that Nirvana was at hand? Is it really possible to turn night into day? to paint the most terrible of concentration camps with utopian hues? Such powers of sorcery strain credibility.

Clayton mentioned Michael Prokes. He belonged to the innermost ruling circle of the People's Temple. Prokes survived the disaster because he had been commissioned by Jones to take the Temple's fortune to the Soviet Embassy in Georgetown. At the height of the killing, Mark Lane and Charles Garry, hiding in the jungle, saw two men running out of the settlement carrying a chest. One of these men was Michael Prokes. They were intercepted before they could complete their task. But Prokes—hardly a cause for surprise—was not detained for long by the Guyanese authorities, who seemed to have no need for material witnesses. Soon he was back home in Modesto, California. In March 1979, after maintaining an unbroken public silence, he summoned the press to a Modesto motel. There he released what is probably best described as his testament, a rambling document some forty pages long. After answering a few questions, he casually excused himself, went to the bathroom and fired a gun into his head. Jonestown had claimed another victim.

Part of Prokes's testament was devoted to a discussion of conditions at Jonestown. "Sure," he wrote, "there were excesses." Jonestown, he conceded, was not flawless. What were the flaws? Prokes, regrettably, did not tell us. In any case, "its bad points were nothing compared to the way it was portrayed by those who left the Temple." The apostates had simply not liked living in the jungle under what he called an extremely structured program. That extremely structured program was made necessary by the types of people with whom they had had to deal. It was important to understand that Jonestown was dealing with all types of social and psychological deviancy. The commune had to cope with ex-convicts, former drug addicts, the emotionally disturbed, the maladjusted, the hyperactive, the mentally retarded—as well as those suffering from more straightforward physical handicaps. Jonestown was a collection of the maimed and the inadequate and the delinquent; cripples who were unable to fend for themselves. ". . . you name it and they were there." Hence the need for a "tight" structure.

Those who had left and slandered the commune, Prokes said, were, in the main, selfish whites who had not been prepared to make the required sacrifices. To paint Jonestown in the darkest colors was one way of stifling the crisis of conscience brought about by their desertion. "Jonestown functioned on a high level of ethical behavior and human devotion you had to see and experience in order to comprehend." Individual rights were respected: that was part of their code. It was the most racially harmonious society he had ever seen or heard about. In his opinion, ninety percent of the people living there loved Jonestown. They wanted it to succeed, and it was succeeding. Jonestown may not have been paradise to the defectors, but it was paradise for those who had been brutalized by the struggle for existence in America's ghettoes.

Prokes admitted that he had never much cared for Jim Jones. "I guess it was his authority that bothered me, although I often saw the necessity for it." But he recognized that his dislike was purely subjective. Ultimately, objective respect triumphed over subjective aversion because he saw Jim Jones practicing what he preached. "Despite how some have portrayed him, he really didn't live above the people—maybe he did in minor ways, but he always had a very modest life-style. I know that the vast majority of Temple members did not feel the dislike for Jones that I felt."

Prokes, despite his believer's fervor, despite his obliquities and elisions, has given us a rather more plausible view of Jonestown than Blakey. Blakey's Jonestown has slipped beyond the reach of reason and imagination. Its utter bleakness, its relentless cruelties are too flat, too extreme. Her Jones is an incarnation of comic-book evil, motiveless and mindless, inflicting misery for its own sake. Prokes offers us a more complex picture. He may not have told us what the excesses were, but he does admit that his utopia was flawed and, without intending to, gives us some idea of how the corruptions, deceptions and cruelties that did undoubtedly abound in Jonestown could set in and be made to coexist with his stridently proclaimed idealism.

His psychiatric characterization of the commune's population is particularly revealing—clashing as it does with the soft-centered jargon of equality and fraternity. At Jonestown, according to Prokes, the aristocrats like himself were not dealing merely with the victims of fascism and racism but, simultaneously, with a group of people who fell into certain cold-blooded clinical categories. They were not simply poor and oppressed and in need of love. They were also emotionally disturbed, maladjusted, mentally retarded, hyperactive and all the rest. Science and sentiment fused. Seen in a clinical light, Jonestown was composed of a few doctors like Prokes and an army of patients who had to be "cured." It was an autocratic conception, and it must have given rise to frightening temptations and actions. Prokes unconsciously strays from the language of socialism and brotherhood to the language of psychiatry. He manages in almost the same breath to talk about an extremely structured program and individual rights. Deeply confused, he did not see the contradiction. The one led in the direction of armed guards, electric shocks and, possibly, gross drug abuse; the other brought him back to tearful love, socialism and racial harmony. The American temptation to categorize clashed with his equally American temptation to sentimentalize.

The excesses and the distortions—interpreted as "sacrifices"—could be consistent with a reasonably high level of devotion to the Cause and Jim Jones. Many, probably the majority, may have been willing captives: Michael Prokes certainly was one. The very rigors of their existence combined with the sense of external threat may have pushed them closer to each other. They who had given up everything to follow Jim Jones out to the jungles of Guyana might be brought close to despair; but despair does not inevitably lead to disloyalty. Revolutionary suicide would have made sense to many of them. To admit this is to go a little way toward explaining some of the elusive ambiguities of Jonestown. The commune may have conspired to fool not only the world but itself.

In San Francisco I met Andrea Walker, a black girl, who had gone out to Jonestown in March 1978 and spent several months there, adopting a Guyanese child in the process. She did not agree with Deborah Blakey's nightmarish portrait.

"Many people got diarrhea, that's true. But it wasn't because they were starving us. It was because of the climate and the strangeness of the food."

Those who were underweight were given special snacks three times a day. Every Sunday they were weighed by the nurses.

"When I got there I was very heavy. I weighed 130 pounds, but my weight dropped to 105 pounds after I had diarrhea. I was pleased because that was what I really should have weighed. Even so, I was given milkshakes and eggs because I hadn't adjusted to the local food. We had to eat things we had never eaten before— cassava, eddoes, dasheen, cutlass bean. But we got accustomed and I started to love it. We also had a lot of cheese, noodles and rice. Once a month we had chicken. We had shark and as much fish as we could eat."

Admittedly, there were days when they had just rice and vegetables. Nevertheless, she said, Deborah Blakey had concentrated only on the bad parts. Children were given eggs twice a week: the Jonestown medical staff paid close attention to their protein intake. Pregnant women had milk as well as eggs. As the months went by, because of the volume of criticism, the quality of the diet did gradually improve. Jonestown was still expanding. Crops were still being planted. It was not difficult to appreciate that the commune would take time to find its feet.

"Blakey wasn't there long enough. She didn't know what Jim had in the piggery and what *we* had. She worked most of the time in the radio room and in Georgetown. I don't know why they want to present Jonestown as if it was a horror. Down there we were trying to cultivate a new land." She looked agitated.

"American reporters were looking for a bad story," her companion put in. He too was black and had spent several months in Jonestown. "They were looking for a quick buck and that was the easiest way. If they saw something good, they wouldn't print it in the paper. They wouldn't print what Martin Luther King did. Only the bad things."

"They looked after us," Andrea Walker said. "Everyone had regular physicals. Dentists came around."

When she had first arrived she had spent two weeks working in the fields. The hours were long, roughly from sunrise to sunset, but they had several breaks and an hour for lunch.

"There were white people working beside me in the fields." She paused. "Some people have said they treated the blacks like slaves. . . . I don't know . . . at times I did feel there was too much white leadership. The people close to Jones mostly stayed in the radio room. But then most of the whites had been in the church for years and everyone trusted them and trusted their judgment —although I did notice they didn't get out with the rest of us and get their hands dirty."

But she was happy. For a while, she was "out of her mind" with joy.

"My husband and I got a cottage. Most married couples were in cottages, and we helped supervise children. We shared our cottage with my best girlfriend. Downstairs was fixed up for the children we supervised. We looked after twelve little girls. They had bunk beds. One of my friends at the sawmill built me a nice table. We got the children up by six and dressed at seven. The parents would escort them to breakfast. Then I went to work in the baby nursery. I worked with year-old babies, teaching them to walk, changing diapers. I loved working with the children. Work ended at six. That was my day."

She had thought she would spend the rest of her life in Jonestown. The children, in her opinion, were receiving an excellent education. They were learning so many different skills—sewing, welding, tractor driving, mechanics, woodwork. They helped out in the fields during the morning and in the workshops for part of the afternoon. Afterward they went to their classrooms, where they discussed their experiences and did their academic work.

It had been lovely until the last four months, when Jones started to sicken.

"Round about August," her companion said. "The last two weeks in August." (Blakey had fled from the commune a few months before that.)

Jones started demanding more of their time. He wanted to hold meetings every night.

"He said he wanted to keep everyone together. He was so sick he would talk to us from his house with a loudspeaker. His voice was slurred. I believed something might be coming to harm us. I believed they were going to come and take John Stoen away from him and take Jim himself away from us and send him back to the United States. For seven days and six nights in September I helped to stand guard, watching out for those people who might be coming . . ."

Yet she was convinced that she and her husband had a future there. (She had returned to San Francisco for family reasons.) Jonestown would have improved. It had the potential.

"I felt it could become a great place, a great community. He never told anyone they couldn't leave. Jim used to say he wanted everyone from the States to come and see what we were doing there." Her face twisted. She fell silent. I understood: she had been terribly betrayed.

Apart from friends and enemies, disciples and defectors, we have another angle of vision on Jonestown—that provided by the staff of the American Embassy. In May 1978, two officials from the embassy (Dwyer and McCoy) went to the settlement. While McCoy performed his consular duties, Dwyer was given the full Jonestown treatment. He toured the nursery, the day-care center, the school, the sawmill, the carpentry shop, the medical clinic; he examined how the senior citizens were housed; he saw an exhibition of handicrafts. Lunch—"a reasonably attractive meal featuring pork"—was served in the main pavilion. Conversation was wide-ranging. Jones confided his worries about what might happen to the Temple after his death. The problem of incentive in a nonmonetary, communal society was discussed. They chatted about forestry and about the difficulties the commune was having with its beef cattle—they, apparently, were not putting on sufficient weight. The Stoen child-custody case was touched upon. Jones once again vowed that he would never voluntarily relinquish his hold on the boy and fretted about the slanders being spread by "Trotskyists." While they ate, the Jonestown band played. Dwyer says he spoke briefly and casually with between fifteen and twenty-five people—apart from those who had been present at lunch and on the tour. Mostly he saw older people and children: the ablebodied were out at work in the fields. He was introduced to several specimens who all asserted that they had been "saved" by Jim Jones and the People's Temple—a drug addict, a prostitute, an alcoholic and so on. Dwyer recognized that this parade of regenerated humanity was no less staged for his benefit than the handicrafts exhibition. Even so, his conclusion remained favorable. Jonestown, he said in his report, appeared to be much more than a Potemkin village.

There was the visit of November 7—eleven days before the mass suicide—of consular officers Ellice and Reece, when Jones, unable to walk without assistance, had appeared with his face hidden behind a mask of white gauze. They also were treated to an extensive tour of Jonestown, seeing all the by then traditional sights. "At no time," they wrote in their report, "did the officers on November 7 see any barbed wire, any guards, armed or otherwise, or any other physical sign that people were being held at Jonestown against their will, nor did any of the conversations by consular officials with People's Temple members at Jonestown reveal any indication that the inhabitants of Jonestown were receiving anything less than normal Guyanese standards of food, clothing, shelter and medical assistance. . . . The members they met appeared to be in good health, mentally alert (considering the advanced age of some of them) and generally happy to be at Jonestown. They all seemed to be absorbed in their various duties. . . . No one indicated any desire to return to the United States."

The U.S. Congressional Report is critical of the performance of the American Embassy. It accuses the officers who went out to the settlement as lacking common sense and skepticism. That Jonestown staged shows for important visitors cannot be denied. Nevertheless, the question remains. To what extent was Jonestown a Potemkin village? If we take the Blakey affidavit as accurate in every detail—and this is generally done—Jonestown, as it was seen by its visitors, was an unadulterated fraud. Jones, it would then have to be admitted, performed on each of these occasions the sorcerer's feat of turning night into day. With a wave of the hand, the joyless would become joyful; the starving would become well fed; despair would become hope; cruelty would become kindness; collective hatred would become collective devotion.

Charles Krause, a correspondent of *The Washington Post,* has given us his first impression of the commune. When he arrived with Ryan he saw women baking bread, others washing clothes, children running about in the playground. No one seemed to be starving. On the contrary, everyone looked quite healthy. Is it possible for hundreds of people to fake good health? Are we to believe that bread was never baked at Jonestown? that clothes were never washed? that children never played? that no one ever laughed? Krause asked Jones whether his people in Jonestown had normal sexual lives. A white woman sitting next to Jones answered the question. "Bullshit. All I have to say is bullshit. People do fuck in Jonestown." Are we, above all, to believe that no one was loyal to the commune and Jim Jones? that no one was prepared to lay down his life for it and for him?

Many things were not as they said. Exaggeration, humbug, downright lies—all existed in Jonestown. It was not a paradise. But neither was it the hell on earth that its enemies made it out to be. Their hysteria goaded it toward extinction. Jonestown, Michael Prokes said, had been backed up against the wall. The Concerned Relatives have never denied that they took Jones's threat of a mass suicide seriously. They made a great deal of it, using it to draw attention to themselves and their campaign. They feared it, and yet, by their words and actions, they helped create the conditions in which it could take place.

On both sides the battle raged out of control. Concreteness rapidly gave way to ideological abstraction. God, America and Freedom were lined up against Atheism, Communism and Slavery. Ryan, for Michael Prokes, was no longer merely an adventurous California Congressman. He was "an arrogant white person representing the American 'establishment' which had failed the blacks and the poor. . . ." Jones, for the Concerned Relatives, was a reincarnation of Satan "employing physical intimidation and psychological coercion as part of a mind-programming campaign aimed at destroying family ties, discrediting belief in God and causing contempt for the United States of America. . . ." Abstraction had turned into a truth-eating monster. Both Jim Jones and

the Stoens were victims of their pasts. Jones was a victim of total-
itarian anxiety, of his hunger for loyalty and obedience which, in
this particular instance, led him to the seizure of a young boy as a
hostage. The Stoens were victims of their "idealism" ("I wanted
utopia real bad," Stoen said on one occasion), their willingness
to serve and sacrifice for the Cause which they thought they
would never desert and which, in this particular instance, led
to the donation of a young boy. Messy human frailties were
lifted up to an exalted sphere. The war between messianic lust
and apostasy became a war between the forces of Good and
Evil.

To my knowledge, not a single defector from the People's Temple has ever admitted any culpability for the carnage that occurred at Jonestown. Not one has ever conceded that past
complicities may have contributed to the Guyana tragedy; that
when, with the flamboyant Ryan at their head, they closed in for
the kill, they were also closing in on their own creation, on aspects
of themselves. That might have bred caution, humility and contrition. But caution, humility and contrition were not conspicuous
among the defectors. They emerged from their years of subser-
vience and loyalty untouched, they tell us, by any moral taint—
the hapless victims of "coercive persuasion" and "mind control,"
heroes and heroines who ought to be applauded for their courage
rather than pardoned for their sins. "The one thing we have
learned," wrote one of their leading lights, "is not to blame ourselves for the things Jim made us do."

"It's over, sister," a man's voice is heard saying on the death tape.
"We've made that day. We made a beautiful day. Let's make it a
beautiful day. . . ."

"We're ready to go," a woman sobs to shouts of approval. "If
you tell us that we have to give our lives now, we're ready."

"Die with respect," Jim Jones pleads. "Die with a degree of
dignity. Lay down your life with dignity. Don't lay down with
tears and agony. Stop this hysterics. This is not the way for people

who are socialistic communists to die. We must die with some dignity."

He sat on his throne, urging them on. The nurses were businesslike, advising parents to calm their screaming children. There was nothing to be afraid of, they said. Death might taste a little bitter, but the bitterness would not last long nor would it be painful. They took their potion, lay down in family groups and writhed to death.

"All they're doing," Jim Jones said, "is taking a drink they take to go to sleep. That's what death is—sleep."

The faith healer from small-town Indiana had come a long way. Many things had gone into the making of this man—credulity, hope, superstition, cynicism, genuine human suffering, the self-sacrificial idealism of scores of people. He had used everything and everyone that had come his way to fashion himself. His had been a patchwork messianism, thrown together from the odds and ends of a dozen disparate therapies of mind, body and soul. The assassins had done their work at the Kaituma airstrip, but there were survivors, and an aircraft was on its way to Georgetown. The last, desperate gamble had failed. He had reached the end of the road and it had turned out to be worse than a cul-de-sac: he could not go back; he could not go forward. He had gone too far, dared too much. Jim Jones had run out of life-giving miracles. Now he could offer only death. That would be the final miracle.

"Take our life from us," he cried. "We got tired. We didn't commit suicide. We committed an act of revolutionary suicide protesting the conditions of an inhuman world."

As it had always been, truth and falsehood were inextricably intertwined in that statement.

The People's Temple died as it had lived.

It is easy to become obsessed with the deaths, with the final moments of Jonestown. The melodrama of the suicides swallows up Jim Jones and the People's Temple. But Jonestown represents more than those nine hundred bodies. They, in fact, obscure the real issues. For the People's Temple as it lived is of much greater significance than the People's Temple as it died. Even then, we must penetrate beyond the People's Temple as such. We must go in search of the ideas it claimed to embody. ". . . there is the fact," observed the U.S. Congressional Report with uncharacteristic insight, "that although he [Jones] controlled considerable wealth . . . he sought out . . . none of the usual trappings of wealth such as fancy cars or expensive houses. In short, Mr. Jones was more interested in ideas than in things."

So, it is to the deadly drama of ideas we must turn—to the ideas and to the milieu in which they took shape, ripened and, eventually, became infected with disease.

That is the American story.

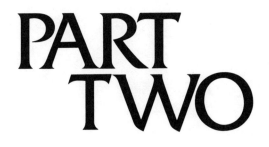

PART
TWO

CHAPTER
7

"... I BEGGED Congressman Ryan not to go; I called his office
... and asked him not to go; I wrote a letter to him telling him
that Jim Jones would see his visit as a provocation ... could they
at least put it off for several weeks. I told them that Jim Jones was
very ill. ... Why did they go? ... Debbie Blakey went to him and
said there are two or three hundred semiautomatic weapons in
there, twenty-five pistols, a homemade bazooka, the lives of the
people are in danger—they practice suicide. ... Why did he go?
Why did the State Department send Mr. Ryan down there after I
begged him not to go?"

So said Mark Lane in a radio broadcast at the end of January
1980.

In San Francisco, it was the season of exculpation, vindication
and explanation.

"It is sadness beyond tears to think of my brothers and sisters
from Jonestown, hundreds of them, not only unidentified but still
unburied. It is significant and tragically symbolic that they have
lain for so long in coffins piled up like so many matchboxes,

waiting for a final resting place. They are back in their homeland, but they have no home. People's Temple was their only home, their only family, their only life. . . . Though I'm white, when I die, I belong with them, for their struggle was mine also."

The voice was that of Michael Prokes, Temple aristocrat, soon to take his own life. He had neither regrets nor apologies to offer.

Those who had died at Jonestown had done so willingly, Prokes said. Their deaths were the result of a collective decision. They had taken their decision to die because they saw that the community they had painstakingly built up from nothing as a labor of love was doomed. Jonestown had been made necessary by the failure of America to meet the needs of its poor and its black citizens. For the hundreds who had died there, it had represented the only possible means of escape from lives throttled by daily misery and oppression in the ghettoes. What the United States had not cared to provide, Jones had given willingly and freely. All that he had done was fill the vacuum created by institutionalized callousness, giving the credit not to himself but to socialism.

But Jones had done more than simply satisfy the material needs of his followers. In addition, he had conferred on them both dignity and freedom. Seeing that freedom and dignity threatened by outside forces, they had preferred to die rather than be restored to the slavery from which they had briefly escaped. It was an act of high moral courage, Prokes insisted, one that he could not expect a depraved society to easily understand. America, inevitably, would do its best to cover up the true circumstances of their martyrdom. They could not find a burial place because it was feared the site would become a national shrine. In death as in life, it was their fate to be dishonored by their country.

It was nonsense to talk of the Guyana martyrs as being no more than semiliterate, brainwashed cultists. That was part of the cleverly orchestrated plot designed to slander and besmirch their memory. The People's Temple was not a cult. It was a socialist movement. Jim Jones had been the exact opposite of a brainwasher; a befuddler of intellect. He could, more fairly, be called a deprogrammer. What he had done was open people's eyes to their real situation, Prokes said. His sermons had been lessons in history. In them he had traced the links of oppression binding the past to the present and disfiguring both. He would "rattle off statistics."

Jones was first and foremost a teacher. The effect on those who had been privileged to hear—and understand—him had been nothing short of therapeutic. "He liberated many minds out of their confused states by demonstrating why there are huge ghettoes in every large city of America and why those ghettoes are populated mostly by blacks." There was nothing in him of either the demagogue or the fanatic. He had preached what many others before him had preached.

At bottom, Prokes asked, had Jim Jones been saying anything different from the panelists of the National Advisory Commission on Civil Disorders who, in their assessment of the causes that had led to the urban insurrections of the sixties, had concluded that the root of the evil was white racism? In the decade since the Commission's report had appeared nothing much had changed. Despite some window dressing, basic patterns of oppression had remained intact. The difference, perhaps, was that Jones had been forceful and lucid in his exposition. Jones understood better than anyone else the sickness that, throughout its history, had debilitated American society. His crime was not only that he had understood and spelled out the nature of that sickness, but that he had offered a cure. This had frightened the establishment.

But, Prokes could hear the Temple's enemies asking, what about the faith healing? How had that fitted in with the socialist message? Prokes was mildly candid. "It is with reluctance," he said, "that I discuss the healing aspect of Jones's ministry, because it will doubtless take away from the credibility of things I say about other areas, at least in some people's minds." He had, he realized, nothing to gain from bringing it up, but he did not want to be accused of avoiding it. He was aware that he would have to depend for a sympathetic response on those few open-minded individuals who were not automatically led astray by prejudice against the paranormal and who, therefore, would not use it to condemn Jones out of hand.

It had to be appreciated from the outset that he—Michael

Prokes—had no intention of suggesting that Jim Jones was in any sense a superhuman being. Far from it. He was all too human. And yet . . . and yet . . . it could not be denied that this all-too-human person had been able to penetrate areas of the mind ignored by most of us. The evidence for it could not be gainsaid. He himself—and thousands of others—had actually witnessed physical transformations taking place during Jones's healings. Those who for years had been crippled by arthritis, for example, had been genuinely helped. He had seen this happen with his own eyes on countless occasions. Jones's psychic talents, his "phenomenal ability" to heal would have convinced the most hardened skeptic. Hundreds had attested to his powers. (Prokes, candid as he was trying to be, did not mention the chicken livers and other props which his master had used to enhance his phenomenal abilities—especially when carrying out his cancer cures.)

But from Prokes's point of view, the crux of the matter was not Jones's paranormal gifts, but his refusal to exploit these talents to the extent that he might have. If he had so desired, Jim Jones could have numbered his disciples not in the thousands but in the tens of thousands. But because the healings were only incidental to his ministry, because the true purpose of that ministry was its social and political message of redemption, he had deliberately refused to succumb to the temptation of being a worker of miracles pure and simple. That would have been the easiest thing in the world for him to do. This abnegation was what those who had accused him of being power-hungry and cynical had failed to understand. Jones, had he so wished, could have surrounded himself with hordes of idolatrous worshipers. For the fact was that most of those who came to the Temple came to be healed, not enlightened. They were not interested in Jones's social and political message. He let them drift away, sacrificing them because his love of socialism was paramount.

It was predictable, Prokes said, that the People's Temple, given its ideological bent, would be subject to a campaign of vilification by the authorities and that the intelligence agencies would use the same techniques they had deployed with every left-wing organi-

zation that had ever existed in America. The harassment had
been constant: their telephones had been tapped; informers had
been planted; their San Francisco headquarters had been burned
down; defectors had been encouraged to be actively antagonistic;
the media had been relentlessly hostile. It had become clear they
were not going to be allowed to survive in the United States. In
order to escape this persecution, to live in peace, they had removed themselves to Guyana. But even there they had been given
no rest by their persecutors. The intelligence agencies had been
determined to bring about their destruction. In the end, by employing tactics of deliberate provocation, they had got what they
wanted. Maybe, Prokes could not resist hinting, they had got, in
the Temple's self-extinction, in those nine hundred corpses, exactly what they had been after. The fascist state, driven by dark
dreams of extermination, had never set any limits to its ruthlessness whenever it had felt itself threatened.

It was not Jones who had caused his brothers and sisters to
drink the cyanide potion. It was, Prokes suggested, the American
Government, in particular the State Department and the CIA,
working through their chosen instruments, Timothy and Grace
Stoen; and, behind them, the shadowy legion of Concerned Relatives. Symbolizing it all was the beautiful boy, the product, as
Jones himself had said, of an unholy union.

"I believe," Prokes wrote, "Tim Stoen was a CIA operative, if
not from the beginning, then certainly long before the end."

Prokes had his own reasons to believe in such a possibility. An
attempt had been made to recruit him before he joined the Temple. At the time he had been working for a television company
and was busily engaged in setting up an exposé of Jim Jones and
his organization. His interest had been roused by a series of articles that had appeared in the *San Francisco Examiner*. These articles had focused on Jones's faith-healing exploits—"The Prophet
Who Raises the Dead" was one of the headlines—and had stirred
a minor controversy. Temple members had responded by picketing the *Examiner*. If, it was suggested, Prokes could somehow
get himself on the Temple staff and pass on whatever informa-

tion of note he picked up, the "Government" would show its gratitude by paying him two hundred dollars a week. The People's Temple, his caller said, was "a revolutionary organization led by a dangerous man, bent on destroying our system of government." Prokes agreed to play the spy. That was in 1972. But Prokes, "starting to identify with the problems and sufferings of the members," was gradually won over to the cause he had come to subvert. Soon, conscience forbade any more betrayal.

When Timothy Stoen left the Temple, Prokes had no doubts as to who had taken his place. If the CIA was not behind the Stoens and those who had gathered about them, where else could they have found the money to finance their campaign? Who had been paying for all those journeys to Guyana and keeping them in the best hotels while they did their dirty work? Why did Timothy Stoen, after so many years of acquiescent silence, begin to insist so vehemently that John Victor was his son? Previously, the Stoens had admitted Jones's paternity. That was a fact publicly acknowledged in the Temple. If Jim Jones was not the child's father, why would he have claimed the boy as his own virtually from the day of his birth? From as early as 1972, Prokes said, Timothy and Grace Stoen had come to detest each other. Grace had actually begun to live with another man. Then, all of a sudden, in the summer of 1977, there they were, proclaiming to the world that John Victor was theirs and that Jim Jones had stolen him away from them. Stoen was perfectly aware when he embarked on his crusade of litigation and harassment, including the threat of mercenary force, that "the child was a point of vulnerability . . . he knew Jim Jones wouldn't give him up even if a court directed him to do so." The conclusion was beyond dispute. Timothy Stoen had not been simply one more traitor to the Cause: he was at the vortex of a set of forces whose single purpose was to destroy Jim Jones and the People's Temple.

Prokes wept for those whose coffins were piled like matchboxes. He saluted his brothers and sisters—those emotionally disturbed, maladjusted, mentally retarded, hyperactive victims of the fascist state—who had died on behalf of all who suffered oppression. Their deaths would not be in vain. Excusing himself, Michael Prokes went into the bathroom and shot himself.

He had done the decent thing.

Grace Stoen was not impressed.

"I was very disappointed in Mike," she wrote to me a few days later, "because he has 'off the record' told reporters he used to work with in Modesto that Jones was a bad person and that he did terrible things to his members. Mike wanted to leave, but the only reason he stayed in the church was because he was counting on Jones dying soon and he wanted to be there to help run the Jonestown commune correctly.

"I think Mike must have had a lot of guilt knowing that he knew Jones was wrong and also *underestimating* him too. I have talked to others who also knew just how corrupt Jones was and even had plans to escape or even help the mass of people down there and they too underestimated Jones—they were just children though so I don't think they can blame themselves.

"Mike cried 'Where are our Human Rights?' at his press conference, yet he saw, he heard and he participated in the violence that was given to the members both physically and mentally in San Francisco, Redwood Valley, Los Angeles and Guyana!"

The colloquium was being held in a Berkeley auditorium. Outside the door, left-wing newspapers and magazines were on sale. The sponsors of the gathering seemed dedicated, as so many American radicals are, to the conspiracy theory of history. I was offered a paperback cataloguing CIA-inspired experiments in mind control through drugs. The long-haired vendor had no doubt that something of the kind had occurred at Jonestown.

"I've examined photographs of the bodies," he said.

"What did that tell you?"

"People who die from cyanide poisoning should be much more contorted. Those corpses were stacked up far too neatly."

"So what do you think really happened?"
"They were probably gassed."
"By whom?"
He smiled broadly.

I paid for the book and went in. The auditorium was about one-third full. Jonestown, apparently, was not a crowd puller. On the platform were Grace Stoen; Stephen Katsaris; the ex-husband of Linda Amos; a journalist from the *San Francisco Chronicle* who had coauthored an instant book on the massacre; a youthful and demure female representative from the Human Freedom Center, a body—now defunct—founded by a pair of Temple defectors and devoted to deprogramming absconding cultists; and—the evening's star attraction—Charles Garry. Slim, silver-haired and wearing a plum-colored jacket, he was a picture of aging elegance.

Garry (he is of Armenian ancestry—his original surname was Garabedian) had come to the People's Temple with sound radical credentials. A lifelong socialist, he had once been summoned to appear before the House Committee on Un-American Activities. But the liaison that had brought him to something approaching national prominence was his association with the Black Panthers: in particular his successful defense in the late sixties of the Party's founder, Huey Newton, on a charge of murdering an Oakland policeman. Since arriving in San Francisco I had tried to make contact with him. All my overtures, however, had gone unacknowledged. I tried to picture this elegant old man who now sat so composedly, palms encasing his cheeks as he scanned his audience, crouching through the long night in the sodden Jonestown undergrowth beside his erstwhile colleague Mark Lane while, not many hundreds of yards away, the People's Temple was butchering itself. It was a difficult image to capture.

The journalist from the *Chronicle*, looking a little bored, spoke first. Jones had cleverly managed to insinuate himself into the San Francisco political scene. He was a masterful social worker and a great self-publicist. In Guyana he had compromised local officials by providing them with the sexual services of Temple women. He had also bribed Customs officials. Jones, he implied, was a thorough scoundrel.

The journalist sat down.

Stephen Katsaris, surprisingly youthful in appearance, followed the journalist. He had once had a daughter. Her name was Maria. She had been killed in Jonestown. At the time, she had been twenty-five years old. He and his daughter had always been close, but after she had been sucked into the People's Temple, they had been distanced from each other. Under Temple pressure she had borne false witness against him, publicly accusing him of having sexually molested her. (A group of women with cropped hair and woolly legs and arms—I discovered afterward they were radical lesbians—sniggered.) Later on, she had accused him of being a CIA agent. He had had many threatening phone calls warning him not to go to Guyana. On the last occasion he had seen Maria, she had behaved in a most hostile manner toward him. He believed she was a victim of brainwashing.

Katsaris sat down.

Grace Stoen announced that she had lost a blood relative at Jonestown, her five-year-old son. (The radical lesbians sniggered.) Looking back on her involvement with the People's Temple, she felt she did not have to reproach herself for anything. She had fought Jim Jones. She had tried to do something. The trouble was that this evil man had had San Francisco in the palm of his hand. He had frightened off criticism because everyone knew he could spend thousands of dollars on lawyers. His long arm could reach, via his friends in high places, into the most unlikely corners. For a while it had seemed as if he was all-powerful and omniscient.

Grace Stoen sat down.

The demure girl from the Human Freedom Center rose. People who came out of cults came out with nothing. They needed love; they needed counseling. The People's Temple was only the tip of the cultic iceberg. Something, she suspected, might have to be done about the breakdown of the American family. The young were looking for affiliation, for meaning in their lives. A lot of counseling was needed. . . .

The demure girl sat down.

Linda Amos' ex-husband was brief. He had lost a daughter in

Jonestown. (The radical lesbians sniggered.) The Temple had made you feel that there was something wrong with you for caring, for bothering about the fate of your loved ones. It was a terrible thing to have happened to Guyana, such a peaceful and gentle place, innocent of political turmoil. The poor Guyanese were still reeling with the shock.

He sat down.

It was the turn of Charles Garry. He rose with a dignified and determined air.

This discussion, he said, was most probably very upsetting. Since that tragic day he had done nothing but think about Jonestown and wonder why it had come to such a sorry pass. The incident raised serious questions. Why had so many people affirmed they had loved it out there? Why had it been necessary for a group of Americans to travel so far from their homeland to create, out in the middle of nowhere and at a cost of several million dollars, a community which he had considered a paradise? Why had the discontent in Jonestown not expressed itself? Those were some of the questions that continued to bother him.

Garry raised an arm. "Fifteen million Americans go to bed hungry in this country every night. Fifty million people live in substandard housing. When a man like Jim Jones comes forward —he called himself God and the Father—to the hungry and the unwanted and the unloved and offers them something, we then get such a situation as existed in Jonestown."

He tidied straying strands of his silver hair; he stared up at the ceiling. The sadness was that nearly a thousand people were now dead. But the conditions that had caused Jonestown were still flourishing. Hunger was all around them. Millions of people were starving in the land of plenty.

He recalled his first contacts with the People's Temple back in 1977. He had been invited to speak to the congregation. Until then he had not heard of the People's Temple. His talk had lasted about twenty minutes and had been enthusiastically received. The audience had been absolutely beautiful and the entertainment absolutely tremendous. A month later he was asked to pay the

Temple another visit, this time to introduce the exiled Chilean
Minister of Finance: the People's Temple, he explained, was active in the Chilean refugee movement. He was summoned a third
time. The occasion was a testimonial dinner in behalf of Jim
Jones. Practically every dignitary in the county was there, including some representatives of the John Birch Society (an eloquent
illustration of Jim Jones's eclecticism). Also among the guests that
evening were four reporters who, not long before, had been jailed
for refusing to reveal sources of information. Garry had witnessed a demonstration of support for the four organized by the
People's Temple. Some eight or nine hundred Temple adherents
had picketed the jail where they were being held. The sight had
moved him.

"I saw all these things and I saw a man—Jim Jones—who talked
about socialism. I personally believe in socialism. I personally believe that the only answer to the world's problems is going to be
socialism with all the democratic rights preserved. Socialism—
American style. So I looked upon the People's Temple as friends,
and then I found that many members of the Temple had been
clients of my law firm and had been active in the Black Panther
Party. So I felt I had a natural community of interest with these
people."

There were those, he was aware, who believed he had taken on
the Temple as a client for financial reasons. That was a travesty
of the truth. The figures would speak for themselves. His office
had expended fourteen hundred hours of labor in connection
with Temple business. All he had to show for it was $13,500. His
involvement with Jim Jones had been based not on any hopes of
princely reward but on the conviction that the People's Temple
was "moving in the direction of a better world and a better society."

In July 1977 four Temple representatives had requested a
meeting with him. One of them was Michael Prokes. Another was
that Eugene Chaikin who, three years earlier, had figured prominently in the advertisement for the Temple's faith-healing extra-
vaganza in Georgetown, asserting that his Pastor was the most

loving, Christ-like human being he had ever met. A third was a young girl named Teri Buford who, in the aftermath of the Jonestown massacre, would become a garrulous protegée of Mark Lane.

Jim Jones, the delegation said, wished to hire him. He wanted a libel action brought against *New West* magazine, which was planning to publish a defamatory article about the Temple.

Garry's answer was that as a fervent supporter of First Amendment rights he did not like libel actions. But even more important than that, no one whose house was not in flawless order should contemplate filing such a suit. He gave strict orders that the Temple was not to put out any form of literature or hold any outraged press conferences when the article—which he had read and thought was "unfair"—appeared.

Something else was worrying him. He felt that there was a violation of law in the Temple's "life care" policy—the process whereby followers signed over all their assets to the Temple in expectation that they would be taken care of for the rest of their lives. The People's Temple might have been moving in the direction of a better world and a better society, but Garry was lawyer enough to recognize that their socialist housekeeping was not entirely flawless. The four delegates seemed to agree to abide by his prohibition. But when the article did appear, they held outraged press conferences and issued statements maligning their critics. The result was two libel actions.

Garry might have been discouraged. His clients had promised him something and then, in the heat of battle, reneged. Discouragement might have turned to defection when Jim Jones fled to Guyana. As it was, he persevered, showing no outward sign of disaffection from the cause.

In September 1977 he had a telephone call from Jim Jones.

"He was hysterical. He did not make any sense. He said the enemy was outside. People were shooting at him. He said they had come to kidnap his son and the enemy in Guyana had taken over because all of the top leadership of Guyana was in Washington, D.C. I said, 'Jim, if you are a Marxist, your present conduct is not consonant with that.'"

After that telephone call, Garry might have been even more discouraged. He might have begun to wonder what was happening to all those people in life care who had been hastily shipped out to Guyana. As it was, he persevered. The chaos in Guyana disappeared as suddenly as it had arisen, and Jim Jones's conduct once again became consonant with his Marxist outlook. In October he went out to Guyana. He spent four days in Jonestown. That was the first time, odd as it might seem, that he had had an opportunity to talk face to face with Jim Jones. He was left at complete liberty to see everything, to question everyone, to wander as he pleased.

"I confronted many of the people who were there. Some of those men and women I had known in San Francisco over the years. And I got the most glorious reports. The attitudes were very affirmative. I talked to Maria Katsaris at length. I talked to every person I could find there to talk to in any way that I could."

He had returned to the United States and had announced that he had been to Paradise. The irony was that since the catastrophe he had spoken to almost eighty people who, at one time or another, had lived in Jonestown; and astonishingly, there was suddenly no unanimity of opinion. While most still believed that it had been beautiful, some now said it had not been beautiful at all. He was at a loss how to account for this. It had proved impossible to bring their conflicting accounts into line.

"I don't know what is fact and what is fiction. I don't know . . ." Garry dried his forehead.

From the investigations he had subsequently carried out, he was now satisfied that Jim Jones had been a master of deceit. He had created a strategy called "diversion." Over the years this practice of deception—which was what "diversion" had amounted to —must have become second nature to Temple members. Who could say, even now, how much diversion there was in the statements of both avowed friends and enemies of the People's Temple?

In September 1978 he returned to Jonestown. The atmosphere was not as pleasant as it had been on the previous visit. Jim Jones was a sick man, incoherent and babbling. Many of his courtiers were "arse-kissing." He advised hospitalization; he advised that the media and the Concerned Relatives be let in.

"I told him, 'If you don't do that, people will wonder why you only allow selected people to come and see this place. You can't run life with such narrowness and bigotry.' That is what I told him."

He could prove he had said that; his message to Jones had been put on tape; that tape was now in his possession. From the beginning of his relationship with the Temple, he had insisted that Jonestown be opened up to the media and Concerned Relatives. He had no reason to reproach himself. But as usual, his good advice had been ignored.

It was on this trip that the battle for socialism, for a better world, became fused with another kind of battle—the battle to retain his dignity, to be acknowledged as the sole champion and defender of the Temple faith. Suddenly, he was a distraught lover fighting to keep to himself the affections of a fickle mistress. As he was about to leave Georgetown for San Francisco, Charles Garry ran into Mark Lane.

"I don't know how he'd got there or what he was doing in Georgetown. He said he was on his way to London. But there must be an easier way to get to London than by way of Georgetown."

However, he thought no more of it. Back in San Francisco he had a call from the press that was to shatter his peace of mind. His informant told him he had heard that Jim Jones was coming back to the United States and was intending to file a lawsuit of gargantuan proportions against the U.S. Government.

"I said, 'Who told you that?' He said Mark Lane had told him. I said I knew nothing about it."

On the day he had been engaged to represent the People's Temple, he had sent for the Freedom of Information files on Temple members. He had made eleven hundred requests. His researches had shown him that there was not a single member of the People's Temple on whom any sort of file was being kept. There was no U.S. Government plan to interfere with Jonestown.

His work with the Black Panthers had given him great experience in such matters. He had looked with practiced eyes and found nothing. So Mark Lane had nothing to go on except his imagination.

(So, come to that, did Garry in the halcyon days before the intervention of Mark Lane. Early in September 1977, he was quoted thus in the *San Francisco Examiner:* ". . . Garry said that the attacks on Jones are part of a seven-year-long conspiracy 'to destroy and eliminate the Temple as a force in the community' . . . Garry said the Treasury and IRS have denied conducting an ongoing investigation and added, 'Government denials don't mean anything.' " Maybe, at that stage, Garry had not completed his search through the Freedom of Information files.)

He asked the Temple what Mark Lane was doing. They said he was "just a friend."

"They told me Mark Lane would not be in the picture. I had told them I was going to withdraw representation from them if he was."

But once again, he had been diverted. One morning he read in the newspaper of Ryan's wish to go to Jonestown and that Mark Lane, now chillingly designated the Temple's attorney, had replied to him in a somewhat negative manner. He telephoned the Temple immediately.

"I asked—what gives? I was told he was not the attorney, just a friend. I said I would not put up with it. I got infuriated."

No preceding occurrence or suspicion of wrongdoing had so ruffled Garry's high-minded imperturbability and determination to serve the Cause—not the illegalities of the life-care policy; not the revelations of extortion, beatings, faith-healing trickery and other unpleasantnesses made public knowledge by the West Coast press; not Jim Jones's flight to Guyana; not the sight of his client, babbling and incoherent, surrounded by fawning courtiers. He could put up with all that. What was absolutely intolerable was the intrusion of Mark Lane into a territory he had staked out for himself; over which he had laid down the scents of his own personal radical commitment.

On November 10, he telephoned the Temple again. He delivered an ultimatum: they had three days in which to repudiate Mark Lane as their attorney; if they did not comply, he would withdraw representation. The Temple was in touch the next day. Jones, he was told, was semicomatose. He was packed in ice. Could Garry wait until he had recovered? But Garry was in no mood to wait. He was stern and uncompromising.

"I said humbug. I insisted on a decision."

On November 15, three days before the massacre, he received a wire. "Jim Jones needs you. Tickets waiting. Come immediately."

Jones needed him! Naturally, he went. But so too did Mar'. Lane, whom Jones also seemed to need. The rest, of course, was now history, including that miserable night spent lurking in the jungle undergrowth beside his rival while socialism, American style, reached its bloody climax.

There was, however, one more thing he wanted to share with us. It would help to throw some light on his tribulations. He had in his possession a memo from the ubiquitous Eugene Chaikin to Jim Jones. That memo said: "Charles Garry is a liberal. If he knew what was going on here and in California he would not represent us. Furthermore, if he was to drop us now it would be disastrous for us. We should make plans to dump him at our convenience so that we do not get hurt by it."

So! It was clear the Temple had understood the kind of man with whom they were dealing. His uncompromising idealism, he seemed to want to say, had alarmed them. . . .

The audience, however, was restless.

"Why do you feel the need to defend yourself for forty-five minutes?" an impatient voice boomed across the auditorium.

The radical lesbians clapped and hooted approval.

Garry fell awkwardly silent, staring up bemusedly at the tiered ranks of seats.

"I would have wished that you, Mr. Garry," Stephen Katsaris broke in quietly, "would have withdrawn as Temple representative much earlier. Why didn't you? You called it paradise and yet, by your own admission, you knew Jones was crazy."

Garry tidied his hair. "I thought the relatives' charges were untrue, exaggerated . . ."

A man in a plaid shirt started to shout: "This is not getting to the heart of the matter. Let's get to the heart of the matter. Let's talk about the ideological struggle. We all know that anybody who challenges this social order—like Jones did—is automatically treated like an enemy. They'll bomb you, they'll shoot you in your sleep like they did the Black Panthers, they'll drug you . . ."

A girl's voice made itself heard: "I want to know what evidence there is of outside forces being at work in Jonestown."

Garry began to say he was busily looking into that, but his reply was lost in the hubbub.

The man in the plaid shirt was on his feet again. "What happened in Guyana is worse than what happened in Nazi Europe. The truth about Guyana is going to make Watergate look like child's play."

Garry nodded sagely.

Somebody raised the question of the extermination of Red Indians. The U.S. Army was supposed to be injecting them with smallpox.

". . . the ideological struggle. Let's talk about the ideological struggle. . . ."

I decided it was time to leave.

In Reno, Nevada, Rev John Moore—for whom Jonestown had evoked the words of Micah and whose two daughters had perished there—was in a more somber and apocalyptic mood than Charles Garry. But he was equally unrepentant.

The people of Jonestown, he said in a sermon, were human beings. They were not cultists, fanatics or kooks. It was idolatry that had destroyed the People's Temple. Yet few movements in our time had expressed, as it had done, Jesus' parable of the Last Judgment. The People's Temple had fed the hungry, nursed the sick, given shelter to the homeless, visited those in prison. They had cared for those whom no one else had cared about. Death had come because there was none among them strong enough or free enough to kick over the vat of cyanide. But should they be especially blamed for that? How many were there who were free enough and strong enough to hurl themselves "against the vats of nuclear stockpiles for the sake of the world?" Because such individuals were few we would all, one of these days, be forced to drink nuclear cyanide. That would be murder; but our passivity would also make it suicide. Death was everywhere. The arms race was death; the abyss separating governors and governed was death; cybernation was death; unemployment was death. Nowhere was death more rampant than in the decaying cities where the sense of community, of human belongingness had been destroyed. That was the significance of Jonestown—it had been an attempt to build a common life, facing away from the forces of death. Its failure was the world's loss.

"I can only compare Jones to Hitler," the Director of the Human Freedom Center said.

She was a plain-faced woman, probably in her early forties; her husband—he had been the official Temple photographer—was a slightly older, plain-faced man. She had spent six years in the Temple, quitting in 1975. It was then that she had made the remarkable discovery—under the tutelage of the mind-control experts—that neither she nor any of the other reformed disciples bore the slightest moral responsibility for anything untoward they might have done during their Temple years. The burden was entirely Jim's.

What, I asked, had Jones been after?

"Power," she said.

"Power to do what?"

"He wanted to rule the world."

"To rule the world! Are you sure?"

"Of course I'm sure." She looked offended. "He was planning to take over the world."

"How exactly did he plan to do that?" I felt as if I had strayed into the lurid plot of a high-adventure comic book.

"He'd gotten hold of an atomic bomb."

"How did he get hold of an atomic bomb?"

"I don't know."

"Did you ever see the bomb?"

"No. But I know he had one."

"What did he plan to do with it?"

"To detonate it somewhere in the U.S.A. Naturally, Americans would think the Russians had done it. So there'd be a war. When they had both destroyed each other, Jim and his followers would come out from the jungle to take over the world."

"You really do believe that was what he planned to do?"

My skepticism seemed to offend her. And why should I have been skeptical? She had merely traded one extremist belief (Jones as Messiah) for another (Jones as Antichrist with an atom bomb). Some months later, I read the book she wrote about her experiences in the Temple. In it she described how the Temple aristocracy would sometimes sit around discussing the best means of preserving the sperm of Jim Jones; out of which, it was hoped, would spring the future master race that would govern mankind. It was a truly comic-book universe.

We began to talk about her work. It was amazing, she said, how quickly human beings developed habits of dependence.

"I could be running a cult tomorrow," she said. "It's the easiest thing in the world to do." She snapped her fingers.

Why did she think it was so easy?

People were searching for "structure." Especially here in California, where so many traditions had broken down.

"You have to teach people how to be free," she said.

"Is it possible to teach that?"

Only if you believed in the one true God and believed in America.

Art Agnos, a liberal Democrat, member of the California State Legislature, had been an admirer of the People's Temple.

"Jim Jones made people feel good about taking his help. Welfare is a bad word in this country. I've come across many older people who would rather die than go on welfare. We've made it into a shameful last resort. But with Jones it was different. It wasn't a shameful thing to do. They didn't lose their self-respect in going to him."

Many of the people Jones had served were from the district he represented. He had referred many of his constituents to the various services provided by the People's Temple.

"We would have people come into this office who had lost their check and the welfare system, because of its bureaucracy, would take one or two weeks to replace it. So you would send them over to Jim Jones and *that day* they would be taken care of. All of the other welfare institutions, public and private, whether it was the Salvation Army or the Catholic Social Services or the Lutheran Social Services, they would all have their bureaucracy. Jones had none. You'd go in if you were in trouble, if you were in need, and they'd take care of you. No questions asked."

It was those of his constituents who had run out of options, for whom no one had anything, that his office had consigned to the mercy of Jim Jones. The Temple was always ready to extend a helping hand. If an older person needed fifty dollars' worth of groceries, a fifty-dollar bag would be delivered. If he needed someone to pick him up and take him to the doctor, the Temple would do that.

"There was a senior-citizen escort service. The Temple gave them five thousand dollars just like that when they were de-funded by a public agency. Jones just gave them five thousand dollars. They had a clinic at their church—excellent health care right there. No tambourines played. No sermons to listen to. They just walked in and were seen to. It was very smart that people would be attracted to that kind of dignified, good service and would go back of their own volition. They didn't need to be proselytized." He stared at me without repentance.

Had Jonestown been debated in the State Assembly?

Agnos shook his head.

Why not?

First of all, it had happened at a time when the Legislature was not in session.

In the second place, by the time it had reconvened in January, all the analyses had taken place. The mystery had been solved.

In the third place, it was seen as a San Francisco aberration.

In the fourth place, the deaths had occurred in Guyana. It was not the practice of the State Legislature to debate foreign affairs.

Jonestown, where it was not simply dismissed as irrelevant, had dwindled to a mere embarrassment. To bring the subject up was to display bad manners, to show a lack of sensitivity to the feelings of one's hosts; but mainly, it was a bore.

When I arrived in San Francisco, Willie Brown, a black Democratic representative in the State Legislature and one of the stars of the city's liberal establishment, was wittily being raffled off among his constituents. The prize: an opportunity to have lunch with him. Some weeks after the raffle, I sat in his law office sipping California wine, listening to him talk.

Yes, he agreed, most people were bored with the subject of Jonestown. Maybe that was because so many of the victims had been black and because there were no votes to be had in it.

Brown was stylishly dressed. Outside in the waiting room his middle-class black clients were drinking wine amid potted plants and leafing through glossy magazines like *Ebony* and *Black Enterprise* which were filled with advertisements that showed blacks drinking Grand Marnier, smoking menthol-flavored cigarettes on the decks of yachts, sprawling dreamily on furry rugs in opulently furnished living rooms.

Brown could not understand how his old friend Jim Jones had been able to make black people kill their children. More than almost any other group, blacks loved their children, cared for them and generally sought every means to protect them from harm. It was strange too that all those very urban people should have wanted to uproot themselves and go to live on a cooperative socialist farm in faraway Guyana. Blacks might have had the rough end of the stick in America, but they were passionate believers in their rights and in the system that, however imperfectly it might do so, offered them those rights. The vast majority, including himself, desired not to shake that system but to work within it. Blacks were good Americans. The trouble was that Jones had had far too much power. No one man should ever be allowed to have that much power. It tended to have a deleterious effect on the character.

How, I asked, had he been able to accumulate that kind of power?

That, Brown said, was one of the mysteries of the whole business. It might have been helped along by the fact that Jones had delivered on many of his promises. He had provided his followers not only with badly needed welfare services but with a sense of belonging and worth. Jones had done what very few were prepared to do. He had picked up the tramps, the lonely, the no-hopers and given their lives new hope and meaning. Nevertheless, he did not think that a Jonestown could ever happen again. The black community was now vetting all its self-proclaimed saviors very carefully. Credentials were being demanded and examined. Blacks had learned their lesson. They were not going to fall for the Jones kind of line anymore.

Brown blinked satisfiedly.

But had the lesson that was learned had to be so drastic? He had been a regular visitor to the Temple; he had seen the ecstatic atmosphere of personal devotion that reigned there. Hadn't Jones's faith-healing exercises ever given him pause?

Brown gestured suavely. It was not his job to tell other people what to believe. He was not going to take it upon himself to deprive old women of their comforts.

What about the beatings and financial exactions revealed by the West Coast press? Why, in the light of those tyrannies, had he continued to be a good friend to the People's Temple?

Because he never credited anything that appeared in *New West*. It was a CIA-infiltrated rag.

There had been earlier articles, earlier hints of the Temple's gross practices, in other publications. Why had he paid no attention to those?

Brown looked a trifle impatient. He didn't have time to read everything that was published; he didn't have a clippings service at his disposal. (In 1972 a series of highly critical articles had appeared in the *San Francisco Examiner*—hardly an obscure source.) He saw what Jim Jones was doing. What he had seen he had liked. Jones, in his opinion, had been doing an excellent job. He, Brown, was convinced that his faith-healing friend had been a genuine Marxist.

There were two of them—Mother and Daughter.

Daughter, who had immediately let me know that she was a militant feminist and not to be treated lightly, sat sprawled in an armchair, her legs spread in masculine fashion. Mother, dressed in faded jeans, was slimmer and altogether better kept. Graying hair reached down to the small of her back. She was standing by a window, eyeing me angrily, her face haloed by the California sunshine.

"Why shouldn't we white radicals suffer from guilt?" she asked. "Why is it wrong to feel guilty at the sight of oppression and injustice?"

"I was just wondering if it was a secure enough base on which to build your convictions."

"I don't care for your European contempt," she said.

"My European contempt?"

"Europeans don't understand Americans. They don't understand our idealism—the kind of *guilt*—that led a lot of brave young people into the Temple." She paced up and down. "I don't like your arrogance at all."

Daughter intervened. "You know," she said, dithering her legs, "I'm not surprised in the least by what happened at Jonestown. It has nothing to do with radicalism gone wrong, in my own opinion . . ."

"Of course it hasn't," Mother interrupted. "That's what he doesn't understand . . ."

". . . it's the obvious result of patriarchy," Daughter concluded.

Even Mother seemed a little taken aback. She stopped pacing and stared intently at her offspring.

Patriarchy, Daughter said, was the curse of Western civilization. Jonestown was no more than an unconscious projection of the male-dominated nuclear family. Every sexist family structure was a miniature Jonestown. "I don't know if you're aware," she added, "that there's a definite link between sexist toilet-training practices and Nazism."

I said I had not been aware of that.

Mother returned to the attack. "I suppose you didn't like the hippies either," she said. "Because they were American idealists too. Their revolt against suburban values and hypocrisy left a lasting mark on the attitudes of this country. They were sickened by the sight of their so-called elders and betters zonking themselves out on martinis before dinner and murdering innocent Vietnamese peasants in their rice paddies."

"But didn't they in their turn get zonked out on LSD before dinner?"

Mother paused, glaring at me. "I suppose you'll be bringing up Charlie Manson next."

"Patriarchy again," Daughter said. "He even called his group the *family*. A totally sexist setup. Manson was your original MCP."

"A condition no doubt aggravated by wrong toilet-training practices," I said.

"That goes without saying," Daughter replied.

CHAPTER
8

IT WAS called the New Earth Exposition. "Living Lightly on the Earth" was how it subtitled itself. San Francisco, whose Mayor had proclaimed New Earth Week, was urged to attend. The New Earth Exposition, the handout said, recognized that the resources of the earth were finite, that all human activities were interrelated and that the balance between man and nature was fragile. For all those reasons, it had dedicated itself to the exploration of ways in which man might live more lightly on the earth and to promoting the general acceptance of a life-style that would enable everyone to live better with less in a nondestructive framework.

The tone, the vocabulary, were unmistakable. Interrelatedness. Human. Fragile balance. Life-style. The handout spoke in the unique accents of California. I had been living in San Francisco long enough to have become almost inured to the singular blend of eco and ego, of technologically minded worldliness and etherealism, of overripe self-consciousness and opulent complacency. Whales were going to be the stars of the show. One could see films of whales, hold aloft balloons shaped like whales, clamber about sculptures of whales, buy whale jewelry, even steep oneself in the language of whales. (Some months later a friend of a friend was to give birth in darkness to the accompaniment of whale sounds. I am informed that the child, as a result, possesses a transcendental calm.)

I decided I would go.

Muddy vans that spoke of their owners' closeness to the soil were plentiful in the streets near the exhibition hall. Out had come the bearded and pigtailed with their backpacks; fecund-eyed girls with babies in slings; shaggy feminists; liberated homosexuals; earnest, mustachioed teachers worried about Energy; divorcées with allergies and lower-back pain. It was a gathering of tribes; of life-styles. Awaiting them were the solar-panel salesmen; the herbalists; the therapists; the purveyors of woodstoves, windmills and earthworms. Close to the entrance there was a stall chiefly devoted to the works of Timothy Leary, the former prince of acid, advocate of the politics of ecstasy, whose psychonautical voyages had once led to Algerian exile. His interest, to judge from the stall, had shifted from inner to outer space: Leary, it seemed, was now "into" planetary colonization. I did not linger, but pushed on, past the giant effigy of a whale, to the big, subterranean hall beyond.

The hall was divided into various sections—Energy and Appropriate Technology; Wholistic Health and Personal Growth; Food and Gardening; Wilderness and Ecology; Shelter; Transportation; Interior Environments. I examined the woodstoves on display in Energy and Appropriate Technology. They were expensive, costing about a thousand dollars.

"Wouldn't getting wood be a problem?" I asked the salesman.

"Not if you live in Oregon," he said. "They have one hell of a lot of trees up there."

"But what happens if I don't live in Oregon?"

He shrugged. "Then you might have some problems."

"I thought it wasn't a good idea to be cutting down too many trees."

"Yeah . . . I guess that's right. I hadn't thought of that. But I reckon they'll develop some quick-growing ones."

For the most part, however, Energy and Appropriate Technology was given over to a bewildering variety of solar devices. I progressed quickly into Shelter and Habitat. The main attraction here was the New Earth Self-Reliant House. This was described as an assembly of homesite technologies. These included such ecological refinements as water recycling, fish polyculture and solar cooking. The aim was complete self-sufficiency in an urban homestead. Self-sufficiency began, suitably humbly, suitably lightly, with earthworms.

Boxes of these creatures were stored beneath aquariums. The earthworms would, apparently, process—i.e., eat—the algae scraped from the sides of the aquariums. The fish would then eat the worms. In turn, the residents of the Self-Reliant House would eat—i.e., process—the fish, previously cooked in the solar-powered oven. The usefulness of the earthworms and the fish did not end there. The water from the aquariums, being rich in nutrients, could be fed to the vegetable seedlings placed above the aquariums. In due course the residents would share the vegetables grown in the solar-heated greenhouse with the chickens and rabbits they kept out in the back. Eventually, they would eat some of those chickens and rabbits. The wastes generated by man and animal would be used to grow more seedlings nourished by the aquarium water whose algae fed the worms that fed the fish. Apart from the occasional trip to a nearby recycling workshop to break down the more intractable by-products, the residents of the Self-Reliant House would never need to leave it and so eliminate any risk of disturbing the fragile balance of Spaceship Earth. They would have established a self-perpetuating ecosystem; a virtually Jain-like purity in their relationship with the environment. Algae, worms, fish, rabbits, chicken and man would all be locked into their respective ecological niches. Over all would shine the beneficent sun. If I had wanted to, I could have embarked on my salvation there and then by investing just under two hundred dollars in a mini worm farm—"Nature's finest waste converter." I resisted the temptation.

I drifted into Food and Gardening. My attention was caught by a new and revolutionary yogurt whose methods of manufacture, it was claimed, did not destroy the environment as other, more traditional methods of manufacture had been doing for generations. Not only did it not wreak untold environmental havoc, but it could be used to feed the starving millions of Asia, Africa and Latin America. Its promoters explained. Ten pounds of milk made one pound of cheese and nine pounds of whey. Most of this unwanted whey was siphoned off into rivers and lakes. Whey, in such quantities, was an ecologist's nightmare. This miraculous new yogurt made use of the whey that would normally be discarded. One gallon of it used enough whey to spare the environment the equivalent effect of thirty people living in a metropolitan area for one day and saved fifty-four thousand gallons of water. In nutritional value, it was surpassed only by mother's milk and eggs. I went away sobered by the awareness of the grave threat ordinary yogurt posed to the planet.

Food and Gardening carried on the theme of self-reliance—growing your own. Organic farming in the backyard was one obvious possibility; and if you did not have a backyard, hydroponic farming in the livingroom was a good substitute.

A change in the planetary diet was another basic requirement of the New Age. Tofu (soybean curd) burgers and tofu cheesecake were on display. Wheat-grass juice was highly recommended. Feeling thirsty, I bought myself a cosmic herbal cocktail.

A clown playing an accordion wandered past me. Children clambered about a whale sculpture. A group of feminists were shouting on the central stage, hairy arms punching the air. The cause of their excitement eluded me. One aspect of their grim evolution was summed up in a document I had been given which set out the rules of nonsexist language to be adhered to by newswriters.

Rule No. 1 stated that news stories about women were to be treated exactly as if they were news stories about men. If the style, tone or concept seemed in any way offensive to women, the item was to be either rewritten or abandoned.

Rule No. 2 was about pronouns. They were, intrinsically, sexist and therefore deeply offensive to women. A good news editor should be able to restructure whole sentences without having to use personal pronouns at all. Ships, hurricanes, countries and nature were now "it," not "she." Male persons should not be first in order of mention more than half the time.

Rule No. 3 was about titles. The introduction of gender into titles was strictly taboo. Traditional sexist labels like "actress" and "suffragette" would have to be discarded. "Housewife" was a particularly offensive term and not to be used under any circumstances.

Rule No. 4 forbade any reference to marital status. To talk about "Miss" and "Mrs." verged on the obscene. But even "Ms." and "Mr." could be offensive and were to be avoided if at all possible.

Rule No. 5 stated that women were *never* to be referred to as ladies, gals, chicks, girls, the fair sex, coeds, divorcées, career girls, housewives or blondes.

Rule No. 6 spelled out the policy to be adopted toward women's struggles and the struggles of all other oppressed groups in the society, especially homosexuals and blacks. These were to be treated with the utmost dignity. The activities of women had to be given the same space as the activities of men.

Rule No. 7 abolished any reference to the sexual orientation of persons in the news. It was an unwarranted presumption to assume that newsmakers were heterosexual.

Rule No. 8 abolished the use of stereotyping words. These included "feminine," "mother" and "husband."

Rule No. 9 announced that the age of "man" was finished. From now on persons would wear synthetic, not man-made, fibers; they would sleep in two-person tents; they would work not man-hours, but work-hours. Gone forever were man-to-man talks and the-man-in-the-street.

Having finished my cosmic cocktail, I took care to stay clear of the howling humans on the stage, skirted a display that labeled itself Women in the Wilderness and penetrated into the gentler realms of Wholistic Health and Personal Growth.

Wholism (sometimes spelled holism) was another term that I had not heard until coming to California. It was explained by one of its practitioners and ideologues, a qualified medical doctor, who was also a Professor of Public Health and Urban Social Philosophy—as well as Director of something called the Dual Degree Option and Integrating Seminars. Anything (I am using restructured, nonsexist language) that is Whole, Whole within itself and working in harmonious conjunction with all the components of its world, is, by definition, healthy. Healthiness, properly understood, is Holiness (Wholiness). Healthiness (Holiness, Wholiness) is to be truly alive—to be, that is, afloat on the River of Life. Aliveness (Healthiness, Wholiness, Holiness) is to be at one with oneself, with one's inner being, with one's dreams, with the world. True healing is the process of making Whole.

The creation or restoration of our wholistic being is not merely the concern of doctors, but that of all humans who have to cope with the rigors of earthly existence. We all have to learn how to be truly Alive (Healthy, Whole, Holy), to unify the fear, love, warmth, pain and hope of existence. When wholeness does not exist—and that is nearly always the case—something is Awry. Some people call this awryness (Unwholeness, Unholiness, Unhealthiness, Unaliveness) illness. But to call awryness illness is to rob the human condition of its meaning and complexity. This is precisely what conventional medical practice does. Conventional medicine confines its attention only to the symptoms of what it calls disease. The contextual issues are ignored. But what illness really connotes is a lack of inner and outer balance—in a word, Awryness. Illness, in fact, is an attempt at personal growth. It is a struggle for harmony and for wholeness. Illness is a creative process. Even dying, come to that, can be a creative experience. The doctors who lock us up in Illness Worlds (hospitals) are stifling the creativity of inner being, frustrating the organism's striving for wholeness. Shamans, faith healers and lamas are authentic mediators between our bodies, minds and souls and the higher planes of spiritual reality. Wholeness will be achieved through art, music, the quest for God; through creative insanity. These are the avenues that lead to totality of being. To be whole is to be reborn.

Each holist, however, has his own version of the thing. Wholistic Health and Personal Growth took up about a third of the subterranean hall. It was a flourishing science. I watched people being massaged, others having their biorhythms monitored, yet others rolling on the ground, testing a grooved, club-shaped piece of wood that conformed to the principles of the Yang and the Yin and was guaranteed to clear up the pains of the lower back. I could have enrolled in the Holistic Life University for a two-year course in holistic health, holistic childbirth and life–death transitions. One entrepreneur offered the Footsie Roller, carved out of cherry wood and finished with the natural oils of the tung nut. It promised to release the tensions I harbored in my feet and to protect and promote my natural energy flow. The Iridology Institute of America boasted of how it had changed the muddy green irises of a sixty-two-year-old man to sky blue in the space of six months. Up on the Wholistic Health stage someone was talking about the positive effects of negative ions on health and house plants. The accordion-playing clown passed and repassed.

I strayed into Interior Environment. Here I saw Creative Lounging furniture, colorful hammocks from Yucatán, Japanese folding beds, an ingenious prismatic device that would flood a room with a dazzling labyrinth of rainbows. I could have bought Unjeans, Shakti shoes, recycled safari clothing. It was impossible not to marvel at the eclectic riot of privileged consumerism that heralded itself as the New Age; and we could live lightly and opulently not only on the earth but under it as well: one entrepreneur was showing off his range of pine coffins.

Interior Environment led to Schools and Communities. Kerista Village advertised itself as a utopian community pioneering a new spirituality, a new family structure, a new economic system, a new psychology—and, most arrestingly, a new sexuality. Several of the men wore their hair in pigtails; the women looked friendly and fecund. I paused for a chat.

Kerista was the inspiration of two Energy Forces, Brother Jud and Even Eve. In 1956 Brother Jud had had a mystical experience which propelled him out of his relatively straight life-style into a search for communal fulfillment and meaningful religiousness. The other Energy Force, Even Eve, after experimenting with the potential of consciousness raising through multimedia art in Vermont, migrated to San Francisco in the flower-power sixties. Even Eve was confused about many things at that time, but of one thing she was sure: the necessity, in some form, of group sex.

It was in San Francisco that the two Energy Forces met and coalesced. Together, Brother Jud and Even Eve set out to found the world's next great religion. Group sex metamorphosed itself into the more elevated concept of polyfidelity. This novel sexual institution became the heart of the Kerista life-style. Its instrument was the BFIC, the Best Friend Identity Cluster. Each BFIC was composed of up to twelve men and twelve women—or, if you prefer, twelve women and twelve men. Sexual gratification was shared by—but limited to—the members of the BFIC. Polyinfidelity—BFIC hopping—was not allowed: sexual relations were to be strictly endogamous. Novitiates, I was disappointed to learn, were not allowed to join a BFIC immediately. They were assigned to the People Pool and were expected to remain celibate while they scouted out a BFIC appropriate to their needs. The atmosphere in Kerista was said to be partylike because polyfidelity permitted the appreciation of many types of human beings, all of whom could be sampled and fully experienced within the BFIC. Despite this, Keristans saw themselves as a new kind of monastic order. Self-admittedly, they were not in the conventional ascetic mold. All the same, they were turned on only by the highest and purest forms of sex. As far as Kerista was concerned, you could be heterosexual, homosexual or bisexual. It just so happened that most of the monks at that moment seemed to prefer heterosexual interpersonal relationships.

But Kerista was more than the sum of its libidos. They had a philosophy. This philosophy was a fusion of scientific rationalism and mysticism. They did, in fact, constitute a recognized church —and thus benefited from the tax exemptions and other constitutional guarantees bestowed by the world of the flesh on the world of the spirit. It was called the Kerista Consciousness Church.

The Kerista Consciousness Church had no authoritarian figure at the head of it. Brother Jud and Even Eve, the founding Energy Forces, were committed to egalitarianism. Their Godhead, a pantheistic essence, was called Kyrallah. The most important attribute—or nonattribute—of Kyrallah was that It was not sexist. Kyrallah was quite definitely an It and not a Him. Although the contemplation of Kyrallah occasionally sent Its devotees into religious raptures, they had found It to be a little too abstract and remote. For everyday purposes, they worshiped a more personalized manifestation of Kyrallah, a goddess they called Sister Kerista. Sister Kerista was Jesus' older sister. She was hip, she was completely liberated, she was black and she wore sneakers. History, in the Keristan view, was a progression toward Utopia. Evil would eventually disappear from the face of the earth when technology reached the necessary sophistication—and when some way had been found to distribute wealth more fairly. Altruism and global concerns motivated them as strongly as their search for a flawless life-style. But, they were quick to point out, Keristans were not angry revolutionaries. They were proud to be American; proud of the freedoms they enjoyed and the benefits conferred by American citizenship.

Harmony was promoted not only by polyfidelity, Kyrallah and Sister Kerista, but by a form of encounter therapy they practiced on each other—the Gestalt-O-Rama. It was a technique of re-education, of psychic surgery, carried out by the group mind, and it enabled the individual to overcome all symptoms of unliberated, insensitive and unloving behavior. Occasionally, the Gestalt-O-Rama brought to light a great chunk of craziness, an outsized neurosis, embedded deep in some individual psyche. It then became the duty of the group mind to extract this chunk of craziness, as you might a rotten tooth. This psychic surgery could be harrowing, but the infected individual emerged from it a liberated, loving and grateful Keristan.

Kerista had many plans for the future. They wanted to expand into rural bases, to set up a network of orchards, farms and eco-villages. In conformity with their altruism and global concern, they hoped to take care of the aged, to provide health services for the poor, to run child-care centers.

Feminism, ecology, pseudo mysticism, communalism, psychic hygiene, philanthropy mixed with commerce, half-baked messianism: Kerista was an eccentric, recycled ragbag of many of the temptations characteristic of the New Age. They were absurd, these men and women; they were also, most probably, quite harmless—as harmless as the germs that go to make up a common cold. But a common cold, given a suitable twist of fate, can turn into bronchial pneumonia. In this hothouse atmosphere of pampered self-consciousness, ideas—or what passed for ideas—floated like viruses. They were a disease you caught; a contamination of the intellect.

I walked on down the line of booths.

"An Idea Whose Time Has Come" announced a bold banner.

It was the stall of the World Hunger Project. I had heard a little about this body, which had set itself the task of ending hunger on the planet by 1997. It was an offshoot of the highly successful consciousness-raising est (Erhard Seminars Training) organization.

"Hi!" A teen-age girl, name tag pinned to her breast, smiled beatifically at me. "Would you like to make a donation?"

I asked her to tell me something about the World Hunger Project.

"We plan to rid the world of hunger by 1997. The ending of hunger is an idea whose time has come."

"That's nice to know. But what does the World Hunger Project actually do?"

"It makes each person realize that he or she can make a difference."

"What does that mean?"

"It means that if you decide you want to end world hunger you can."

"I still don't understand. How does my deciding I want to see world hunger end make world hunger end?"

The beatific smile was becoming edged with impatience. "I'll get someone who can explain it better," she said.

She went off, found a young man and brought him to me.

"Hi!" The young man grinned and shook my hand. "What's the problem?"

"I can't get him to understand the idea behind the World Hunger Project," she said.

The young man laughed pleasantly. He looked into my eyes. "What's your name, sir?"

I told him.

"Quite simply, Shiva, we feel it's an idea whose time has come."

"I'm aware of that. What I'd like to know is how you plan to implement that idea."

"Well, Shiva, if you and millions of other people like you want to see world hunger end, you can make it happen."

"All I have to do is *want* world hunger to end? Nothing else?"

"That's about the size of it, Shiva."

"But what does the World Hunger Project itself do with all the millions of dollars it has collected? Has it actually helped to feed anyone?"

"You're missing the point, Shiva," he said gently. "It's not our aim to actually feed anyone."

"Then why do you need to collect money?"

"Our job, Shiva, is to spread the good news. That's what we use the money for, Shiva."

"What good news?"

He too was beginning to show signs of impatience. "The good news that hunger can be ended by 1997 if millions of people like you decided that they wanted it to end. We collect signatures, Shiva, of people who have made that commitment. We spread the idea—the good news."

"I must say it's a very elusive idea."

He signaled over another—and older—man.

"I'm experiencing some difficulty explaining the World Hunger Project to my friend Shiva," the young man said.

"Hi, Shiva! That's an interesting name you've got there. Like it! Like it!" The newcomer beamed at me. "What aspect of the World Hunger Project is troubling you?"

"All aspects."

He did his best. Since the beginning of time there had been hunger. The attitude throughout the ages had always been that it was inevitable. Malthusian economic doctrine had helped to reinforce that fatalistic attitude. The World Hunger Project was reversing that traditional pessimism. It was saying that where there was a will, there was a way. Using modern technology, the planet could produce enough to satisfy the needs of four billion people. If the majority of people wanted to end starvation, starvation would be ended.

We had been joined by a third man.

"Can I share Shiva with you?" he asked.

It was agreed that I could be shared.

"You see, friend Shiva, it's all about commitment," he began. He spoke of Karl Marx, the French Revolution, the Russian Revolution, the program to land a man on the moon, the campaign to eradicate smallpox. Those had all been acts of will, acts of commitment. The Hunger Project was in the same mold. It had been praised by the Indian Government and by the United Nations. True, they were not ending hunger as such. What they were doing was creating a *context* in which hunger could be ended.

He put a hand on my shoulder. "I can see you're a pretty negative type, Shiva," he said, gazing compassionately into my face. "You're hung up on logic and all that kind of bullshit. To understand the Hunger Project, Shiva baby, you've got to forget everyday logic. For some of us, I know, that's difficult. It took me about a year to get the hang of it. But, man, when I finally did, it just sort of blew my mind, you know?"

"How about a donation?" the girl asked.

"I think I'll get the hang of it first," I said. "Wait for the idea to blow my mind."

"Sure, friend Shiva. Sure. Take your time. Let it sink in. That's okay by us. Nobody's forcing you to do anything."

Looking around, I discovered another devotee of the Project, a woman of pensionable age, on the point of persuading my five-year-old son to commit himself. I seized the enrollment card he was holding. "The Hunger Project is mine completely," it said. "I am willing to be responsible for making the end of starvation an idea whose time has come. As an expression of my participation, I will do the following: (1) I will fast on the 14th of ———; (2) I will enroll another individual or individuals in the Hunger Project; (3) I will donate the following amount to the Hunger Project: $10, $25, $50, $100, more . . . ; (4) I will create my own form of participation."

"He's five years old," I said. "How do you expect him to create his own form of participation?"

The woman apologized and retreated.

Fatigued by the chimeras of the New Age, I went out into the gloomy San Francisco afternoon.

They often call it the twenty-first century. California, in this view of things, is something more than merely the richest and most populous state of the Union, the first among equals. It is a state of mind; a state of being. The dogma has it that what California is doing today, the rest of the United States will be doing tomorrow; and, of course, whatever the United States is doing tomorrow, the whole world will be doing the day after. According to one of its devotees, it is a seminal ground for new ideas, one vast laboratory of the human spirit. Californians are the ultimate pioneers, a chosen people living in a golden land flowing with milk and honey, whose precocious self-consciousness makes them more than ordinarily human.

It is not accidental that its Governor, Jerry Brown, should have a sophisticated spiritual life replete with a cortege of Zen gurus, should talk of "planetary realism" and should have an amateur's enthusiasm for the colonization of outer space. (In California, to avoid confusion, one must always make clear the kind of space that is being referred to—inner or outer.) But the legend does not stop there. It is not simply a matter of adventurousness fueled by great wealth, of people playing with privilege. Land and man, we are further invited to believe, are bonded together in a mystical unity. California is uniquely what it is because the land itself is magical. Its vibrations enter into the soul and irrevocably alter it.

". . . After a while," write the editors of a book typically titled *The California Dream*, "one notices something different about otherwise familiar objects. Colors are deeper, metals are shinier, the air is cleaner and the brilliant California sun seems to jump from every surface. Before long, everyday scenes begin to look like Technicolor scenes." Sometimes the worship takes on a more aggressive tone, as in an essay by the Los Angeles–based writer John Gregory Dunne. A defector from New York, Dunne expresses himself with all the vehemence of a convert. His essay is aimed at the supercilious Eastern Seaboard. "I do not think that anyone in the East," he wrote, "truly understands the importance of this idea of space in the West. The importance of that emptiness is psychic. We have a sense out here . . . of being alone, of wanting more importantly to be left alone, of having our own space, a kingdom of self with a two-word motto: 'Fuck Off'." Dunne hymns the "narcosis" to be found on the freeways. He contemplates with rapture the arabesques formed by off-ramps, on-ramps and intricate lane interchanges, emblems of a mobility that is both physical and spiritual. He is entranced by the subtle tricks played on him by the subtropical light. For him, refineries gleam and glitter like extraterrestrial space stations. "It is the end of the line. It is the last stop. Eureka! I love it."

Such an attitude lends itself to extremism, to frenzy: we often become victims of our legends. For many, California is indeed the last stop; the end of the line. The triumphant cry of Eureka! must wither and die on a multitude of lips every day. Heightened consciousness, heightened expectation can aggravate as well as liberate. A girl brings a gun to her high school and shoots several of her fellow pupils dead; a man finds his parking place usurped and he too goes on a murderous rampage. Californian crimes tend to have a spectacular quality. That is only to be expected. If colors are deeper and metals are shinier, so, in proportion, are the derelictions of failure and madness more vividly expressed than elsewhere. They stand out starkly in that clean, golden air. "Here," an acquaintance said to me, "you either reach for the stars or you crack up and run amok with a chain saw."

But that is overstating the case, an excessively romantic extension of the legend. California, it has to be admitted, has its fair share of outwardly normal people. You see them by the hundreds in a suburb like Sunnyvale, not many miles south of San Francisco. On weekends, mothers and fathers herd their children to the Little Leagues of soccer and baseball and football. From the sidelines they exhort and criticize, instilling the orthodox reflexes of competition. These mothers and fathers are conservative and patriotic and hate big government. They are fearful that the presence of too many blacks in the neighborhood will drive house prices down. One woman I met mentioned with embarrassment that her first marriage had ended in divorce. She was fearful that if her marital history became widely known in the community it might cause her neighbors anxiety.

Conformity was the first prerequisite of happiness in Sunnyvale. It was unthinkable that a child should not be an enthusiastic member of one Little League team or another. A man whose work kept him at home—a writer, for instance—would be regarded with suspicion. The people of Sunnyvale are really no different from those you meet in Des Moines, Iowa. They would eat the same convenience foods (Americans hardly seem to cook anymore), watch the same mass-audience television programs, read the same syndicated columnists. In Des Moines, as in Sunnyvale, American flags will grace neat front lawns. Perhaps the lawns are neater and the flags more plentiful in Des Moines, but at bottom, all belong to that vast, featureless prairie of well-nourished, clean-thinking humanity known as Middle America, whose chief cultural monuments are the self-contained shopping plaza and the cavernous discount store. Middle Americans, whether Californian or Iowan, are as alike as Chinese. "I resent the energy crisis," I overheard a middle-aged San Franciscan saying. "Do you know why I resent it? I resent it because I am an American. I resent it because as an American I have a right to do as I like." His audience did not disagree. A remark like that takes one several light-years away from planetary realism and the New Age.

But that having been said, it is also to be conceded that California is unique. The legend does have its effect, creating its own special lure and vulnerabilities. Iowa does not, as a rule, attract the vagrant and the restless. Its neat farms and lush meadows discourage fantasy. America's wilder dreams have always rolled to the Far West. Fantasies flourish best in a warm, sensual climate. In 1967, during the summer of love and flower-power, the hippies rolled West to San Francisco's Haight-Ashbury district and Golden Gate Park. Charles Manson, cradling his murderous dreams, rolled West from Cincinnati, Ohio. The colonies of trailer homes, harboring an anonymous population of adventurers, have rolled instinctively West and come to a halt, face to face with the Pacific Ocean. America's homosexuals, rolling West in search of fulfillment, have laid siege to San Francisco. Predicting a nuclear holocaust, Jim Jones and a handful of disciples rolled West from Indiana in 1965.

"I would say without hesitation," a woman in New York said to me, "that it was the more unstable members of my family who chose to settle in California."

She may have had a point. In San Francisco I ran into a couple of her cousins. One, a mild, soft-spoken creature, had joined a Zen sect. He had, he said, become a Buddhist in reaction to the hypocrisy he saw in society. For a while, he had been moderately active in behalf of progressive political causes. But he had come to the conclusion that it was no good doing anything about anything. Whatever happened did so of its own accord, when the time was ripe for that thing to happen. His only aim in life now was to empty his mind. The other cousin was involved in a cult of (I believe) Indonesian origin. But he would not talk to me about it. What about the girl, a disciple of an Indian guru, who claimed she was following his teachings by working as a dancer in one of

San Francisco's topless bars? "My guru says everything is holy, everything comes from God. It doesn't matter what you do. Everyone must follow his own path. I dedicate my sexuality to God." Would her family in Wisconsin have understood that?

Some are driven to desperation, like the "cocktail waitress" from New Jersey who had rolled West to San Francisco to make her fortune and had ended up as a common streetwalker. She had offered me her services for a mere fifteen dollars.

"Why so cheap?" I asked.

"I just want to get out of this place," she said. "All I want is the bus fare *out*. They're all as crazy as hell." She started to weep. "I don't even know who's a man or who's a woman anymore. It's crazy."

I looked around the bar. "It seems fairly easy to tell," I said.

"That's what you think. But most of the women you see in here are really men. They've had that operation. And a lot of the men are women. It's crazy, I tell you. A normal girl like me can't make a living in this town."

California sucks in America's loose ends. It twists and tangles them in a hundred different ways.

The legend crops up in some of the most unlikely places. I was being driven around Los Angeles by a black journalist, a man who, all so typically, had migrated West from New York after his marriage had broken up and he had begun to feel that his life was falling apart. He had discovered that California—Southern California—was the paradise for which he had always been unconsciously yearning.

"This sun! This sun! I worship it. It does things to you, man. It melts you down. It loosens you up. You have to experience it yourself to truly understand how people who live here feel about this place."

We drove into Watts, the ghetto that had been the scene of some of the most violent black rioting in the 1960s. Traces of that violence could still be seen in the many empty lots once occupied by businesses that had never been rebuilt. From Watts, the hills of Hollywood are plainly visible, the name etched out in giant letters on a hillside: HOLLYWOOD. Those who lived up on those hills would have seen the glow of the fires raging on the asphalt plains below. But on that bleak, if light-filled, Southern California morning, my companion's thoughts roamed far from memories of insurrection.

Did Watts, he wanted to know, conform to my preconception of a ghetto? He pointed out the streets of neat bungalows, the trim lawns. Was this anything like Harlem? Chicago? Boston? Compared with those, Watts was anything but a slum. Even misery acquired a gloss in Southern California. The weather made everything possible. Cars lasted longer. Houses remained in better repair. You spent next to nothing on heating. Every harsh winter in the Northeast brought in new floods of refugees—you could tell what was going on by the number of out-of-state license plates that suddenly appeared. His paean broadened its scope. Southern California had managed to create a genuinely open society. Everything was new. There were no rigid traditions about anything. It was a free-form, extemporaneous universe in which nothing was sacred and everything was possible to those who dared.

We passed a Mercedes-Benz without a license plate.

"That means *new*," he pointed out helpfully. "That Benz is probably fresh from the showroom. Somebody has just made his pile and he's letting the world know. That's how it goes in L.A. Maybe six months from now he'll have blown it all and be back in a Ford subcompact. That's how it goes in L.A. too. Easy come, easy go."

It was different in San Francisco. Money there was hidden, used more discreetly. It was an older town, with a long-established aristocracy. San Francisco was another ball game. His California, his magic kingdom, was unambiguously southern in complexion. John Gregory Dunne, in the essay already referred to, is also anxious to make the distinction between the two cities. "Perhaps it is easier to define Los Angeles by what it is not. Most emphatically, it is not eastern. San Francisco is eastern . . . Yankee architecture and Yankee attitudes boated around the Horn and grafted on to the Bay . . . Small wonder Easterners feel comfortable there. They perceive an Atlantic clone; it does not threaten as does that space-age Fort Apache five hundred miles to the south."

Again, there is exaggeration. The uniqueness of Los Angeles (Southern California) can be as overplayed as the uniqueness of California itself. How different is Los Angeles from the pride of Texas—Houston? Houston too might describe itself as a space-age Fort Apache. With justification: it is the headquarters of NASA, the National Aeronautics and Space Administration. It has all the un-Eastern virtues that Dunne admires. Consider the introduction I was given to Houston by the publicity brochure I picked up in my hotel:

> Houston is a Boston Brahmin's nightmare. It's got hundreds of miles of freeways, a gas station on every block, countless cars, no buses, subways or trains, a brash attitude that won't be put in its place. . . . Houston has got what everybody else in the world wants: money, guts, untold prosperity, vitality. . . . If Ulysses had had a choice of Houston or the sirens, he'd have picked Houston. *That's* how strong the lure is. It's even stronger for an American, born and bred on the ideals of the West. Free men. No nonsense. Don't waste time. Don't tread on me. Liberty or death. Don't fence me in. If you don't like it where you are, move on. . . . If there's any city that seems to have a monopoly on the American Spirit, that city has got to be Houston. . . .

This apocalyptic vulgarity is shared by Los Angeles.

That San Francisco does have more orthodox pretensions to sophistication and refinement is undeniable. One need penetrate no further than the all-male preserve of the Bohemian Club with its impeccably dressed clubmen, its wood-paneled walls and its elective exclusivity to understand that. But San Francisco, while it may not be a Boston Brahmin's nightmare, is also the city that pioneered topless bars, est and the hippie movement. Marin County outside San Francisco is as laid-back, as mellow and as experimental as anywhere in the cosmos. Los Angeles and San

Francisco offer different versions of the California legend. In the latter, Eastern sensibilities are refracted into the more inward-looking neuroses of the New Age. The languages are different, but they spring from a common root—the California "dream." In the south, that dream, turning into nightmare, spawned Charles Manson and his Family; in the north, it spawned Werner Erhard, the synthesizer of salesmanship and Zen, upon whom Enlightenment descended as he drove across the Golden Gate Bridge.

That common, legendary root goes even deeper—to America itself, to the New World dream of rebirth and self-realization in a spacious land uncontaminated by memory, tradition and restraint. California became, as it had to, the New World's New World, its last repository of hope. In California, you come face to face with the Pacific and yourself. There is nowhere else to go. Just as both Los Angeles and San Francisco are, in their separate ways, recognizably Californian, so is California recognizably American. All that California does is magnify what is brought to it; and often, under the strain of magnification, there occurs a sea change. It seems that those whom the gods wish to destroy they first send to California.

They come from everywhere—from Pittsburgh, New York, Chicago, South Dakota. Enraptured by their good fortune, they expect you to be enraptured too. The demand for admiration is tinged with totalitarianism. Go to any party. Once it is discovered that you are a stranger, the conversation turns to California and its wonders. Isn't it just too marvelous for words? All those years spent in Pittsburgh seem like a punishment now. How could they ever have tolerated it? Heads shake in perplexity. Those Chicago winters! That New York rat race! That South Dakota tedium and nothingness! You walk out on the sun deck. The sky is flawless blue; the vegetation shines with a hard, precise sparkle. In the distance is the blue expanse of San Francisco Bay, lazily alive with the colorful sails of pleasure craft. California wine foams into your glass. Sun-soaked flesh glows. Languid eyes gaze at the red towers of the Golden Gate.

Isn't it just too marvelous for words? How can you bear the thought of having to return to London? If you are rash enough to keep silent or even, God help you, murmur a few words of mild dissent, you are done for. Conversation lags. Your hosts become remotely polite. It is unlikely that another invitation to participate in the splendor of it all will ever be received. To be reticent about California is to insult your hosts and their friends. Their individuality, their identity, has been absorbed by the sun, the space, the color. Their lives and their life-styles are one. They are incestuously bound up with the land and its legend. That seductive view from the sun deck is, at bottom, a narcissistic projection; a mirror of the imagined self. When they look at it, they are looking at their alter egos; when they adore it, they are adoring themselves; when they invite you to praise it, they are inviting you to praise them. The California dream cannibalizes the personality and ends by taking its place.

"One meets here," observed William Brewer in the 1860s (he was a member of the California Survey), "people apparently out of their station." The remark was prompted by his meeting with a raggedly dressed prospector in a rough mining town. Their conversation revealed that the man had come from a solid middle-class background in the East. A graduate of the U.S. Naval Academy, he was well traveled and cultivated: a Boston Brahmin. However, he had lost his fortune and come out to California in the hope of remaking it—and remaking himself. Hardly unusual in 1860. What is remarkable is that the impulse to seek regeneration in California has persisted with such strength.

"I left my home in Georgia," sang Otis Redding in the 1960s, "and headed for the Frisco Bay/I had nothing to live for . . ." One continues to run into people who, literally and metaphorically, are out of station. California is thronged not only with seekers of fame and fortune but seekers of new selves who have deliberately severed their ties with the past. It is a vagrancy that knows no class barriers: it can be discerned in the doctor who threw up a lucrative practice and came West to paint and dabble in Zen; in an academic like Timothy Leary who turned to the chemical ecstasy of LSD and made himself an outcast; in the young waitress from New York who now called herself a radical lesbian; in the businessman who turned to consciousness raising and took up full-time work with est; in the kind of tramp about whom Otis Redding sang. The out-of-station are to be met with at every twist and turn.

Away from the East, it is said, restraint seems to fall away. The gravitational force exerted by tradition weakens. Life, to use the fashionable word, becomes unstructured. Men and women become ripe for conversion; ripe for revelation. Culturally, the California atmosphere is lunar. Insecurely anchored by that weak gravitational field, one finds it all too easy to float off into absurdity and extremism. The nuts and bolts of the personality are loosened, and a certain promiscuity of thought and practice becomes endemic.

One comes across Sears, Roebuck–type catalogues catering exclusively to seekers of the exotic. A publication titled *Common Ground* is one of these—"a directory," it proclaims itself, "of growth, healing and spiritual experiences in the Greater Bay Area." It lists in alphabetical order over two hundred organizations. You can, through the Accelerated Personal Growth Program (forty dollars for one and a half hours), achieve rapid personal transformation and growth in self-awareness and self-integration. This will involve body work, "clearing," dream work and participation in group processes. The program will transform the way in which you perceive your reality by freeing you from the past and putting you in present time, thereby releasing your infinite abilities. Actualism (no price supplied) will actualize your untapped potential for creative self-expression and enable you to communicate joyfully with all forms of life by awakening the inner light-fire. And so on and on through the pages of the catalogue. These organizations are not the inventions of unfriendly fabulists or satirists. They exist; they have hourly rates. One must assume that to some extent, supply mirrors demand. Intellectual and spiritual adventurousness becomes indistinguishable from intellectual and spiritual collapse.

It is a sobering thought that in 1974 six and a half thousand predominantly white, middle-class people paid forty dollars each for the privilege of attending a seminar set up by the est group in San Francisco's Civic Auditorium. The theme: Making Relationships Work. Six and a half thousand people listening raptly to the words of a former encyclopedia salesman! Six and a half thousand people in search of a revelation. Six and a half thousand of the most affluent and privileged humans in the world willing to be taught how to live. More recently (in 1978 and 1979), thousands of whites from the Bay Area were attracted to a sect called the Church of Hakeem, founded by Hakeem Abdul Rasheed (alias Clifford Jones), a handsome and enterprising black from Detroit. "I feel good! I feel great! I feel terrific!" his disciples chanted. Hakeem said he was in touch with the World Mind and that diseases like cancer and tuberculosis were the results of negative thinking. "Wow!" responded his listeners. "Amen!" The Church of Hakeem also promised wealth: donations made to its "Dare to be Rich" program would, because of divine intercession, be multiplied fourfold and, in this enhanced state, be restored to the donors. When Hakeem finally came to court, one of his unrepentant disciples recited her version of the Lord's Prayer: "Rasheed is my shepherd, I know what I want, he maketh me to lie down in pastures that are crisp, green and clean."

Theodore Roszak, a bright star in California's intellectual firmament, has written a book titled *Person/Planet*—a fusion, as the title implies, of ecology and self-discovery. He advocates "the open, organic textures of small towns, rural hamlets, agrarian cooperatives and family homesteads. . . . What yearns to be big in us, to be vast beyond reckoning, is the adventure of self-discovery. The larger that grows, the more lightly will human society rest upon the earth." Education, in the new order, will be largely introspective, a coming to terms with the inner motions of mind, body and soul. We must develop a sense of kinship with all things; a religious respect for the earth.

The ideas float like ghosts. So do the men and the women who cling to the ideas. A swirling vapor of assorted "idealisms"—ecology, feminism, heightened consciousness—clouds the brain. The gurus wait with open arms. You can get a good deal at the Anubhava School of Enlightenment: room, board and Illumination all for one hundred dollars. ". . . Authentic enlightenment experiences occur for some and mental, physical and emotional barriers to the truth are cleared, enabling one to make swift spiritual progress. Recommended for seekers of truth."

One evening, out of curiosity, I went to an event that billed itself the "Men Together Conference." The venue was the gymnasium of one of San Francisco's public schools. I half-assumed that, this being San Francisco, it might be a homosexual gathering of some kind. It was a wrong assumption—or rather, only marginally correct.

Men Together turned out to be the masculine equivalent of the feminist movement. Sexism, it seemed, had been oppressing men as well as women. Those one hundred and fifty men gathered in the gymnasium, all white, nearly all middle-class, had set themselves the task of breaking out of the masculine stereotype. This led, in one direction, to what one might call radical homosexuality. One member of the movement had decided to stop being attracted to women because that oppressed them. He should get all the emotional support and physical affection he needed from men and stop ripping off women. To achieve that result, he went into therapy. He came out of therapy with a strong sense of being a man, a musician and a Jew. With that there came an access of love for and sensitivity to Third World cultures, Jewish culture and Women's culture. This led in turn to what one might call radical bisexuality. After having repressed his sexual attraction to women for over a year, he had discovered that opening up emotionally and sexually to them had helped him in his efforts to open up emotionally and sexually to men. Radical bisexuality was the apex of human happiness.

Traditional concepts of maleness, it was noted elsewhere, were, essentially, anti-ecological. The feminist movement was helping to undermine a chauvinist system which had always been inimical to life and the earth. Hence the need for men to think and act along similar lines, to rid themselves of the destructive attributes of maleness. "We affirm that men are capable of loving, nurturing and supporting other men. We have been taught to fear and suppress our feelings of affection for our brothers and to deny our need to touch and hold one another. We are struggling to overcome the effects of this destructive conditioning, and we affirm our need to openly express our feelings for each other." Men, to put it another way, had to become liberated women.

The Men's Movement had dedicated itself to self-exploration, growth and change in a supportive, caring environment. Men, like women, now needed a safe space, a separatist environment, where they could learn how to relate intimately with each other, understand their role as oppressors and cultivate their vulnerability and softness. Men Together hoped to provide that supportive, caring environment.

It did not matter where one started or what the alleged problem was: you always ended up in roughly the same place (space) and with the same solutions. The New Age, whatever the circumstances, whatever the hang-up that had to be rooted out, would produce the same printout. I came to understand that in the twenty-first century one was not dealing with the rigors of intellectual struggle but that the intellect was dead and its place taken by a set of shared pathological obsessions which, given the chance, would infect every department of life. Ideas had indeed become viruses. In California one constantly had the feeling of being trapped, of endlessly crawling along the surface of an outsized Möbius strip. No wonder there was so much frenzy, so many promiscuous couplings of ideas and bodies—these people had nowhere else to go, nothing left to do. Spiritually as well as physically, they had come face to face with the blue emptiness of the Pacific Ocean: the ocean without had its counterpart in an ocean within. They had made a jail for themselves and did not know it. The search for "structure" was a search for the lost self.

Their language tells much. Despite the ostentatious obsession with the inner life, with "wholeness" and "self-realization," it is a language of fragmentation, of mechanistic self-degradation. Perpetually externalizing and abstracting, it becomes the perfect tool of a robotized spirituality. "I have learned to accept my body," a woman said to me. "I feel much more comfortable with it than I used to." I was new to California and her phrasing took me by surprise. She might have been talking about something only fortuitously connected with herself, an appendage she had got casually saddled with along the way. As with the body, so with the mind—or soul. "I find I'm liking myself more these days. I'm really getting *into* myself, you know?" Or: "You can tell that he doesn't really feel mentally comfortable with himself." Mind and matter are spoken of in more or less the same way. Both are externalized and fragmented into categories. Social life breaks down into a welter of "relationships" which, for a mere forty dollars, you can tuck under your arm and take to Mr. Erhard to see if he can help you make them "work." There arises a curious and disturbing impersonality of expression, a distancing of the individual from himself/herself—or, as the rules of the new feminist language specify, itself. (From Stricture No. 2 of the Anti-Sexist Code: "Many sentences can be restructured to avoid using a personal pronoun at all.") Intellectual life becomes a matter of being "into" something or "turned on" or "turned off."

You become your abstractions—a bio-energy mass, a set of relationships, a Growth Process, a higher-consciousness machine, a Gestalt. You can talk about the self as if it were an alien object whose component parts are perpetually being flashed up—externalized—on a monitoring screen. From time to time, as need, mood or fashion dictates, the components are tuned up, altered or exorcised. If you are a Keristan, big chunks of craziness can be extracted by the group mind. We are faced, then, with a language of disintegration, not integration; the new humanism ends by dehumanizing us. It encourages its practitioners to see and treat themselves as things, as mechanisms to be tinkered with in hopes of regeneration. Given time, the self will die. It will have been reduced to its various taxonomic indices. All that will remain will be the abstractions flitting across the screen; one endless voyeuristic trip.

I strolled around the gymnasium. The topics of the various seminars being offered were posted up on the walls—Masculine Belief Systems; Our Fathers, Our Selves; Hero Myth in Masculine Psychology; Embodying Male Roles; Components of Sexual Identity; Relationships Between Men Through Guided Imagery; Male Sexuality: Myth and Reality; Men's Transformation: Overcoming Rivalry and Learning How to Share.

"Which one are you thinking of choosing?"

A melancholy-looking, bearded man of middle age smiled at me.

"I'm not sure," I said. "How about you?"

He pointed at Our Fathers, Our Selves. "Are you married?"

I said I was.

"Is . . . is yours an open marriage?"

"I don't think so. . . . Is yours?"

"Oh, yes. My wife and I lead independent life-styles. We have an agreement."

"What kind of agreement?"

"Well, we each have a night set aside when we don't have to come home—you know, no questions asked and so forth." He smiled shyly. "Tonight is my night to do as I please."

"Does your open marriage make you happy?"

"Oh, yes! We have quite a wonderful relationship now. Very caring. Very sincere. I've grown a lot."

His hand strayed toward mine. But I cruelly denied his need to touch and hold me.

The room darkened in preparation for a film show.

"I've really enjoyed sharing with you," he said.

He moved away, rubbing his hands, looking lost and sad.

Sometimes, when one thinks about California, there comes to mind H. G. Wells's futuristic fantasy *The Time Machine* in which the hero of the tale transports himself to the year 802,700. He finds himself in a land of gardenlike beauty where the sun always shines, the trees are laden with delicious fruit and flowers are resplendent. He meets a beautiful race—the Eloi: graceful, delicately formed creatures clad in soft robes. They seem very open, very laid-back, very up-front. Their life is an endless round of innocuous pleasure. The Eloi spend their days playing childish games, fashioning garlands for one another, splashing in warm, sparkling streams and making gentle love. Bountiful nature appears to have showered on them every blessing.

But slowly the Time Traveler begins to realize that this Eden conceals a nightmare. The Eloi, he discovers, have no capacity for concentration or for any other kind of strenuous mental activity. Human intelligence in the year 802,700 has all but atrophied. These gorgeous, charming creatures have even forgotten what fire is. When night falls they crowd into the ruined palaces of a long-vanished civilization and huddle together for mutual protection and comfort, showing great fear. For in tunnels deep underground live their counterparts, the mutant Morlocks, lemurlike descendants of a once-oppressed proletariat who, transformed by darkness and confinement, can no longer bear the brightness of day. At night, ravenous with hunger, they emerge from their caverns to feed at will on the defenseless, fruit-eating children of light. Paradise turns to horror.

Eloi and Morlocks: the New Age is replete with both.

CHAPTER
9

FOUR MONTHS after the Guyana massacre, it was announced by the San Francisco Superior Court that the assets of the People's Temple were to be put up for auction. The event would take place at the Temple's headquarters in the Fillmore district, one of San Francisco's black ghettoes.

On the eve of the auction, the Temple once again hit the headlines with the suicide of Michael Prokes. Whether or not the auction had anything to do with the timing of his suicide is a matter of conjecture. Prokes may have seen it as the final, unfeeling indignity perpetrated not only on the Jonestown dead, his brothers and sisters, who were being denied proper interment, but on the living, the marooned and dislocated survivors, who tended to regard themselves as the rightful heirs to Temple property. For Prokes, the auction may have been one more act of fascism and racism— that, no doubt, is how his master would have interpreted it. But for the U.S. Government it was one way to underwrite the costs of a macabre airlift and show taxpayers that it was not heedlessly spendthrift.

As perhaps befitted the occasion, the March morning was gray and dismal. Geary Boulevard—on which the Temple was located

—looked bleak. It and the surrounding streets were a desert of inner-city decay compounded by planning blight—fenced, rubble-strewn lots, crumbling tenements, hangdog bars and cheap eating places. Young blacks, as ever, stood on street corners, looking with apathetic intensity at nothing in particular. "PEOPLE'S TEMPLE OF THE DISCIPLES OF CHRIST DENOMINATIONAL BROTHERHOOD. JIM JONES, PASTOR." The sign above the entrance could not have been much more modest in either design or content. Considering the claims the Temple had made for itself, this quiet announcement was uncharacteristically self-effacing. The building, a former auditorium, was solid in construction and charmless. Wrought-iron grilles over the windows and the heavy wrought-iron main doors hinted at the fortress mentality that had been sheltered by it.

A musty smell pervaded the lobby. "Victory," said a sign which lay propped against a wall near the entrance, "is not easy, but it is not impossible, it is sweet because it is so difficult." The Temple had had a liking for uplifting sentiments and stirring exhortations: Jonestown had been littered with quotations. The sale was being well attended. Scores of people milled about, going from room to room, examining the treasure on offer. The atmosphere was businesslike. Intimidatingly so. Most of these people were not ghouls in search of ghoulish mementoes. They were small-time, serious-eyed businessmen—secondhand dealers, professional bargain hunters. This, as far as they were concerned, was just another auction. The fact that they were picking over and fingering the bric-a-brac of a community, many members of which remained frozen in cold-storage chambers, was not a deterrent. Two hours later they would be somewhere else, doing much the same thing.

There was a great deal available to them. They could buy office chairs, desks and filing cabinets; they could buy hospital carts, dental equipment, oxygen tanks, oxygen tents, stretchers and blood pumps; they could buy stationery, mothballs, sanitary pads and coffee urns; they could buy sewing machines, television sets, a Hammond organ and Honda motorcycles; they could even buy

Jim Jones's oak pulpit (lot 209), an American flag (lot 58) and the People's Temple sign above the entrance to the building (lot 217). Nothing had been spared. The Temple was up for grabs.

I bypassed the main auditorium, where the bidding was being done. To the rear was a large room which looked as if it might have been used as a refectory. Here there was another sign, this one forbidding smoking because, it said, the Government had determined it was detrimental to health—it is possible that this was the only official U.S. Government statement ever accepted unreservedly by the Temple—and because, in addition to that, smoking showed disrespect for the senior citizens and set a bad example to the children.

I wandered out into the large, fenced-in compound at the back of the building. On display here were the Temple's buses, cars, trucks and trailers. (The buses would be acquired by a Chinese entrepreneur for use in San Francisco's Chinatown, which, he said, was not adequately served by public transport.) There were several big wooden crates, rumored to contain grain, their intended destination boldly stenciled "PEOPLE'S TEMPLE AGRICULTURAL PROJECT, PORT KAITUMA, GUYANA." I went into one of the buses.

It was on these buses that Jim Jones had taken members of his flock on "vacations" which had crisscrossed the North American continent. "Pastor Jones goes on no vacation," said the Temple newspaper in 1973, "without giving every person . . . the chance to go with him." These vacations, according to the writer, left a trail of goodwill in the communities fortunate enough to be included in the path of their progression. The Temple received "enthusiastic praise from people across the nation into Canada and Mexico" because they cleaned up the parks in which they camped and picked up litter wherever encountered. Scores of letters had been received expressing appreciation and gratitude for the assistance Temple members had given those whom they had met in distress on the roads and highways of the nation.

But for the vacationists themselves, the buses often evoked memories of physical torment, of the rigorous evangelical schedule imposed on them by their Pastor—the long weekend journeys from Redwood Valley to San Francisco, from San Francisco to Los Angeles, from Los Angeles back to Redwood Valley. The buses were so crowded that they had to sleep in the aisles, the roof racks and the luggage compartments. Jones and his intimate lieutenants traveled in greater style, in a bus specially fitted out to meet their needs. Nor were the vacations all they were cracked up to be. Bonnie Thielmann, who left the Temple in 1974, described one such vacation in her book *The Broken God.* Food was sparse and not inspiring—cold noodles, cold tuna and Kool-Aid. They camped in fields infested with mosquitoes. The air-conditioning system broke down and it became intolerably hot. Misery was compounded when the toilet went out of commission and began to smell. Children were not permitted to relieve themselves as they wished and were, in general, subjected to the harshest discipline: food was forcibly stuffed down the throat of a boy who said he was not hungry; when he vomited, he was made to eat his vomit. One of the main images left by that vacation was the long lines of Temple disciples waiting to use public toilets during the infrequent rest stops.

Leaving the bus, I strolled across the compound to an outshed heaped with junk: lot A34. Set amidst dusty mattresses and broken furniture was a group of drawings done in colored chalk on strips of board. The themes were grotesque—grinning skeletons and death's heads. "Death is waiting," ran the caption to one. Who had done them? When? Were they meant as some kind of terrible joke? I returned to the compound. There I ran into a former Temple member whose acquaintance I had made some weeks before: a young white girl who had married a black. She looked vaguely distraught, vaguely resentful.

"I expect you heard about Mike," she said. (She was referring, of course, to the suicide of Michael Prokes.)

I asked her what she made of it.

"I don't want to think too much about it," she said. "You never know what you might do if you start thinking too much about certain things."

She clenched her fists, staring dully at the milling bargain hunters. "I keep working. I'm concentrating on my child. What else is there? I have to remain strong."

Her husband, eyes hidden behind dark glasses, leaned against one of the buses, watching us.

"It's very bad for a lot of us at the moment," she went on. "Some of the others are very depressed. What with Mike yesterday and *this* today . . ."

She stared up at the building, to where some pigeons were squatting on a sill below a line of broken windows.

"I can't afford to give in," she said. "I have to remain strong. Rear my child . . ."

I asked her why she had come.

"Just to have a look . . ." She shrugged. "See what's happening, you know. There was a time when this place was home to me. It was all I had and all I thought I would ever need . . ." She stopped speaking.

The pigeons flew up suddenly from their roost on the window-sill, circling in the dirty sky.

In Guyana she had lost her mother, a brother, a sister, a grandfather, a grandmother, an uncle.

Our awkward conversation ran dry. Excusing herself, she wandered back to her husband.

Inside, in the auditorium where Jim Jones had once healed by faith and rained curses on capitalist injustice, the bidding went on apace.

Lot 31, six boxes of adding-machine paper, fetched twenty dollars.

Lot 32, one box of file folders, fetched ten dollars.

Lot 33, a batch of miscellaneous envelopes, fetched fifteen dollars.

Up on the podium, Jones's oak pulpit occupied what I assumed was its appointed place. Across from it was a curving staircase leading to a doorway set high in the wall. I imagined Jones making his dramatic entrances through that doorway, materializing, as it were, from on high and hovering momentarily above the heads of the assembled multitudes, before descending the stair-case and moving across stage to the pulpit. Close by drooped Lot 58—the American flag.

It was a reminder that Jones's attitude toward the fascist state he had so excoriated had always been edged with ambiguity. I thought of his odd association with the John Birch Society; his frequent attacks against Trotskyite provocateurs who, he said, were trying to bring the Temple into disrepute; his repeated as-sertion that by looking after human junk he was saving taxpayers' money; the grants he gave to the widows of slain policemen; the Temple's claim that it supported U.S. policy in the Caribbean and around the world. Mark Lane says that at one point, Jones had toyed with the idea of doing roughly what Eldridge Cleaver had done when he had begun to tire of his Algerian exile: he would return to the United States, renounce socialism and declare him-self a reformed and repentant son of the soil. The idea of revo-lutionary suicide was as provisional a commitment as the rest of what he said he stood for; as applied to himself, it was probably even more provisional. One searches in vain for the authentic revolutionary voice of Jim Jones.

In the packed auditorium, the bidding went on.

Lot 38, a Victor adding machine, fetched twenty dollars.

Lot 39, an Allan Wales adding machine, fetched twenty-five dollars.

Lot 40, a box of staples and punches, fetched fifteen dollars.

In early 1977, just a few months before the exodus to Guyana, a journalist from a Bay Area weekly newspaper attended a People's Temple service, one as typical as any that the public was ever allowed to witness. The auditorium was crowded, every seat taken. He estimated that there might have been nearly three thousand people packed into the hall where I was now standing. The atmosphere was electric. Jones was late that evening, because he had gone to deliver the main address at a banquet for the Officers of Justice, a group composed of mainly "minority" po-licemen.

Eventually, Jones arrived, but even later than expected. However, he had a good excuse. He told the congregation that he had been counseling a woman who was threatening to commit suicide. He was sure they would understand and forgive him his lateness. They did indeed. The congregation sang "Oh Freedom!" and "We Shall Overcome." Two groups of teen-age dancers, the Soul Steppers and the Africano Dancers, sang and danced. The atmosphere, the journalist said, was as ebullient and as joyous as a civil rights rally in the early 1960s. Jones did his best to blend into the happy scene, moving his arms "stiffly, almost mechanically, in an only partly successful attempt to keep time with the pulsating African rhythms." When the entertainment had run its course, Jones embarked on the night's sermon. It was already past eleven o'clock; but no one, we are assured, showed the least sign of fatigue or restlessness. A feverish excitement took hold of the congregation when he mounted the platform.

His theme that night was the subordination of personal desire in the pursuit of human betterment. Questions were solicited. Someone raised the issue of capital punishment.

"I think it's wrong," Jim Jones said, "for a society that wants to eliminate crime to kill people in such a brutal manner. It seems very wrong to help someone to commit suicide."

He attacked apathy as being one of the major diseases of American society. It was apathy that allowed the CIA to support tyrannical regimes in Chile and Iran. It was apathy that had created one kind of justice for the rich and another for the poor. It was apathy that was currently permitting the resurgence of Nazism in America and around the world.

"The way I keep myself straight," Jim Jones said, "is to live here in the Fillmore. I am at war with this system."

He would never condone a system that placed emphasis on material things and neglected human welfare. Love of money was the root of all evil. That was why he did not eat in expensive restaurants and avoided luxury.

"I do not feel good about being in a restaurant," Jim Jones said, "when some people are not warm. The only thing I feel good about is work."

Did that mean, he was asked, that he was acting out of guilt?

"I have a lot of guilt," Jim Jones said. "I have guilt to know my taxes have gone to the Shah of Iran and to Chile. Some people are not guilty at all about these things and I sure do not want to end up like they are."

Afterward there was a "seniors' " dance, the old folks jigging to the jazz that was pounded out on a piano. One ecstatic blind man of ninety several times came close to tumbling off the stage. Soon, the old folks were joined by some of the younger folks. The journalist was deeply moved by this scene. "Where else in our society," he wanted to know, "do old people get up to entertain younger people?"

He talked to a white member of the congregation, a woman in her early thirties, who came from a wealthy family. She had been a member of the Temple for nearly ten years.

"I tried to figure out," she said, "what his angle was. You could watch what he did all the time. He was an open book. Why did he adopt all those children? What does he have to gain? What does he have to gain by taking in senior citizens?"

She had finally decided he had no angle, no ulterior motives other than those prompted by the goodness of his heart and his sensitivity to human suffering.

He talked to a black man in his forties.

"I was thinking of blowing up police stations and a few other things. He convinced me that blowing up police stations would not change the system or deal with the injustice. . . . It's like the inner person was taken out of my shell and put into another one."

At every turn, the journalist heard stories of revelation and redemption; and praise for the man to whom everything was owed.

Jones, when he spoke to him, exuded humility. By nature, he confided, he was a recluse. He was doing what he did only because something of the kind had to be done by someone. He liked people. But it was hard to be so badly needed by such a desperate cross section of people. If he had had a worthwhile successor, he would have retired from the battlefield of human salvation. He was terribly overextended. But physically and psychologically, he could cope with the strain. He would endure. In his opinion, nobody but a masochist would ever try to create another People's Temple. What kept him going was the satisfaction he derived from seeing one more human life rehabilitated. Occasionally, though, even he became discouraged by the magnitude of human suffering. But these dark moods did not last long. Why, in any case, should he complain about his life? He had nothing better to do with it. Recently, he had been freshly inspired by the example of Laura Allende, wife of the murdered Chilean President, who had paid a visit to the Temple.

"I have seen sainted people," Jim Jones said, "people that are living epistles. And I think Laura Allende is in that category. You see other people making sacrifices, as she is, and you say to yourself, "What less can *I* do?' "

While Jones talked upstairs, his old folks jigged downstairs. The People's Temple, the journalist reflected, was the Christian ideal made flesh. Jim Jones, no less than Laura Allende, was a living epistle.

Like so many others, he came, he saw and he believed in what he saw.

In March 1977, when the journalist published his findings, the People's Temple was close to—or at—its apogee. Earlier that year, in January, Jones had been one of the recipients of the Martin Luther King Humanitarian Awards. (He had been named Humanitarian of the Year the previous January by the *Los Angeles Herald-Examiner*.) The event had been celebrated at the Temple with rock music, inspirational political sermons and ardent audience participation. Present were the Governor of California, Jerry Brown; the Mayor of San Francisco, George Moscone; assorted members of the state legislature; a host of clergymen. The master of ceremonies praised the recipients of the awards for "breaking the barriers that separate, segregate, destroy the lives of people."

The following month Jones was named Chairman of the San

Francisco Housing Authority. His appearances at the meetings of the Authority were carried out with flair. Jones presided flanked by his bodyguards (the local Nazis, he had said, were out to get him), and his every act was cheered by members of his congregation, who would turn up en masse to provide a supportive ambience for their Pastor. At one of the meetings, he collapsed. This was attributed to his hard work and dedication: he had been up most of the night before, it was explained, counseling a drug addict.

The Temple continued to attract prominent visitors. In June 1977 it welcomed the now deposed Prime Minister of Grenada, Eric Gairy, hailing him as "the valiant black leader arrested fifty-one times for resisting colonialism, internationally respected and recognized for his achievements." Ideologically, Eric Gairy could not have been further removed in political outlook from another of Jones's Caribbean friends, Forbes Burnham. Gairy was a militant antisocialist. His presence at the Temple provided one more example of Jones's flexibility. Or, maybe, all black men looked alike to him. Another visitor of note was Jane Fonda, the activist-actress. The Temple's work had been praised by Walter Mondale, Vice President of the United States. Its deep involvement in the major social and constitutional issues of the country had been, he said, a great inspiration to him.

The fund set up for the families of policemen killed in the course of duty was only one of the many worthy causes to benefit from the Temple's largesse. Donations were made to the National Association for the Advancement of Colored People, the American Civil Liberties Union, the American Indian Movement, the Ecumenical Peace Institute, Cesar Chavez' United Farm Workers. Money was given for research into cancer, heart disease and sickle-cell anemia. When four Fresno journalists were detained for refusing to reveal sources of information, the Temple rallied to their support, a thousand of its members engaging in round-the-clock picketing for several days. "As a church," a spokesman of the Temple said, "we feel a responsibility to defend the free-speech clause of the First Amendment, for without it America will have lost freedom of conscience and the climate will become ripe for totalitarianism." Relations with the press would not always be so amiable.

The Temple's welfare operations were widely advertised and praised. Its medical clinic was supposed to treat, on average, eighty people a day. There were special facilities for sickle-cell anemia (a disease to which blacks are specially susceptible) and for the analysis of Pap smears. A physical-therapy unit was available to senior citizens and the handicapped. In San Francisco alone the Temple's drug program, using the "cold turkey" method, was reputed to have rehabilitated three hundred addicts. A legal-aid service offered its help to anyone in trouble with the police. They ran an employment bureau, nursing homes and a day-care center. Fourteen hundred free meals were allegedly served each day. Their newspaper, *People's Forum,* was said to reach six hundred thousand people in the Bay Area. Community groups had free access to the Temple's printing press. Outsiders who managed to penetrate the Temple's fortress fastness (all visitors were searched by armed guards) found it bustling with purposive activity. They might see the elderly eating a breakfast of bacon and eggs, a nurse examining a patient, a physical therapist at work, children playing in the day-care center, the print shop busy.

Rehabilitation, Jones had said, gave him his greatest satisfaction. It was his reason to be. But the jewel of the Temple's rehabilitational endeavors, consuming one-quarter of its annual budget, was something very few of its admirers had seen, could see or would ever see: the twenty-seven-thousand-acre farm (or "ranch," as it was occasionally called) in distant, cooperative Guyana, where Temple pioneers, the glad tidings would have it, were growing cassava in quantity as well as one hundred and seventy other exotic crops of the tropics. It was not in San Francisco but out there, in the middle of the Guyanese wilderness, that the Temple, by all accounts, was creating something akin to an earthly paradise; was having truly miraculous successes in human redemption and transformation.

"Today," said a 1977 publication, "you will find a little band of misfits from the streets of San Francisco trying to start a new life." In Guyana, you would find a purse snatcher feeding pigs, a shoplifter hoeing corn, a transvestite driving a tractor, a prostitute and some dope addicts sewing their own clothes. You would find other types as well in Guyana, not only the run-of-the-mill losers from the street trying to make a go of it. Among these were the embittered son of a CIA agent; a school arsonist; a boy whose chief gratification had come from decapitating cats. The youngest inhabitant of the settlement was five years old. This infant was both a certified sociopath and a genius. Guyana had precipitated the discovery that in the field of rehabilitation, nothing worked so well as a change of scene. (A change of scene could, in certain cases—the Temple admitted—be supplemented by physical discipline. A good beating in a wrestling match had been observed to produce "the necessary change in behavior.") The results achieved, even with clearly sociopathic individuals like the five-year-old boy, were "fantastic."

In the wholesome, natural atmosphere of the farm, new skills were being imparted, responsibility conferred, leadership qualities stimulated. Their Guyanese experience had made them confirmed "environmental determinists." In Guyana, everyone—arsonist, transvestite, sadist, dope addict, prostitute—was metamorphosed into an ideal human being. No one was kept on the farm against his wishes; yet since the inception of the project, not a single individual had ever asked to leave or shown the smallest sign of discontent. Testimonials from grateful parents were cited. "My own son lives and works there," said a Mrs. M. "He was unable to cope with life in the big city. At fourteen, he was a drug addict. At seventeen, I put him in a mental hospital for observation. Nothing helped. He was a lost cause until he met Pastor Jones and went to the farm in Guyana." If, it was said, Jim Jones and his followers were suddenly to disappear, the moral and economic loss to the city of San Francisco would be unimaginable. The politicians believed and applauded; and responded by sending their "underclass" constituents to Jim Jones. Whatever he did with them—or to them—was fine.

They also had a healthy respect for the more worldly powers of the man whose daily deeds seemed to re-create the life of Christ. In the battle for votes, Jones's support could make all the difference between victory and defeat. Nobody could scour the precincts in behalf of favored candidates with more regimented determination than the rehabilitated squadrons of the People's Temple.

"Everybody talks about the labor unions and their power," a Moscone campaign worker said in 1975, "but Jones turns out the troops."

It is accepted that Moscone (who won by the slim margin of four thousand votes) would not have been elected Mayor of San Francisco without the support of Jim Jones. The Mayor would remain his faithful patron to the end. Nor, equally probably, would the candidates for District Attorney and Sheriff have been successful in their hunt for office.

"In a tight race like the ones that George [Moscone] or Freitas [District Attorney] or Hongisto [Sheriff] had," Willie Brown remarked, "forget it without Jones."

When a crowd was needed, Jim Jones could always be depended upon. In September 1976, when Rosalynn Carter came to officially open the San Francisco Democratic Party headquarters, the organizers, fearing too small a turnout for the occasion, called on Jones. He responded generously. Of the nearly eight hundred people who turned up, six hundred were provided by the People's Temple.

"You should have seen it," a witness told *New West:* "old ladies on crutches, whole families, little kids, blacks, whites. Made to order."

When the trouble came in the summer of 1977, Jones would not be bereft of support. "We applaud People's Temple. . . . We are familiar with the work of Reverend Jones and People's Temple and have no hesitancy in commending them for their example in setting a high standard of ethics and morality in the community and also for providing enormous material assistance to poor, minority and disadvantaged people in every area of human need." That statement was signed by, among others, Willie Brown, Jane

Fonda, Tom Hayden (Fonda's husband and a radical luminary of the 1960s), Dennis Banks (leader of the American Indian Movement), Art Agnos and Charles Garry. Later, Angela Davis and others would broadcast lively messages of socialist solidarity to the beleaguered Jonestown garrison. But now, on this gloomy March morning, it was all over. The rotting bodies had been counted and tagged, and the talk—when, that is, there was talk—was of brainwashing, of cults, of charismatic evil geniuses, of CIA conspiracies. No one accepted any measure of personal responsibility for what had happened. Soon, thoughts would gratefully turn to the accident at the Three Mile Island nuclear plant. Once again, stirring words would echo abroad, championing the cause of outraged humanity.

There was much Jones's admirers could neither have known nor suspected; but there was also much they could have known, could have suspected, had they taken the trouble to look. They could, for instance, have read the free newspaper distributed by the People's Temple. It would not have told them everything, but it might have given them pause.

"Jack Beam squinted into the morning sun as the rays spread across the windshield of the giant semi-truck he was driving. Pressing eastward across the Arizona desert, he thought to himself how very beautiful the desert was, slightly tinged with green from newly awakening buds of early June. He turned to his fourteen-year-old daughter, Eleanor, who was riding in the seat beside him, and smiled a reassurance that the Temple caravan was on schedule and would arrive in Philadelphia on time. . . ."

It was then that the accident occurred. The truck somersaulted, the roof of the cab was crushed. All the passengers should have been killed instantly. As it was, the occupants emerged with hardly a scratch. Was the survival of these Temple members merely a freakish happening? Or was there some more profound explanation for their improbable escape from injury and death?

When the accident took place, Jim Jones was not even in the

country. He was many thousands of miles away, visiting the Temple's mission in Guyana. There had been no contact with him for several days. Yet when the Temple radio operator finally managed to get hold of him at the mission, Jones's first words were "How is Jack Beam?" The astonished radio operator could only reply, "He's fine, Pastor Jones."

Once again, the Temple newspaper said, Jim Jones had demonstrated his superhuman powers. The miraculous escape of Jack Beam and his passengers had been no freakish happening. Over thousands of miles, Pastor Jones had been able to interpose himself between them and disaster by means of his premonitory gifts. Exactly how his telekinetic powers of intervention worked no one, including Jones, had ever been able to say. What, however, was beyond dispute was that Pastor Jones was able to save from disaster and misfortune those who had placed themselves under his semidivine protection.

The most generally accepted interpretation was that it arose out of the fathomless wellspring of his compassion for people of all races and from all walks of life. His was the power of supreme, disinterested Love, expressed in a life devoted not to the satisfaction of his own needs but to seeking out opportunities to be of service to others. The power of his love did not stop at man but encompassed all creation. For many years, inspired by the example of its Pastor, the church had been tending all animals brought to it, "even every wounded little bird." Only those who had been fortunate enough to witness the practical effects of this Love, those who, because of it, had escaped disaster in their personal lives, could truly understand how that Love—Pastor Jones's love—was literally all-conquering.

His personality cult, even in the earliest issues of the Temple newspaper, was already well established. Jim Jones was the axis about which the Temple revolved. The Temple was not devoted to abstract ideals and principles. It was not love as such or compassion as such that redeemed, but Jim Jones's love, Jim Jones's compassion. Even a casual reader of the Temple newspaper must have been aware that adherence to the organization—especially on the part of its educated white elite—involved regression to a more primitive intellectual state.

The Temple, we are told, based itself on the Judeo-Christian tradition. They held that Jesus Christ was the saviour of mankind. His teachings had played the greatest role in the evolution of human consciousness. They, however, were inspired by the spirit rather than the letter of the Bible. It was impossible not to agree with Tom Paine, who said that much of the Bible was an unedifying chronicle of violence and atrocity which had only helped to further corrupt and brutalize mankind; and that the churches had been no more than human-derived instruments of enslavement. The Bible was riddled with error. Men, seizing on the word, had always misunderstood and misused Jewish and Christian teachings. "Just last month, for instance, newspapers carried the story of a religious cult . . . in which the adult members beat to death a three-year-old child believing he was 'possessed by the devil.' " That kind of evil was the direct consequence of Biblical literalism. They, on the other hand, had grounded themselves in the ethical, humanist teachings of Jesus Christ. People's Temple aimed to establish the great kingdom of Jesus Christ on a troubled globe. They had taken the spirit of the Scriptures to heart.

Their task was not an easy one. The world in which the Temple found itself had long ago turned its back on Jesus Christ. For the poor, the minorities, the deviant, it was becoming an increasingly treacherous place. They knew just how far the rot had gone because of the opposition their work aroused. From all points of the compass the Satanic legions were closing in. Every day hate letters poured in from their Nazi enemies. They did not hesitate to provide front-page samples of these.

"First of all let me say at this time your paper 'the peoples Forum' is really *sick* . . . you say that the Nazi party is, or does teach, Hate, well you got it all backwards. The Nazi party is teaching *Love* for ones own kind, not Hate of others. They are but a few Aryans left, you Niggers want us white people to mix with you, and you white Nigger loving punks make me even *sicker* . . . If you are still reading this letter the next Reich will be here in the USA. And this time there are not going to be any of your kind left to write this Kind of Shit. . . . Heil Hitler!"

The writer (if he was genuine—to one who knows the methods of the People's Temple, it is possible they might have written the letter themselves) need not have worried about being ignored by the Temple. It did not dismiss effusions like this. They constituted the very essence of its case. This is the point at which one begins to catch glimpses of the shadowy regions that lay beyond the brilliant circle of lamplight cast by the Temple's welfare-oriented propaganda.

Nazi takeover was imminent. The Temple alone could see the danger and they alone were standing up against it, laying their lives on the line. A photographic montage showed the skeletal survivor of a Nazi concentration camp; a Southern lynch mob leering up at the pendent bodies of two blacks swinging from the branches of a tree; a young white boy parading in a Chicago suburb, carrying a swastika-decorated placard bearing the legend "Who Needs Niggers?" They had, they tell us, been considerably harassed in recent days (1977) both by telephone and in writing by abominable racists. The Nazis were boasting that their "abhorrent and inhumanly depraved ideology" was catching on fast; that they had gained the sympathy of a majority of whites. Time, the Temple remarked portentously, would tell if that was true.

But whatever the extent of their sympathy, the Temple would never be cowed. They were putting the Nazis on notice. This time around, Niggers and Jews were not going to be quietly exterminated. The Temple had always been pacifist. They had never inflicted violence on any human being. For many years, they had patiently tolerated the taunts and provocations of sick racists, self-avowed Nazis and other equally hated-filled elements who went under more innocuous designations. Some of these groups, perhaps emboldened by that tolerance, had even attempted to infiltrate their church, to sow division in its ranks and promote violence within the congregation. That was going too far. Even their patience had its limits. They wanted the Nazis to know that the Temple would relish their coming by the church *at any time* and trying to start something. The days of their being bullied were over. They were perfectly able, willing and prepared to defend themselves. America, though it might very well be heading that way, was not yet the Third Reich. Adolf Hitler, though he might very well be waiting in the wings, had not yet taken over. Not everyone was goose-stepping—yet. But even if all that were the case, it would not make the slightest difference to them. They would resist with their lives! They would resist down to the last man, woman and child!

The growing Nazi threat to American society had only strengthened their determination to expose fascist insidiousness and cowardice. Every aspect, every ploy of Nazi infamy would be tracked down and boldly catalogued in their newspaper. No threat would deter them from producing it and delivering it free of charge. Hundreds of thousands would come to know that there was a committed opposition to those who recommended the use of violence against people of color and against those who professed different creeds. They would not, they repeated again and again, lie down passively when faced with the threat of genocide. Freedom of expression, as the whole world knew, was a right they had always held dear. Their devotion had been noted in the Congressional Record. "But when racists begin harassing us on the telephone, threatening us with extermination and other demoniacal actions, *they have gone beyond the realm of free speech.*" They would not be intimidated. They would not be silent. They would not be caught off-guard. Fearlessly and whatever the personal cost, they would expose to the world the plans that were actively afoot to implement an updated version of the Final Solution.

In issue after issue of its newspaper, the Temple wrestled with shadowy devils, torturing and tormenting the black disciples with visions of doom. "No. It couldn't happen here. We are a freedom loving people after all. White power? Nazism? Dictatorship? I mean this *is* America. We have to let people have their say. But do you *really* think they can . . . I mean, like in *Germany*? No, that was different . . . no, not here . . . [but] . . . the poison begins to work. Maybe we should stop these 'niggers' and 'riff-raff' from terrorizing our neighborhoods, driving down 'property values,' eating up our taxpayers' hardearned dollars on welfare checks, spreading crimes, drugs, mayhem, corrupting our children . . . maybe send them all back to Africa or just get *RID* of them somehow, as Hitler rid Germany of the Jews and all other minorities . . ." Another gory photograph drove home the message: a black teen-ager lay on a street, his head split open, his brain spilling out from his shattered skull.

Evil was everywhere. The Great Society had failed. The War on Poverty had failed. Unemployment was running at between fifty and sixty percent in the ghettoes. Racist feeling was everywhere on the rise. This was shown in the callous indifference to the plight of the poor, the black, the elderly, the delinquent. Minorities were being cast as scapegoats in the building drama of fascist takeover. The unwanted and unwashed were giving way to despair. Economic distress, already evidenced by shortages and joblessness, was bound to get worse, bound to create the kind of political climate in which a racist demagogue would take power. Slowly but surely the stage was being set for a re-enactment of Hitlerian genocidal policies. Would Americans—white Americans—be tempted to yield to the lethal expedients that had ended in the slaughter of millions a generation ago?

The omens were not good. There could be no doubt about the capacity of white Americans to murder on a mass scale. The newspaper referred to some experiments conducted by a Yale psychologist. He had shown that there existed an extraordinary willingness to obey orders. The subjects of his experiments had been able, without any apparent twinges of conscience, to inflict torture on perfect strangers for no other reason than that they had been commanded to do so by an "authority figure" who had assured them that he would take full responsibility for their actions. The experimenter was forced to conclude, according to the Temple writer, "that ordinary Americans were perfectly capable of carrying out genocidal acts such as those devised by Hitler and his henchmen." The writer was suitably appalled at the power that could be wielded over subordinates by an unchallenged authority figure.

But there was more. A poll conducted by the *Ladies' Home Jour-*

nal in 1976 had asked schoolchildren about their heroes and heroines. Charles Manson had emerged as one of their fifty top idols. Yet another experiment, this one carried out by a high-school history teacher among his pupils, had pointed in the same disquieting direction. The teacher had acted out a charade of dictatorship with his pupils, replete with salutes, slogans and so on. His charges had responded with unnerving enthusiasm, falling completely under the sway of the fantasy. Thus it was proved that even pink-faced cherubs were capable of taking part in mass slaughter. Moral and religious values, the Temple writer pointed out, counted for nothing when subjected to a determined fascist onslaught. Fascism would face no obstacles in its conquest of the American personality. A passage from *Mein Kampf* was quoted: "A state which, in an age of racial pollution, devotes itself to the cultivation of its best racial elements, must someday become the master of the earth . . . we all sense that in a far future mankind may face problems which can be surmounted only by a Supreme Race supported by the means and resources of the entire globe." That future was at hand; America was teetering on the brink.

One had only to look at the kinds of ideas that were being bruited about in the scientific and intellectual communities. Cliometric theories were preparing the way for an inhumane assault on the powerless. The cliometrists were now saying that plantation slavery had been a fine way of life for the blacks. Some of them were even proposing the restoration of slavery for up to forty percent of the black population. That was horrible enough. But what were they planning to do with the remainder? Elsewhere, the sociobiologists were idolizing self-interest and genetic inheritance, discounting the operation of environmental factors. Sociobiology was rapidly gaining adherents and respectability. The dangerous possibilities of cloning did not escape the Temple's attention. Cloning could be used to weed out inferior and undesirable types from the population. Lobotomy and other psychosurgery were knives pointed at the brain of every deviant, every black. These genocidal temptations were not fantasies.

Hadn't the U.S. Indian Health Service sterilized nearly four thousand Indian women without their consent? (How delighted the Temple would have been by the recently enunciated views of the chairman of the agency in charge of Texas' welfare programs. He said that recipients should be compelled to have abortions and, on top of that, be forcibly sterilized. "I'm a little discouraged and irritated," he said, "at the welfare-recipient families growing in size all the time and those of us who work and pay taxes all the time having to pay for them.") Hadn't black prisoners been infected with syphilis for experimental purposes?

Research was well advanced into biological-warfare techniques that would eliminate targeted populations and leave others unharmed. "Imagine that a military power, in pursuit of global conquest, could pinpoint genetic differences between the races and design chemical agents to ATTACK AND VIRTUALLY DESTROY ETHNIC OR RACIAL GROUPS!! Science fiction, you say? On the contrary, the creation of ETHNIC WEAPONS presents a terrifying present-day threat." For example, black and Asian Americans were vulnerable to lactose. If high concentrations were introduced into the water supply, these two groups would be incapacitated. Others would remain unharmed. Antibiotics were another potential ethnic weapon. Nerve damage had been inflicted on Egyptians and Jews by a particular antituberculosis drug. The same drug had no effect on Japanese and Chinese. A project called Population Genetics had been financed by the U.S. Army. Its aim was to map the distribution of human blood types in the United States. A child could work out what they planned to do with this information. Ethnic weaponry was being designed for use *among our own ethnic populations.* The message of genocidal doom was reinforced by the "psychodramas" acted out during Temple services: Ku Klux Klan lynchings were a popular theme. One can only guess at the effect these edifying spectacles must have had on the hundreds of black senior citizens compelled to watch them and, sometimes, participate.

Deep racial terror was mercilessly exposed and exploited in the

People's Temple. Jones stripped bare his following and left them naked and defenseless. He did not liberate: he assaulted and traumatized those who believed in him. One can sense at a certain level his raging hatred for the blacks whose God he claimed to be; a hatred so deep-seated, so tormenting that, in its fury, it turned itself inside out and called itself Love.

It was the 1930s. The Depression was at its height. One day, in the descending dusk of a spring afternoon, a tramp wandered into the little Indiana town of Lynn. A young boy, sensing the man's confusion, immediately went up to him. Where, the boy asked, had he come from? What was he looking for? The tramp said that he did not have a single friend in the world; that he was ready to give up.

The young boy refused to listen to such defeatist talk. "What do you mean, mister?" he replied. "God's your friend and I'm your friend. And Mom will help you get a job!"

The boy was as good as his word. He took the stranger to his mother. She did exactly as he'd said she would: she found the tramp a job in a Lynn factory.

That was Jim Jones's earliest recorded act of charity.

"I was alienated as a child," Jim Jones said in a confessional tape transcript picked up at Jonestown and published by the *Guyana Chronicle*.

I was considered the trash of the neighbourhood, because in those days they referred to you as white trash. . . . They liked my mother less than my Dad because she was unconventional, and not religious. So, the fact that I sought approval so damned much and couldn't get it enabled me to work through that at a very very young age. Finally decided to be true to my own conscience because the frustrations of trying to be accepted, meet the norms, and still not being accepted, relieved me at an early age of a lot of the pressures that a lot of people still have to deal with.

The story about the tramp is mentioned in an article published in 1953 by an Indiana newspaper. Jim Jones was twenty-two years old, working as a student pastor at a Methodist church. It was his love for humanity and his desire to help the unfortunate, he told the reporter, that had led him toward the religious life. The newspaper had decided to draw him to the public's attention because he had embarked on a campaign to set up a recreation center for the children of Indianapolis' South Side ghetto. In keeping with his nondenominational outlook, the youthful pastor had set up a program in his church which had become a wonder of the local religious community. In his teaching there, he had thrown aside all sectarian strictness. He did not preach dogma, but drew out the unadorned moral content of Bible stories. But there was another side to the idealistic young pastor:

> I was in a coma when the Rosenbergs were being executed. I was ready to die, infectious hepatitis. My mind was so dim . . . It was in summer. Marceline was standing behind a screened partition. Jesus Christ! I kept thinking—they can't kill these people, they can't kill these people. I'd marched till there was holes in my shoes trying to get petitions. The fucking Pope, we got even the Pope. And their children came up and kissed them through the screen, oh God. I just died a thousand deaths. I wish I could have died then. Hell, you can only have so many revolutionary deaths, you care for people—you die, you die. So hell, death isn't any problem for me any more. . . . I really don't understand why I lived. I thought, "It's futile, an inhumane system that kills people based on a bunch of scrap paper, just because they had Communist affiliations." . . . I hated that system. . . . I wept till those goddamned sheets were just soaked. Some place along the line I quit crying. Don't cry any more. Rough being a communist. . . . I'd get picked up hitch-hiking, talking communism—car would come to a screeching stop, and I'd be ordered out of the car, middle of nowhere. Happened not once, but dozens of times. I mean it must have happened two dozen times. But, equally, I'd convert people. So there were those redeeming moments. But shit, where's it got now?

I'm wandering down the street, stopped at a used car lot, and I met a man, and I find out he's a Methodist Superintendent—and I think, oh shit, he's a religious nut. I started knocking the church, just raising hell, knocking the church. He said, "Why don't you come to my office?" He must have been a communist . . . Here I am, raving against the church, knocking the church, ridiculing God, all this shit, and he says why don't you come to my office. I thought you fucker I'm not coming to your goddamn office. But I did, for some instinctive reason I went. He said I want you to take a church. I said, you giving *me* a *church*? I don't *believe* in anything. I'm a revolutionary. He said, why don't you take a church, why don't you take a church. And he appointed me, a fucking communist, to a goddamned church, and I didn't even meet him through the Party, I met him in a fucking used car lot. This was in 1953, I think. I take this goddamned church as a communist who believed in nothing—that is how religious I was and still am. And I preached to Marceline, I said what am I going to do with this goddamned thing. This guy, he's obviously a communist and he wants me to do something with this goddamned church. That is how the church wandered into it. The church fell in my lap. He's the one who started it. I hope he's dead. . . . I took this church. I remember I thought I was going to die a thousand deaths when I got up in that pulpit. Preaching the first day, I had people in turmoil—integration. . . . On it went. I finally brought blacks into the church. Three or four weeks I brought a black singing group in. . . . I'm going on with all this bullshit, bringing all these people in—losing all the old timers . . ."

Religion had always fascinated Jim Jones. When he was a child one of his favorite pastimes was to conduct mock services. Maybe from the very beginning it was the raw power of the preacher figure that attracted him. Even in those juvenile enactments he was much more strict than merciful. He would beat his congregants with a stick. God, in the Bible Belt, is power, not love. He intervenes as much to punish as to save.

How, on top of his fascination with preaching, Jones acquired his racial passions is not certain. Lynn was a conservative town, not the sort of place that encouraged the presence of blacks. Jones's father was a member of the Ku Klux Klan—whose national headquarters was in nearby Indianapolis. Gassed during the First World War, he was a permanent invalid and led a sequestered life. It was Jones's mother, Lynetta, who held the family together. One suspects, from the few hints we have, that she and her husband were an ill-assorted pair; the maimed, useless devotee of the Ku Klux Klan and the "unconventional, not religious" dark-skinned woman who had once shocked Lynn by smoking in public could not have had a great deal in common. One can imagine her accumulating bitterness and contempt. Jones never had much to say about his father. His mother, on the other hand, would be incorporated into his hagiography.

> Integration was a big issue with me. An inclusive congregation, that was the first big issue, a big, big issue. What a hell of a battle that was—I thought I'll never make a revolution, I can't even get these fuckers to integrate, much less get them to get any communist philosophy. . . . I'd get the Pentecostals in and all the Methodists would leave. [The new Methodist superintendent] said, "What's going on over there?" . . . I decided we'll piss on you, man. You didn't put me in this church, and I'm not going to let you put me out. So I conspired with the whole goddamned church to withdraw from the Methodist denomination. . . . I got a whole bunch of people together to vote the goddamned church out of the conference, and named it another church. . . . Church was nothing, handful of old bigots till I brought in some blacks. And that is how the goddamned religious career got rolling. I was preaching integration, against war, throwing in some communist philosophy. Got a bunch of Pentecostals in there and they were going crazy. . . . It was a circus. So the Methodists saw that as a weak moment and they pulled in and told us to get our ass out. . . .

Accusing the Methodists of lacking love, Jim Jones, now settled in Indianapolis, branched out on his own. His raw material was at hand. Some of the black sections of Indianapolis bring you back to the Third World. What Jones saw in the early fifties you could still see in the late seventies—the decaying cabins and row houses; the rutted, unswept roads; listless blacks sitting out on collapsed front porches; half-naked children playing in dust and dirt; young men with matted hair standing on street corners, drinking from bottles encased in paper bags, shouting at you as you go by. I was there on a hot summer's afternoon. The sky turned yellow. Lightning flashed, distant thunder resounded and big drops of rain began to fall. On every corner there seemed to be a little church, sometimes as small and as run-down as the houses themselves; page after page of the Indianapolis Yellow Pages is taken up with the listing of religious establishments.

> ... I heard all these healers and I thought well if those sons of bitches can do it then I can do it too. And I tried my first faith-healing. I don't remember how. Didn't work out too well. But I kept watching those healers; I thought, these assholes, doing nothing with this thing. I couldn't see nobody healed. But crowds coming ... so I thought there must be some way that you can do this for good, that you can get the crowd, get some money and do some good with it. Ended up in Columbus, Indiana. Trying my best to get something started along those lines and I wasn't getting very far. I remember a little old lady ... she called me up to her and said, "I perceive you are a prophet, that you shall go around the world, you shall be heard around the world." I thought, Okay, honey, you said it. I didn't know what the fuck she was talking about. And then she said, "and tonight you shall begin your ministry" ... and I got up in that damned pulpit, and my mouth wouldn't open. I closed my eyes. And all this shit flies through my mind and I call it out. And I had people coming up, screaming and hollering ... and the *second* night you couldn't get in the goddamned building. And I'd just call people out and they'd get healed of everything. Much like I do now, with help, but they didn't have no help, really, nothing. Just closed my eyes and call. Such a drain, it got so heavy. Jesus Christ! I thought, I can't stand this. Wasn't long before I started taking little notes, for years and years and years, it was me, my gift and whatever I could take down.

Packed out the biggest auditoriums in Indiana and Ohio. I should've left it that way. But I'd have been dead. People pass growths and then by sleight of hand I'd started doing it—and that would trigger others to get healed. But I never had anybody to help me, not even Marcie. Marcie never knew there was one thing but reality. Carried the entire operation on by myself [for eleven years]. And I don't know how the hell I got by with it. . . . Didn't trust people and I should have kept it that way. It wasn't days before people were saying, "You're Jesus Christ." Hell, it didn't make me believe any more in living deity than I did before, I can tell you that. But people give me more bullshit, I don't know. "You are Jesus Christ." Hell, it didn't make a difference to me one way or another. I didn't know how to explain how people got healed of every goddamned thing under the sun, that's for sure, or *apparently* got healed. . . . I was a dogged person; I'd fight every goddamned case. I was different from every other healer; I wouldn't ignore hardship cases —I'd tackle them. Lost some, but I'd win enough. . . . I'd fill the places—goddamned places would be packed. You couldn't be so stacked, you couldn't squeeze in. Climbing in the windows. You never seen crowds in our day like it. Be thousands outside crawling through every window. But you see, nobody gives a shit as long as you don't become political. . . . I'd hold meeting in Ohio, travel some other town and hold one at night. Three meetings a day in some places; three meetings on Sunday and beat the roads Thursday, Friday and Saturday. Get home, I'd drag ass home, nine o'clock Sunday. Sometimes it got so bad on me physically that I'd strap my wrist to the side of the car door, and Jack Beam would drive the car at a running pace, so I'd be forced to run alongside the car—to get my system back in balance, get me going again. I'm amazed I'm alive today. . . .

In 1956, after a number of sorties, Jim Jones finally established a church he called the People's Temple. During this period, his rainbow family was growing: he was putting his ideal of racial integration into personal practice. It was in these early Indianapolis days that the basic Temple pattern was set. Everything it was ever to be existed there in microcosm. The ecstasies of faith healing were balanced by religious unorthodoxy, social commentary and the provision of welfare services. The Temple ran a soup kitchen, an animal shelter, a job-rehabilitation program, a scholarship scheme for impoverished students, nursing homes for the elderly. The Temple congregation became noted for its energy —members devoted more of their time to church affairs and raised more money than other equivalent groups.

It was also in Indianapolis that Jones began to develop his demands for unquestioning personal loyalty, the earliest expression of which was a so-called interrogation committee whose function was to unearth and punish the disobedient and disloyal. This would evolve into the Temple's catharsis meetings, characterized by the accusations of informers, self-incrimination and publicly administered beatings. The desire for total control may, in part, have been stimulated by his long-held Stalinist fantasies.

> . . . I loved Stalin. I never would accept that Stalin was all that bad as he was portrayed. . . . I don't switch in the middle of the stream. Stalin, who I'd read of and heard reports of, that stood on the outskirts of Moscow; who lived in humble surroundings. Purged, yeah, sure he purged. The goddamned allies had infiltrated his high command. Enough to drive anybody insane. And all of a sudden along comes Khrushchev, and Stalin is a son of a bitch. . . . I couldn't accept what the hell they would want to discredit Marshal Stalin for. I know I wasn't there, I wasn't there, but to me it was too instilled loyalty, instilled, and I just could not reconcile that break. That loyalty is still down deep in me today. Stalin did great things for the Soviet Union. If it hadn't been for Stalin Russia would never have won that fucking war. The Man of Steel persevered. The people fought not for Mother Russia; they were fighting for Stalingrad, Leningrad and Stalingrad by God. . . . Nine hundred or eleven hundred goddamned days at Leningrad eating dead flesh. And then at Stalingrad, by God . . . That battle lives in my mind. I met a guy at the University, a former Nazi who was there. . . . He saw that mass, it actually dimmed the rising of the sun. . . . All this mass

coming, they were singing, singing the Internationale. Old people, he thought, this is laughable. But they kept coming on and
coming on. They ordered to fire on them. Bodies splintering in
the sky and the people kept on coming . . . couldn't stop them.
Mowed down bodies . . . and then at the end he said . . . here
come the young. . . .

Jones did not hide his views from the congregation. He would
cast doubt on the Virgin Birth, fling his Bible to the floor, spit on
it and encourage others to do the same. "When this preacher
Jones advised my aunt to throw away her Bible," one Eugene
Cordell told an Indianapolis newspaper in 1972, "we started
fighting." But it did not do any good. His seventy-year-old aunt
remained steadfast in her devotion to Jones. Her nephew believed that he had practiced some kind of sorcery on her; that she
was literally under a spell. His aunt was one of those who, in 1965,
would make the hegira to Redwood Valley. Thirteen years later,
she would be listed among the Jonestown dead, faithful to the
end. Jones's "charisma" was already well developed by the time
he left Indianapolis. "Just the sound of his voice made you feel
like you had power," recalled a girl who had joined the Temple
when she was sixteen. Until she heard Jones preach, she had felt
herself to be no more than a "single ant in the whole world. I was
nothing, going nowhere." Jones changed all that. She too would
follow him out to California.

It was also in Indianapolis that Jones first demonstrated his
ability to charm the liberal political establishment. When, in 1961,
the city began looking for a director to head its newly created
Human Rights Commission—who more natural to choose than
Jim Jones? "As a result of his efforts," the Mayor said, "many
second-class citizens for the first time in the history of this city,
have become first-class citizens. . . . I have the greatest confidence
in his integrity, ability and true affection for his fellowman."
Then, as afterward, his faith healings and other eccentricities
would prove no stumbling block.

And it was also in Indianapolis that the pattern of persecution, real and imagined, began. The Joneses' children were threatened, Marceline was spat upon while queuing for a bus with her black son, dead animals were thrown onto the church premises. Someone, Jones said, hit him on the back of the head with a milk bottle. Their house was stoned. Jones's name was often in the newspapers—the embattled humanitarian, under siege by the forces of darkness.

It was at about this time that the idea of wholesale removal of himself and his congregation first occurred to Jones. He had, it has been said, a vision of a nuclear holocaust in which it was revealed to him that Indianapolis, because of its special wickedness, would be completely destroyed. Jones, subsequently, would deny that he had ever predicted any such thing. What is certain is that in 1961 *Esquire* published an article listing the places that would be safest in the event of nuclear war. One of the areas mentioned was the Belo Horizonte region of Brazil. Early in 1962, Jones and his rainbow family suddenly turned up as "missionaries" in Belo Horizonte. It is possible that his fear of nuclear war was genuine. But there were probably other reasons for the sudden move. The harassment of his church and his family was real. This, together with his own messianic temperament, may have implanted in him the germ of the desire to found a domain of his own. The voyage to Brazil can be interpreted as a confused foray in that direction.

> . . . same thing as always—search out a place where an interracial family could live. Interracial mixture of my family and my church—I thought America was incompatible. And I really felt that more, more than anything—interracial family was just fundamentally at odds with the capitalist development in the U.S. The thermonuclear reality was there too. I thought how people could be mad enough to make such weapons and then sane enough not to use them. I didn't give a damn about living, but I thought children should be given a chance. The hemispheres were somewhat separate in wind currents and in that period there was some chance of more likelihood of survival. . . .

Bonnie Thielmann was sixteen years old when, one day early in 1962, a clerk in the Belo Horizonte post office called to her father and asked him to translate the requests of a black-haired American who could speak no Portuguese. Thielmann's parents were missionaries and had been living in Brazil for some years. Her father was only too happy to be of help to this fellow American who said his name was Jim Jones and who told him that he was the pastor of a rapidly expanding congregation in Indianapolis. He had only just arrived in town and was staying in a hotel. It was a matter of course that he should be invited to dinner.

Bonnie was not enthusiastic. Her inside knowledge of the American missionary community in Belo Horizonte had not endeared the breed to her. One of the things that most distressed her was its racism. She was personally affected by this because her boyfriend was a dark-skinned Brazilian. Her liaison had scandalized her father's missionary colleagues. She had no reason to expect anything different from this freshly arrived black-haired preacher from Indianapolis and his overly blond wife.

She was to be most delightfully surprised. There was, to begin with, the Joneses' rainbow family, one of whom was "undeniably black." Here, obviously, was no run-of-the-mill missionary imbued with cultural and racial arrogance. She was to have further cause, as the evening progressed, to be enamored of these unusual strangers. When, as was inevitable, the subject of her Brazilian boyfriend came up, the Joneses did not react in the predictable way. In fact, they did not react at all. They went right on eating. The conversation moved on to more general topics. Jones told his hosts a little more about himself. He had come to Brazil partly to recuperate from the strains of his ministry and partly to scout out a refuge from the nuclear war that was bound to come. American racism was another topic with which he seemed preoccupied that evening. He mentioned that when one of his Korean children had been killed in a car crash, he could not find a single white undertaker in Indianapolis who was prepared to bury her. How could such an evil society escape annihilation?

The more Jones talked, the more Bonnie was charmed. She began spending much of her spare time with the Joneses, who had moved into a modest three-bedroom house. Eventually, she became part of the household. They lived simply. Most days, they ate bread, rice and beans. Meat was a rare treat. But everyone was happy. To the tune of "I love Paris in the springtime," Jones would sing, "I love Polly in the morning" to his parrot. He showed his abundant love and tenderness in other ways. Once, moved by the austerity of their diet, some friends gave them a duck. Jones could not bring himself to slaughter the animal. Instead, it was kept in the backyard as a pet. It was not long before the beggar children of the neighborhood discovered that they would always be met with kindness—and food—at the Joneses'. They would come by the dozen and be fed in the kitchen and on the veranda. Bonnie was so enthralled by all this goodness that she decided to take Marceline as her new "role model"—until then her role model had been Brigitte Bardot. Her goal was now the pursuit of "inner beauty."

Nevertheless, Bonnie—who was, after all, a missionary's daughter destined for Bible college—could not help noticing the oddities of her new friends. For one thing, the Joneses did not keep a Bible in the house. Nor was grace said at mealtimes. She was mildly puzzled when Jones showed her a photograph of himself and Marceline flanking Fidel Castro—the Joneses, apparently, had met him during a brief stopover in Cuba en route to Brazil. Why should a missionary be posing with Fidel Castro? Equally unsettling was his permanent state of agitation about nuclear destruction: he would see missiles in steeples and begin to rave. His theology was also worrisome; but even worse than his theological skepticism was his open fascination for Brazil's numerous African-derived spirit cults. All in all, Jim Jones was a most singular missionary. In the autumn of 1962, Bonnie departed for the United States and Bible college. She was not to see the Joneses for another nine years.

Despite its favorable wind currents, Jones became disenchanted with Belo Horizonte. He took his family two hundred miles

south to Rio de Janeiro, where, making use of a recently acquired
Bachelor of Education degree, he got a job in the American
School.

> Brazil . . . One day we got to the beach, and we swam. I had
> my kids, and we were playing in the water. It was the closest
> thing we had to a moment of freedom, sheer freedom, from
> worry, until I looked up over Copacabana, saw the hills. Tier
> after tier of shanties put together with the barest of wood, car-
> tons, cardboard . . . which would always wash out at any major
> rain . . . how those people endured . . . Brazil was a painful
> chapter in my life. Remember catching Jim [his black adopted
> son] when he nearly fell out of a seventh-floor window. What
> goes through your mind at times like that . . . I remember
> thinking, "Well, being Black in America had been so rough on
> him, and to have to go back there, maybe I'm doing him a
> disservice. . . ." But grabbed I did, just before he would have
> fallen seven stories to his death. . . . I did a lot of humanitarian
> work, orphanage, two orphanages, I was feeding, getting
> the food and other supplies for them. Always short of needs
> and supplies and I had an ability to get that kind of thing to-
> gether.
> That led to the final painful chapter—at one point it looked
> like all my money was cut off . . . I had to scrape it together.
> . . . That's where the Ambassador's wife came in. She took a
> shine to me, and we had all those kids to feed, they were looking
> forward to it, to the food, and there was no funding. . . . So the
> Ambassador's wife offered me a pile of money if I'd fuck her,
> so I did. There is nothing to compare with the kind of revulsion
> felt when you are lying next to someone you loathe. And I
> loathed her, and everything she stood for—for the arrogance
> of wealth, the racism, the cruelty. I puked afterwards, it was
> that bad. But I got the money and I bought food and took it to
> these children only I made that bitch go with me so she could
> see the other side of life. And when these half-starved black and
> brown children reached out to touch her dress, she snatched
> her skirt away lest they contaminate her lily-white self. . . . I
> could've killed that bitch, could have killed her. . . .

Money was not the only problem Jones had. In 1963, Brazil was on the verge of a right-wing military takeover. His thoughts turned homeward as the political climate worsened.

> . . . there was nothing more I could do there, nothing more. . . . Got out of there just in time . . . they came by the school asking what happened to this missionary Jones, and it was the right-wing police, who did their own vigilante work. . . . I'd given assistance to various people, underground people, given them tangible help so they could defend themselves, defend their lives, and I preached communism openly. . . . I got out of there just in time. I remember leaving the airport wondering whether I wouldn't get in trouble for what I was doing revolutionary-wise *there* when I got back to the United States. And I was sick because I knew how that affected my family. In those days I was still careful about guarding people's lives . . . it was clear that in the States my duty was laid out for me—my church was in a hell of a mess. Been taken over by an opportunist and if the good people in that church were in any way going to be saved . . . and Kennedy was just murdered and it looked to me like fascism may be about to take over the country. And it would be better for me to fight fascism in my own country, rather than in Brazil, where my roots were not that well established, and my following wasn't that extensive. So, that was the decision. . . .

Toward the end of 1963, Jim Jones returned to Indianapolis. He had learned how to use himself, how to combine primitive sentimentalism about race and justice with ruthlessness and self-aggrandizement; he had learned how to identify himself—his body, his powers—with his message. The two had become indissolubly linked. Thinking instinctively in terms of a "following," he would be satisfied with nothing less than kingship and a domain to go with it. His "idealism" had sunk its roots in personal and ideological corruption. That corruption was not something which developed with time—as Jones became more power-mad, paranoid or whatever—but was contained in the very premises on which the Temple was founded: the cult of the superman equipped with paranormal powers; the idea of a preacher who did not believe in God and a church that was not really a church but a secret society; the abasement of the self in the name of the Cause—all of this was already in place when Jones left Indianapolis for Redwood Valley. Those who were received into its inner circles knowingly recruited themselves into corruption. From the inception, devotion and self-contamination went hand in hand. In a society like the United States, aggressive doctrines of racial brotherhood as exemplified by the People's Temple are often stamped on the same spiritual palimpsest as their polar opposites. Both arise from a similar torment: an intolerably aggravated race consciousness. A body like the Ku Klux Klan and groups like the People's Temple write their obsessions on different sides of a single sheet of paper. Behind the images of genocidal doom so relentlessly evoked by the Temple's propagandists there shines through the wish-fulfilling glow of flaming crosses. The Temple was the disease it claimed to be fighting. In that lay its most hopeless corruption.

In Indianapolis, Jim Jones had gone about as far as he could go. He was too well known, had too many enemies. A full-fledged kingly domain would be almost impossible to carve out in so public and inhospitable an environment. Another area *Esquire* had pinpointed as being safe from the effects of nuclear war was the region around Eureka in Northern California. Toward the middle of 1965, Jones, together with about one hundred and fifty of his hard-core faithful, headed West.

In 1971, Bonnie Thielmann saw her old friends again. She went to one of the Temple's services in Los Angeles and afterward took a Temple bus up to Redwood Valley. The Joneses welcomed her with affection. But Bonnie blushed when Jim, recalling the old days in Brazil, told how the wife of a diplomat had paid him five thousand dollars to have three days of nonstop lovemaking with her? Poor Marceline. How could he talk of such a thing in front of her. But Marceline, whose inner beauty the years had not dimmed, did not even bat an eyelid. That, however, was only the first of the evening's surprises.

The Joneses revealed to her that she had been their daughter in many previous lifetimes.

Bonnie nearly choked. But then she remembered something. Some time before, she had read a book titled *Youth, Yoga and Reincarnation*. This she had done rather nervously, because to read such a book did not seem entirely in keeping with a Christian life. Still, she had persevered; and while reading the section on reincarnation she had gained the distinct impression that she had been the Joneses' daughter in another life.

Thus Bonnie, though taken aback, was not utterly astonished. Her ancestry was distinguished. Jones had been the heretical Egyptian Pharaoh Ikhnaton, who had tried to introduce a new religion based on worship of the sun. Marceline had been his wife, Nefertiti. One of their daughters had become the bride of the boy king Tutankhamun. But whether or not she was that daughter, they did not say. In previous lives, it emerged that evening, Jones had also been the Buddha, Jesus Christ and Lenin. Bonnie had to admit that none of this sounded very Christian. But her confusion was matched only by her fascination. Before she went up to bed, Jones, descending from these high planes of revelation, inquired after her sex life. Did she, like so many other women, fake her orgasms? Bonnie assured him that she never did. Jones giggled and said that he had figured as much.

Next day, she attended one of his sermons. Jones appeared in dark glasses and a black robe. With his jet black hair (we now know he dyed it), he cut a commanding figure. The atmosphere was thick with iconoclastic passion. Jones went through his routine. He shook his fist at the American flag, flung his Bible on the floor and spat on it. He raved.

"We can let nothing stop us from building a just and living society right here on earth. . . . We must tear down the Sky God and all this talk of the sweet by-and-by. If there's a God up there,——— you, God!"

Ikhnaton's daughter fled from the church.

Marceline wrote her a thoughtful letter. Everyone, she said, had to live through his karma. Bonnie got in touch with a pastor friend. She told him about her doubts and confusion. He told her that such skepticism was perfectly normal; he also told her that he would like to take her to bed with him. Bonnie lost her faith in the Sky God.

In the summer of 1972, ten years after she had first been entranced by Jim Jones and his rainbow family, Bonnie joined the People's Temple.

The Temple, claiming an active membership of four thousand, had blossomed in the seven years that had elapsed since its migration from Indianapolis. It had, to begin with, encountered some hostility from the Redwood Valley locals. Many of them, migrants from the Deep South, were rednecks. The rainbow-hued urbanites of the People's Temple were an exotic addition to their pastoral landscape. Many did not take kindly to the sudden infusion of color. "Local Group Suffers Terror in the Night" was the headline of one story in the *Ukiah Daily Journal.* Jones armed his bodyguards and built a watchtower. Once, there supposedly occurred an attempt at assassination. Shots rang out and Jones, in full view of his followers, fell to the ground, blood streaming from his chest. Apparently mortally wounded, he was carried away by his nurses. A few minutes later he re-emerged, unscathed and smiling. Another miracle.

But Jones's policy was not only defensive. He assiduously courted the conservative sentiments of the community and set out to demonstrate what a civic-minded body the Temple was. The Temple newspaper published laudatory articles about the California Highway Patrol; the local sheriff was praised. It was during this period that the Temple set up a fund for the families of slain policemen. The Masonite Corporation of Ukiah was congratulated for its sound ecological practices. Citing his trumped-up Cherokee ancestry, Jones did good works among the depressed Indian community. His volunteers painted the Redwood Valley school, saving, it was said, nearly three thousand tax dollars. He successfully wooed the editor of the *Ukiah Daily Journal* and his wife, the free-lance journalist Kathy Hunter—who, one day, would go to Guyana in search of him. As early as 1967, Jones was beginning to get his rewards: in that year he was made foreman of the Mendocino County Grand Jury. Other honors would follow. Within a few years, the Temple had become a power to be reckoned with in and around Ukiah.

In the midst of all these successes, Jones did not forget Indianapolis. He continued to maintain a presence in the city where his organization had first seen the light of day. In October 1971, for instance, hundreds packed the Temple church to listen to and be healed by the man who now advertised himself as the "Prophet of God." Not only, he told them, could he cure all kinds of diseases, but he was even able to resurrect the dead.

"With over four thousand members of our California church," he said, "we haven't had a death yet. I am a Prophet of God and I can cure both the illness of your body and the illness of your mind."

In December he was back in Indianapolis, railing at those "faith healers and fundamentalists" who "call for the coming of Christ and go out to meet Him in a brand-new Lincoln Continental." He, on the contrary, was penniless, a point emphasized by a sign placed near the pulpit which described him as using only "modest and worn" clothing. But the grace of God was with him. This was shown when he and his band of faithful disciples had first arrived in California in 1965. For many months they were left out in the rain, and yet, not a drop of water had ever touched their heads. The credit was due to the Christ within him, which was able to reach out and touch the Christ within others who believed in him.

Redwood Valley could not contain the ambitions of the People's Temple. More and more it was looking south, to the lush pastures of San Francisco and Los Angeles, but especially to San Francisco. Jones's technique was to make inroads into the congregations of black rival ministers; to first infiltrate their ranks and then outsell them. Hannibal Williams, a black Presbyterian clergyman, was one of those affected.

"I never tried to compete with Jones. That man was the Devil himself." He didn't like it in the least when outsiders cast him as a competitor for souls with Jim Jones. Rev Williams stressed his theological respectability. Velvet curtains were draped across the windows of his chic wood-paneled office. A portrait of himself decorated one of the walls. On another wall was hung a sculpture of Christ on the Cross. He might, he said, be just a small man with a small Presbyterian church—"But we Presbyterians are the same people that landed the *Mayflower* on Plymouth Rock." (I was reminded of Malcolm X's remark that the blacks did not land on Plymouth Rock but, rather, it had landed on them.) Given such an ancestry, was it likely that he would so lower himself as to compete with a man like Jim Jones?

Jones had good reason to woo Hannibal Williams in those early days when he was still trying to establish himself in San Francisco. Williams was active in the Western Addition Community Organization (WACO). The Western Addition, a relatively run-down area of the city harboring a substantial population of blacks, had been scheduled for urban renewal.

"Urban renewal," Williams said, "means that you'll tear down low-rent housing and put up structures the longtime residents can't afford. Urban renewal means black removal—that was one of the WACO slogans." He and WACO had agitated ceaselessly. "During that time I became so famous I was the subject of doctoral theses. Girls from Vassar, you know, were coming down here to find out about me."

Jones's emissaries came to see him, regaling him with glowing tales about their leader. But he had steadfastly opposed Temple infiltration of the movement in the Western Addition. They had no need for some out-of-town Messiah coming and telling them what to do.

"You must know," Williams added, "that when a man begins telling his followers he is Jesus Christ, I get immediately suspicious."

Jones approached a Rev Bedford, a friend of his, who ran the Macedonia Baptist Church. Bedford was in the habit of letting other preachers use his church. Without too much reflection, he let Jones in. It was to be his undoing.

"Lo and behold, that man began straightaway to subvert Rev Bedford's congregation." Rev Williams shook his head. "He did it right under his nose."

One hundred members of the Macedonia Baptist Church deserted their old leader and joined the People's Temple.

"That was quite a blow to Rev Bedford, I can tell you." Rev Williams buried his face in a handkerchief and blew his nose loudly. "He was a pretty old man by then as well. It kind of broke him."

Williams continued to receive stacks of letters from the People's Temple saying that Jim Jones had "taken note" of his good work and many other flattering things. Each letter would contain a small money order—five dollars, eight dollars, ten dollars. "So I sat down and wrote a general letter to the folks at the Temple, saying that I felt in all conscience I couldn't accept all this money they were sending me for my own use."

Exactly the same strategy—flattery, money, praise for Jones and his work with poor blacks—was used, Williams said, on nearly every black leader in the community.

Jones, meanwhile, applied to the Board of Education. They gave him permission to use the auditorium of Benjamin Franklin Junior High School for his services.

"Next thing I hear is that Jones is raising people from the dead. Making them spit out cancers. I became really suspicious then, as you would imagine." He saw old black women preparing large amounts of food—all at their own expense—and taking it up to Ukiah to be sold for the Temple's benefit. "I heard they had a swimming pool in the church up there and that people liked that." Williams sighed. "I can't help thinking we black people can be very gullible."

The Temple, as it grew more confident, ceased its flatteries. "Jones began to denounce the black preachers. He called us Cadillac-driving and chicken-eating. Every church, you know, has its malcontents. Jones pulled in those malcontents." Rev Williams

rose from his large desk. "But look at me, sir! Look at my old car!
It ain't no Cadillac!" He opened a drawer, pulled out his last tax
statement and showed it to me. "I, sir, make the biggest contri-
butions to this here church. Look at this statement. *Two thousand,
five hundred and thirty-nine dollars and thirty cents* I gave of my own
money to this church. Who am I exploiting?"

Jones's accusations still rankled.

By late 1972, courtesy of the Board of Education, Jones was
playing to capacity audiences in the auditorium of Benjamin
Franklin Junior High School. The religious correspondent of the
San Francisco Examiner attended one of those services. Marceline
sang a song titled "My Black Baby." While she sang, her black
adopted son stood at the foot of the stage, gazing up at his blond
mother. Jones carried out a couple of healings. Old black women
jigged and shrieked and swooned.

"Pastor Jim Jones is God Almighty himself," someone shouted.

"You say I am God Almighty?" Jones asked.

"Yes. You are."

"What do you mean by that?" Jones replied. "If you believe I
am a son of God in that I am filled with love, I can accept that. I
won't knock what works for you, but I don't want to be interpreted as the Creator of the Universe. If you say, 'He is God,'
some people will think you are nuts. They can't relate. . . . I'm
really a messenger of God . . . I have a paranormal ability in healing . . ."

Nineteen seventy-two would be the year when, confident of its
appeal, its strength, its numbers, the Temple would make San
Francisco its headquarters. But 1972, paradoxically, was also the
year it received its first major unfavorable publicity. This took the
form of a series of articles written by the *Examiner*'s religious
affairs correspondent. He described succinctly and unambiguously the prophetic pretensions of the Temple's leader, his res-
urrective activities, the vaunted welfare programs, its murky
property dealings and other odd ways of raising money (including the sale of fetishes blessed by Jones), the pistol-toting armed
guards. He also drew attention to the backup services that en-

abled Jones's extrasensory faculties to function so faultlessly. A
defector told of the visits paid to the homes of those the church
considered potential members. These spies would scour the
house, noting the medicines they saw in the bathroom, reading
letters, studying photographs and riffling through wastebaskets.
No act was too humble or too despicable for the young, idealistic
Temple aristocracy. An interesting letter from Timothy Stoen to
the *Examiner* was reproduced. "Jim [wrote this utopian socialist]
has been the means by which more than forty persons have literally been brought back from the dead this year. When I first came
into the church, I was the conventional skeptic about such things.
But I must be honest. I have seen Jim revive people stiff as a
board, tongues hanging out, eyes set, skin graying, and all vital
signs absent. Don't ask me how it happens. It just does. . . . Jim is
very humble about his gift and does not preach it. . . ."

The Temple was stunned by this attack. Its foot soldiers began
to picket the *Examiner,* carrying Bibles and placards. Jones was
given the right of reply. It took the form of an interview. Jones
explained that his resurrections were spontaneous events, involving no magic words, no special prayers. All he did was radiate his
love. It was an extremely democratic business. "I would say, 'This
is Jim.' That's my title. No 'Reverend' or anything." Corpses responded well to this mixture of love and egalitarianism. If he had
had no previous acquaintance with the corpse, he might say,
"This is Pastor;" but such pulling of rank was rare. The People's
Temple was not like other faith-healing outfits. It encouraged
both those it had healed and those it had brought back from the
dead to go and see a doctor. If they could not afford to do that,
the Temple paid for them to do so.

A rational, humane reviver of the dead. This was Jones at his
most urbane. But the Temple newspaper adopted a different
approach, a characteristic mixture of innuendo, slander and
threat that was devoid of all urbanity. The persecution to which
the church had been subjected of late, they said, had been the
work of worldly, materialistic and carnal minds. Hostility had
been aroused because certain people became jealous when they

saw a successful church composed of people from so many
diverse backgrounds and races. But nemesis would always strike
down those who had the temerity to cross the Temple. "Ironically
enough, that reporter, our one critic, has been demoted from
being religious editor of a big city newspaper to representing
some newspapers in Idaho and Wyoming."

His source is then discredited. This source had been seething
with resentment because he had been asked to leave the church
—the only person ever asked to do so. They had taken this unusual step because he had refused to seek psychiatric help after it
had been revealed that he had once sexually molested his daughter, a mere child at the time. The Temple was reluctant to cause
that individual any more pain by naming him, even though his
daughter had begged them to do so in order to demonstrate the
malice motivating his lies. Still, the charge of sexual assault was
true, the man having confessed to it in writing while he was a
member of the church. Believing that the community must be
protected from his perverted lusts, the Temple had supplied the
police with all the necessary details. Anti-Temple sentiment, however, did not arise only from the malice of mentally disturbed
child molesters. Their journalistic foes had also made use of informers who were certified racist bigots. Reverend Jones, fortu-
nately, was not easily provoked, despite the evil consequences
flowing from their racist natures, consequences that included "the
brutalization of little animals."

As it was, the storms of 1972 blew away. In the autumn the
People's Temple moved into its new headquarters in the Fillmore
district of San Francisco and entered—with the help of a Vice
President, a Governor, a Lieutenant Governor, a Mayor, two
Prime Ministers, assorted Assemblymen, communists, socialists,
Black Panthers, ministers, feminists, ecologists, friendly journal-
ists, social workers, Chilean martyrs—the most glorious phase of
its career.

CHAPTER

10

NOT MANY miles away from San Francisco is the distinct metropolitan entity of Berkeley, home of the biggest, most sought-after and most notorious of the campuses that together make up the University of California. Berkeley—the cradle, in the sixties, of violent student protest, of every conceivable strain of radical politics, a town whose magical potency could transform well-brought-up girls from the Midwest into terrorist soldiers of the Symbionese Liberation Army; Berkeley—whose militants were beaten, tear-gassed and shot at; Berkeley—the *bête noire* of Governor Ronald Reagan's administration. "In the streets and cafes of Berkeley," wrote Elinor Langer, a young reporter from the East, "people walked with a bounce, dressed roughly, carried their babies in canvas sacks on their backs or breasts. Perhaps it was the ancient attraction of Bohemia. All I knew was that I felt at home." That was how it was and seemed in the glorious days of 1965. For the young journalist from stuffy Washington it was a revelation. She threw away her Italian knit suits, her high-heeled shoes, her leather briefcase, and plunged into the "Movement."

Compared with the sedate, country-club atmosphere of Stanford University at the southeastern end of the Bay, Berkeley is distinctly raffish. The broad avenue that takes you into town when you come off the freeway is lined with motels, gas stations, heavily curtained massage parlors, fast-food restaurants. On Telegraph Avenue, the remnants of Berkeley's once-famed "street people" —aging hippies, dropout students, drifters—offer for sale a gypsy variety of knickknacks. You can buy necklaces, rings, lace shawls, blankets reputedly woven by Guatemalan Indians. Kiosks sell pies, hamburgers, soft drinks, fruit kebabs. A spaced-out, barefooted street girl wanders along in the luminous sunshine playing a flute. Nearby, shaven-headed, saffron-robed Hare Krishnas dance, chant and beat their tambourines. Students sunbathe or lounge in the shade. Unswept leaves form drifts in the gutters. Newspapers are blown along grimy pavements. Up on the spacious plaza in front of Sproul Hall, the administrative heart of the campus, a few stalls are set out with sunbaked paperbacks and magazines of a predominantly left-wing, antinuclear and feminist flavor.

It was here, on Sproul Hall Plaza, that many of the most stirring events of the Berkeleian sixties were enacted. Here the students had rallied, sat in and been arrested by the hundreds. It was sunbaked stalls or tables like these, symbols of the students' conviction that they had a right to engage in political activities on the campus, that had led to the original showdown with the administration in September 1964. Many of the rebels had been tempered that summer by personal involvement in the campaign for civil rights in the South. In the autumn they came to Berkeley, imbued with the tactics, heroics and hectic self-righteousness of the Southern battlefields.

"They [the students of the 1960s] think and demand justice for all humanity, with no exceptions," Buckminster Fuller was proclaiming, lending a pronounced messianic gloss to the twin conditions of Studenthood and Youth. "The world students," Fuller continued, "are the world revolutionaries." These were the most literate students in all history, the most world-minded, the most free of national and class bias, the most healthy. He brought in sociology to back up his claims of special election. They were Second World War babies, many born while their fathers were away fighting. Their mothers had worked in munitions factories. Most crucially, they were the first generation to be thoroughly exposed to the influence of television, the "third parent," and as a result, they were steeped in the affairs of the global village. They were (almost) a higher species of humanity. "Unlike any previous generation, the students think 'world.' They will settle for nothing less than justice and physical advantage for all, everywhere around earth . . ." What pusillanimous, middle-aged politicians and the cowed wage-earning masses would never dare, this freewheeling aristocracy would. Theirs, Fuller declared, would be "the most powerful and constructive revolution in all history. . . ." They alone possessed vision; they alone could save mankind from certain destruction. With such encomiums resounding in their ears, why should anointed Studenthood, anointed Youth not be arrogant? intemperate? uncouth? The autumn of 1964 was ripe for confrontation.

Trouble there was; trouble on a scale no one could reasonably have imagined was possible—except, perhaps, in America's fermenting ghettoes. Mario Savio's frenetic oratory echoed across Sproul Hall Plaza and Telegraph Avenue. "There's a time," he declaimed, "when the operation of the machine becomes so odious, makes you so sick at heart, that you can't take part, you can't even tacitly take part. And you've got to put your bodies upon the gears and upon the wheels, upon the levers, upon all the apparatus, and you've got to make it stop. And you've got to indicate to the people who run it, to the people who own it, that unless you're free, the machine will be prevented from working at all."

By the spring of 1965, the Free Speech Movement had turned into the Filthy Speech Movement—or Dirty Word Movement—after someone had stood on the steps of the Student Union opposite Sproul Hall, displaying a placard adorned with the single word "Fuck." The offender was arrested. Demonstrations and brawls followed. As the sixties wore on, the original issues were obscured, and then finally lost altogether in the ideological logjam of Vietnam anguish, Third World anguish, feminist anguish, alienation anguish, drug anguish. Riots, police, tear gas, shooting, hippies, National Guardsmen, Hell's Angels, Allen Ginsberg—Ginsberg, hoping to avert a clash between the students and the Hell's Angels, led the latter in a recitation of the Buddhist Prajna-paramita Sutra—all became, at one time or another, participants in the Berkeley mélange.

Matters came to a head in April 1969 over a plot of waste ground. The University wanted the land either for playing fields or for building on; the rebel students wanted it to be a "People's Park." A newspaper article urged the rebels to direct action. Go out on Sunday. Make the park happen. "Nobody supervises," the writer said, "and the trip belongs to whoever dreams." The dreamers went to make a park; the forces of law and order went to stop them from making a park. The trip was not a good one. One man was killed. Hundreds were arrested and roughed up while in detention. A Sikorsky helicopter, standard equipment in Vietnam, sprayed the campus with a chemical called pepper gas. Governor Reagan declared a state of emergency. For three weeks the town was under martial law, patrolled by two thousand National Guardsmen. Anointed Youth, Anointed Studenthood had, after a fashion, committed revolutionary suicide.

"Some people think of the sixties in Berkeley as an exhilarating time," an elderly professor said to me. "I'm afraid it is an opinion I cannot share. For me, it was a deplorable period. Really quite deplorable." He recalled how the rebels would march through buildings, breaking windows, setting fires. "It wasn't socialism they were cerebrating upon. Most of them didn't know what socialism was. They merely wanted to destroy whatever was in existence." He laughed. Trying to understand it was like trying to understand why epidemics broke out. "What did they use to say? If you weren't part of the solution you were part of the problem. I guess I was part of the problem. Anyone in any position of authority was part of the problem. It was deplorable and distressing, not at all exhilarating."

Hysteria had bred hysteria. Student extremism was often

matched by the extremism of faculty and administration. "I was really surprised by the irrationality of a lot of people under pressure," Clark Kerr, former president of the University, said to me. "I was shocked by the behavior of some people I had really respected and thought had good judgment."

Americans, he had decided, felt much more threatened by Freud than by Marx. The development at Berkeley that had most outraged the Californian public was the Filthy Speech Movement. He had had more letters and phone calls about that than about anything else. That one four-letter word had aroused a much more violent response than any of the radical rhetoric that had been pouring out of the campus. The Board of Regents—the body that oversees the running of the entire University of California—had held a special meeting to discuss the Filthy Speech Movement. It had been a stormy affair.

"One of the board members," Kerr said, "got up there in the room, his face red. *'Do you know what that word was?'* he shouted— and then yelled it at the top of his voice. It was much more obscene than this deranged kid holding a sign."

One of the Regents would have been Catherine Hearst, wife of Randolph Hearst, mother of Patricia Hearst, notorious for her conservatism. A decade later her daughter would be seized by the Symbionese Liberation Army, a remnant of the Berkeleian sixties, and be transformed into Tania, the People's warrior and bank-robbing revolutionary feminist, whose liberated speech would crackle with four-letter words.

By 1965, according to Kerr, both the left wing and the right wing had gone "absolutely crazy." The left wing saw in a confused student revolt a revolution that was going to transform not only the university but American society; the right wing behaved as if it would soon be fighting on the barricades.

During most of those years, I was a student at Oxford. The news from distant Berkeley filtered through in a spasmodic fashion. Television showed us American cities on fire, tanks and soldiers in the streets. Across the water in France, an alliance of workers and students would almost bring down a government.

Oxford was quiet; the sixties glowed as faintly and as disappointingly as Kohoutek's comet. Not that we escaped the contagion entirely. I believe that there was a talk-in about the Vietnam War and that a hairdressing salon alleged to practice racial discrimination was picketed. Mostly, though, what came through to us was the style rather than the substance of revolt. Hair was grown long; a certain amount of drugs was consumed by the self-consciously avant-garde. But very few of us, I think, felt anointed. We may have heard of and even read R. D. Laing's celebrated celebration of schizophrenia, but Buckminster Fuller was virtually unknown. At best, the student revolution was a curious and romantic abstraction, peddled by isolated cognoscenti.

Never having shared in its excitements, I could approach the "most powerful and constructive revolution in all history" only as a stranger. Walking around Sproul Plaza, looking at the students peaceably sunning themselves on lawns, I wondered what had happened to that bright dawn. "There's a time when the operation of the machine becomes so odious, makes you so sick at heart . . ." The last echoes of Mario Savio's oratory had died away a long time ago. As for Savio himself, he too had dropped out of sight a long time ago. It was rumored that he had had psychological troubles, that he was a broken man. No one seemed to know where he was or what he was doing now. Worse than that, no one seemed to care.

"These students?" The young man tending one of the bookstalls on the Plaza made a gesture of disgust. "They're interested in nothing, man, but saving their asses. College degree, nice job, civilized divorce—that's about the size of it these days."

"Aren't you a student?"

"Me?" He looked as if I had insulted him. "I'm a worker. A member of the proletariat. You dig that? I earn my bread in a factory. In my spare time I try to raise consciousness around here." He stared grimly about him. "Trying to do that is like . . ." Words failed him.

"Can you," said a scientist with unconcealed contempt for the bodies sprawled in the sun, "can you believe that once upon a time a revolution almost happened here?" In the sixties, he had been one of the more ardent faculty radicals. He was still looking for an igniting cause, but, as the years had worn on, with diminishing hope and diminishing energy. He described how, at the beginning of the semester, he had tried, in an introductory lecture to a class of freshmen, to raise certain broad ethical issues that might arise from the pursuit of certain lines or emphases of research. They had watched him sullenly. Sullenness had turned to open impatience. They had yawned, scraped their chairs, examined their fingernails. He had abandoned the attempt, vowing never again to risk himself like that. The story was the same everywhere. Universities across the country had been hit by a backlash of realism. Students were dull, uncurious and apathetic, minds narrowly focused on their course of study and their personal futures. It was only that in Berkeley, given its colorful past, the change stood out more starkly.

But it is possible that dullness, uncuriousness and apathy are the wrong terms to use in describing the phenomenon. Their negative ring conceals the positive content of the reversal that took place in student sentiment during the seventies. Most of the students I came into contact with were profoundly content with their condition and took enormous pride in their philistinism and aversion to larger issues. They saw themselves as worldly-wise and practical; they had their heads screwed on the right way. Any mention of the sixties brought dismissive and knowing smiles. For the crazies of that era they had nothing but scorn.

The positive nature of the change was nowhere more clearly shown up than in the reaction to the seizure in November of 1979 of the American Embassy in Teheran. Outbursts of militant patriotism, symbolized by bonfires fueled by Iranian flags, occurred on several college campuses. Rednecks and students could not be distinguished in their response to that drama. There were calls for mass deportation of Iranian students studying in the United States; for military invasion; even, in a handful of cases, for the use of nuclear weapons. "All Iranians should be arrested," said a UCLA student; and those who protested this treatment should be

deported. At San Jose State University there was wild cheering at
a demonstration when a photograph of John Wayne was held
aloft. These reactions cannot be described as apathetic. They suggest, rather, the occurrence of a powerful—and deeply patriotic
—counterrevolution. The prodigal sons had come home.

What had happened to the student revolution?

"It's something that still puzzles me," Kerr said. "It's almost
unbelievable that you could go from May of 1970, when there
was the greatest wave of student unrest in American history by a
very substantial margin, and in September it was quiet. Quiet!
And it has remained quiet for ten years."

It was not that the world had, all of a sudden, become a much
better place to be in. The war in Indochina went on after 1970. It
even intensified. Student outrage, however, was muted and spo-
radic. One is led to the cynical conclusion that most students had
been opposed to the draft rather than to the war itself; passionately dedicated to saving their own skins. There was Watergate.
Barely a murmur arose from the students. In many ways, the
seventies were as stressful a decade as the sixties. Nor was it that
all of a sudden the universities had decided to reform themselves.
Indeed, as Kerr pointed out, many had gone back to being what
they were before the start of the unrest. Some of the more progressive reforms were even rescinded. Berkeley today is bigger
and more bureaucratic than it has ever been. At Berkeley, before
the 1970 summer recess, there had been mass meetings discussing
the reconstitution of American society. The idea was that the
students were going to dedicate themselves to reconstituting the
University and turn it into a mechanism which would reconstitute
society. They were supposed to spend that summer organizing
for the Congressional elections to take place in the fall of 1970.

"And what happened?" Kerr asked, spreading his arms. "They
went to the beaches and the mountains and to Europe."

The Revolution had run out of steam; the pleasure principle of
the consumer society had been rediscovered. A number of things
had happened during that fateful summer. There had been several deaths—an explosion at a bomb-making "factory" in Green-

wich Village; a bombing at the Madison campus of the University
of Wisconsin in which a graduate student had been blown up;
and as a background to such misadventures, there had been the
shootings at Kent State and Jackson State universities. Protest, it
was discovered, could get you killed.

Earlier, the struggle for civil rights—a concrete struggle for
concrete justice—had provided a broad unity of purpose. By
1970, that had gone. As black militancy blossomed, friction had
developed; the blacks wanted to be in charge of their own liberation. Deprived of a vocation, tired and disenchanted and bored,
many whites fell away from the Movement. The factionalized
remnants were pushing on to wilder shores. Here and there scattered elements would stumble into the wilderness of terrorism;
many more would turn to ecological and mystical fancies; most
would simply cut their hair and go home.

Even the scientist, who had gazed scornfully at the inert bodies
sprawled on the sunlit lawns, had in the end fallen prey to Consciousness Raising, to the enticements of est. The experience, he
said, had "changed" him. Est was based on very simple but very
sound science. But what was it all about? What had it actually
done for him? He had some trouble explaining. The experience
had been a very private one. It was all about the essential you, he
hazarded. Culture and habit hid from us the truth about ourselves. They overlaid and colored our desires. How, I asked, did
these insights connect with his radicalism? Est, he replied, had
given him a context for action. It was a familiar phrase. The
trouble with most Americans, he felt, was precisely that: their
actions did not occur in a context. There was a lot of activity but
no meaning. People were unable to link one event with another,
one idea with another. He thought it wrong to say that the infusion of quasi Eastern philosophies had seduced people away from
social involvement. The heightened appreciation of individual
powers, or, to be more precise, the individual's potential powers,
took one directly back to society and to battle with the forces
which thwarted those powers. That was a strange radicalism. The
self is a swamp. Once you become trapped in its quicksands there
is little likelihood that you will ever re-emerge.

In retrospect, Kerr said, it was possible to see more clearly the self-indulgence, the elements of play that had been at the very heart of the student upheaval. He mentioned a cartoon that had appeared in one of the local newspapers. It showed a young girl arriving in Berkeley, wearing a blank button: not knowing what the issues were going to be that semester, she was taking no chances.

"They'd try things on for size. They'd pick an issue and if it didn't catch on, they'd quickly drop it and move on to another one. It was a great big circus. Many of those who've written about it said they'd never had such a great time in their lives."

For some, demonstrating, sitting-in and rioting became a form of therapy: at Berkeley, during periods of disturbance, the University hospital would log abnormally light intakes of psychiatric cases.

It was an explosion rather than a movement, a big bang against authority and convention, that sent a middle-class generation scattering out from the center of acceptance. For a while, it was a constantly expanding universe of dissent, experimentation and improvisation. These affluent young people said they wanted to change the world. But the world did not want to be changed—or was too difficult to change. Those who believed ended up, for the most part, trying to change themselves, to alter their "consciousness." The Revolution was lost in the individual. One of Marx's most famous dicta says that the point is not to philosophize about the world but to change it. The sixties substituted the self for the world.

That modification freed the participants from restraint. The Movement was whatever one chose to make of it—a drug trip, a sexual trip, a musical trip, a political trip, in varying degrees and combinations. "Trip" is the key word, emphasizing, as it does, the egocentric nature of the exercise. Drugs, music, sex and politics merged into a single experience. Categories were blurred and often disappeared altogether: a desire to lace a city's water supply with LSD could be treated as a political stance; chemical ecstasy could fuse with Marxist fervor. For Timothy Leary, the dope dealer was ". . . going to be the Robin Hood, spiritual guerrilla,

mysterious agent . . ." of the New Age. He had the key to turn
you on, to make you feel good, to unveil visions of the celestial
paradise. The dope dealer was indispensable to the revolutionary
impulse. "I think that this [dope dealing] is the noblest of all
human professions and certainly would like to urge any creative
young person sincerely interested in evolving himself and helping
society grow to consider this ancient and honorable profession."
Many would take his advice. Liberation came, more and more, to
mean personal, not social, transformation. Or at any rate, social
transformation, it was said, had to be preceded by personal transformation. This came to be called consciousness raising and was
eagerly picked up by the emergent feminists toward the end of
the decade. This doctrine had all the additional advantage of
having a good Marxist pedigree: sorting out false from true consciousness would become an obsession.

Hence the self-centered nature of the fallout produced by the
explosion. After the initial frenzy, entropic exhaustion was bound
to set in, overheated consciousness cooling into self-absorption.
The current febrile concern with sexism (substituted for racism,
much to the relief of everyone) and ecology do not contradict this
evolution. Both are tied to the new, naked consciousness of self,
of thwarted potential; both are inward-looking. "We regard our
feelings," a militant feminist stated in a 1969 declaration of her
principles, "as our most important source of political understanding." As a result, groups of women gather in rooms all over the
United States dredging up feelings and having them analyzed
and exorcised. The turning away from the world and its problems, America and its problems to the self and its problems was
inherent in the indulgence of the sixties. The Me Generation, as
the seventies have been labeled, is not a betrayal of the sixties, a
falling away from its ideals, but its predictable outcome.

For Elinor Langer, who has published a long, thoughtful essay
describing her involvement with the Movement, the sixties were
rooted in small, highly personal feelings of dislocation and unrest.
Seeking to trace the source of her discomfort, she subjects her
childhood in Massachusetts to delicate and introspective dissec-

tion—her days as a Brownie, summer camps, patriotic parades
on the village green. She remembers a speech she delivered at a
benefit dance for cerebral palsy. That performance continues to
irk her. "Where was I in it? Who was I? Who put that prosperous,
corny and sentimental suburban matron in my sixteen-year-old
body, and why?" In much the same way she recalls how, in a
school essay, she referred to Léon in *Madame Bovary* as a "sensual
coward." What could she possibly have meant by that? Where
could all that nonsensical verbiage have come from?

Somewhere, somehow, she had been robbed of something.
Robbed of what? Of a truer self, perhaps; of any vital connection
with the living world. She did not even know there were poor
black and Italian communities not far from where she lived.
Much had been hidden from her. She was being bred into a
predetermined role, a set of predetermined dispositions, by a
smothering culture which behaved as if all the world's problems
had long ago been solved. College claimed her for a number of
years. After college she married and went to live in Washington,
D.C. She gave cocktail parties; she entertained black activists resting from their labors in the South. To the outward eye, her life
seemed comfortable and secure. All was exactly as it should have
been. But still she was nagged by an unformulated dissatisfaction.
Guilt spoiled her pleasures. She began to feel that she was in
"emotional and moral jeopardy." Then, in the spring of 1965,
with the Free Speech Movement in floodtide, she went to Berkeley.

It was a revelation. In Berkeley, the anointed young dressed
carelessly, slung their babies on their backs and breasts and
walked with a jaunty step. Here was freedom! Here was longed-
for authenticity. At last she had found a milieu in which she might
flourish.

Up to this point, the narrative is plunged in introspection. Hers
had been a Proustian odyssey. We are not dealing with someone
looking out at the world, seeing its sufferings and injustices and
responding in a direct way to what she sees. We are dealing with
someone who is meticulously charting small motions of anxiety,

frustration and obscure desire. Most of the time we are confined in the prison of private consciousness. Only the most tenuous correspondence exists between inner sensation and the outside world. But in Berkeley, during that Bohemian spring of 1965, a connection of sorts was effected. Langer read an FSM pamphlet which made a deep impression on her. This pamphlet laid bare the commercial interests that controlled the University of California—the big banks, oil companies, aircraft makers, railway companies, landowners and so on. Suddenly, those inner sensations acquired a context. They could be translated into a political stance, a radical allegiance, a change of life-style. She was now ready to help make the revolution and change the world. But many others, perhaps the majority, would never make the connection. For these, the sixties would become a style, a Saturnalia, played out against the festive, permissive backdrop of the Vietnam War. Vietnam, indeed, would become an extension of the psychedelic imagination, its excesses mirroring the excesses at home. During San Francisco's summer of love, the higher consciousness was simply a brute chemical process. In the domain of love, the drug dealers were crowned kings.

But for Langer, consciousness—introspection—remained the central reality despite her conversion to radical politics. The personal had been made political and so the political could be assessed only in personal terms. Thoughts and actions had to be given "periodic check-ups for symptoms of co-optation as if to a mobile X-ray unit. That blemish of the brain was one of the known danger signals of revolutionary demise." This was only to be expected with a revolution that was being made largely in the head. With this reflexive psychoanalysis there went another introspective tremor—a feeling of worthlessness. Contaminated by privilege, white radicals like herself did not consider themselves pure enough to be the vanguard of the revolution. So, mired in the swamp of self, they searched for the true agents of change. With that, the revolution in the head made contact with mystical abstraction. It was this search which led the middle-class whites of the Symbionese Liberation Army to an escaped, semiliterate black prisoner. They renamed him Cinque Mtume, a title which, they said, meant the Fifth Prophet. One of their communiqués explained that they had so named him because of his keen instinct and senses, his deep love of all people on earth and his advanced spiritual consciousness. They adopted as their symbol a seven-headed cobra. It signified, they said, God and Life, and had a history going back 170,000 years. The unity of those seven heads in one body, they added, defined the essence of cooperation and socialism.

Marxism was merely a medium in which the unchained self was temporarily refracted in its long journey in pursuit of satisfaction. For a while, it provided a vocabulary and an outlook. But fundamentally, it was no more than a plaything of evolving consciousness. It was the drama of the individual voyage that mattered— the search for what was described as wholeness, balance and self-realization. The imperious self flowed like a river, onward, ever onward. By the end of 1970 it had traveled a long way. Bernadine Dohrn, one of the leaders of the terrorist Weather Underground, could write thus: "People have been experimenting with everything about their lives. . . . They've moved to the country and found new ways to bring up wild, free children. People have purified themselves with organic food, fought for sexual liberation, grown long hair. People have learned . . . that grass and organic consciousness-expanding drugs are weapons of the revolution . . . a tool—a Yaqui way of knowledge."

Purity, drugs, feral children, sexual liberation, ecology, Yaqui wisdom . . . what would Karl Marx have thought of all that? The sixties had finally exploded. Consciousness, ultimately, was like a fragmenting bomb planted in the heart of the Movement. In 1973, Elinor Langer was living in rural Vermont, surrounded by long-haired men and women who, she remarked, could not by any stretch of the imagination be called revolutionary. To do so would have been to mock history. But neither could she, by any stretch of the imagination, be called revolutionary. In 1973, she was seeing for the first time the rings of energy around rocks and trees and had come to comprehend that the Universe was Holy and One. Not far away, in Boston, blacks and whites were murdering each other over the issue of school integration and busing.

There are those who would turn the conventional view of the sixties on its head and see the decade as an attempt not at revolution but at restoration, at refurbishing old-fashioned American virtues and values, concealing behind its waywardness a deeply conservative yearning. The authors of a recent book, *Woodstock Census,* say that feminism, environmentalism and political activism were all indigenous American traditions; that the do-your-own-thing attitude (they call it an "ethic") of pot smokers and consciousness expanders bore a close resemblance to the rugged individualism of the frontiersmen who detested taxation, politics and bureaucracy. "The counter-culture was based on *traditional* not radical values, so it is no wonder that [it] was so rapidly absorbed into the American mainstream." This is an amusing interpretation of events. It is like watching a conjurer change the color of a scarf. So—they were all Goldwaterites under the skin; they were, despite vociferous indications to the contrary, good American boys and girls, thwarted patriots, who, in their heart of hearts, wanted their own psychedelic home on the range; not, as we foolishly believed at the time, citizens of the global village thirsting for universal justice.

But the sixties talked—did it not?—about humanism, gentleness, sharing, caring and community. It did not, as far as I am aware, talk the language of rugged frontier individualism. Rugged frontier individualism—the flight from taxes, politics and bureaucrats—is a flight from social responsibility and the burdens of citizenship. Let the ghettoes disintegrate. Let the poor live short and brutish lives. Let the police, when they get out of hand, shoot and kill. (In the last ten years, six thousand Morlocks have been shot dead by the police.) Wasn't it these attitudes which, allegedly, had got America into trouble in the first place? which had ruthlessly plundered and contaminated a continent? which had bred capitalist greed and materialism and corrupted the "relationship" not only between man and man but between man and himself? Weren't the flower children agonized waifs alienated from a cruel world? It is confusing to discover them suddenly surfacing as traditionalists.

But there is really no need for any of this confusion. What we are confronted with is an attempt to rescue one brand of cant—humanism, gentleness, sharing and caring—by magically transforming it into another brand of cant; an attempt to coat a phony revolution with the sheen of romantic reaction. The fact is that neither brand of cant quite describes the less than heroic, frequently tawdry realities of the sixties and their equally uninspiring evolution during the course of the seventies.

In the sixties, some of the children of a prosperous middle class exploded into a semblance of revolt. They were well nourished, they were more or less educated, they were sentimental, they were spoiled, they were bored, they were looking for kicks, they were touched with half-digested idealisms, they were scared of dying in a war in Southeast Asia. They constituted, one might say, a *lumpen-bourgeoisie*. Their revolt was underpinned by privilege. They could afford to revolt—to buy the drugs, the clothes, the books, the records that were the indispensable accouterments of that revolt. Their parents, when the need arose, could bail them out of jail. When the money ran out, or the trip became too heavy or they couldn't be bothered anymore, they could nearly always return to the suburbs out of which they had come, pick up on the privileges they had temporarily discarded and carry on as if nothing had happened. Every hippie knew that when the chips were down he could be rescued from the bazaars of Kabul, New Delhi and Katmandu. Civil-rights volunteers knew they could stop being nigger lovers and withdraw, as George Jackson put it in 1971, to "... organic food gardens and a life of sex, music and drugs." Unlike the objects of their concern, they could go to the mountains, to the beaches of California and Goa, to Europe. Those brought up on fads do not have long attention spans.

Not many took themselves beyond the point of no return. The tradition out of which they had fled was never too far away. In adversity, it could quickly reassert itself: old reflexes, like protective scar tissue, could grow over and cover the raw, painful areas exposed by idealism. "I used to picket and march in Civil Rights demonstrations back in the sixties. But things have changed. It was one thing to want to help little Liza, but when it's a big, strapping guy . . . On the subways now you can see the hate in their faces. Blacks see whites as the enemy—and whites see blacks as a threat. I've been mugged twice and my son four times—always by blacks. It can't help but change you."

What a conservative institution a university is, Clark Kerr had remarked. It could live through a revolt and come out of it even more like what it had been before the revolt had started. Something similar can be said for the majority of those who lived through the sixties. When idealism tires, even the little Lizas must tread with caution.

Southward from Berkeley, the roads become bleaker and emptier. Street after forlorn street is lined with rows of peeling, Southern-style cabins standing in grassy lots. Many of the shops look as if they had gone out of business. There are many liquor stores, battened down behind elaborate vandalproof grilles. As numerous as the liquor stores are the ramshackle storefront churches calling sinners to repentance. Grass sprouts between the paving stones. Drifts of refuse are heaped up everywhere. Fading, tattered political posters adorn walls and lampposts—a call to join a demonstration against the Chilean regime, an attack on the Shah of Iran, exhortations by the Revolutionary Communist Party to free American political prisoners and make the revolution now. Groups of blacks stand on corners, doing nothing, watching the cruising police cars. The sun shines goldenly, mocking the decay. You are in Oakland, another distinct metropolitan entity of the Bay Area, another world; original home of the Black Panthers, the most aggressive of the black groups to arise during the sixties.

The Black Panther office building shares in the general air of decay. A photograph of Huey Newton, former Minister of Defense of the Party, decorates one of the plate-glass windows. It shows him dressed in the Panther regalia, beret and black leather jacket, sitting erect on a thronelike cane chair, holding a spear in his left hand. He stares at the camera with warrior intensity. But the glory is of a previous time. At the back of the office hangs another large portrait of Newton, this one done in oils. A photographic montage of comrades fallen in battle with the police occupies one wall.

The office, though, is empty and looks as if it has not been used for a long time. A few dusty, out-of-date pamphlets are scattered about. A petition solicits signatures in behalf of Newton, who is facing yet another trial for murder. It is easy to lose count of Newton's trials. Is this the third or fourth? Over the years they have become routine legal events. I stare at the warrior photograph.

"My name is Ozymandias, king of kings:/Look on my works, ye Mighty, and despair!/Nothing beside remains. . . ."

No one answers my knocks. I go around the side of the building, down a street lined with wooden cabins, to the rear entrance. The back door opens a crack. A black face scrutinizes me. I state my business (I have an appointment) and am allowed to enter. The woman who will talk to me leads me to an upstairs office. Works of black writers fill the bookshelves. The room has a musty smell. It must be used only rarely.

True, she says. Things are not what they used to be. The Panthers no longer had the mass following they had had ten years before. All the Progressive Left movements of the sixties had been systematically destroyed by the FBI and other government agencies. It had been J. Edgar Hoover's declared policy to leave the blacks leaderless and confused.

"The U.S., you must understand, is a very difficult country in which to work for freedom. Very difficult. It's hard to struggle here. People get tired after a while. It is also very easy for them to be bought off by material possessions, window dressing."

America was too big, too powerful, too overwhelming. Nevertheless, the Panthers were neither completely routed nor daunted by the magnitude of the task facing them. They were survivors.

But the would-be liberators had had to scale down their

dreams, to rethink their strategy. Their main source of pride now was the Oakland Community School, started in 1971 and considered to be a model of its kind. It had one hundred and fifty pupils and a waiting list of over four hundred. Those parents who could afford it paid twenty-five dollars a month; those who could not paid nothing. The Community School was not the only example of their good-works policy. They had set up a free-food program and a medical clinic—the George Jackson Clinic, named for the convict turned Marxist ideologue who was killed in 1971 during an alleged escape attempt at San Quentin prison.

"Health care in this community is atrocious for the poor. So we try and do what little we can. All our programs are survival programs, founded in the day-to-day needs of the community we serve."

Since most prisoners were poor black men, they also provided a free bus service out to the prisons so that wives and children could see their husbands and fathers who were locked away.

Yet, though one heard so much less about them, the Panthers had not given up their basic aims.

What, I ask, are those basic aims?

"To be the vanguard of political change in this country. To raise the people's consciousness."

Did she believe that a left-wing revolution—any kind of left-wing revolution—was possible in the United States?

She gazes out at the sunlit street below us. "As I look outside, I see that we are in for some very hard, very difficult times. But as long as it's only black people who are doing the suffering, not too much is going to be done about anything. That's the way it always has been and that's the way it will be in this country for the foreseeable future."

In Oakland, unemployment was running at about fifteen percent. Among black teen-agers, the figure was probably twice as high. Relations between the police and blacks, a major cause of so many of the sixties insurrections, were as bad as they had ever been. Just a few days before, the police had shot a black boy dead —one more summary street execution. She notes the resurgence of the Ku Klux Klan; the growing demand for the restoration of capital punishment; the triumph of the tax-cutting campaign; the successful attacks on affirmative-action programs. All those developments were directed against poor and black people.

"Who will get sent to the gas chamber? Who will be most affected by a loss of public revenue? Who will lose if there is to be no more affirmative action? Us! Us! Us! Who do you think killed all those beautiful black people in Guyana? Why did those beautiful black people leave this country of ours which they tell us is so wonderful and choose to go to the jungles of Guyana?"

The CIA killed them. America killed them. They had gone to the Guyanese jungle because they wanted to live a life free of racism, sexism and poverty. Many had come from Oakland, from those bleak streets lined with wooden cabins.

But why would the CIA want to kill old black women and black children?

Because the Temple was a socialist organization; because the CIA did not want it to set an example; because the CIA did not want to see consciousness raised. The Black Panthers had felt a very close kinship with the People's Temple. Huey and Jim had been good friends.

How did faith healing raise consciousness? How did it fit in with the theories of scientific socialism espoused by the Panthers?

She looks uncomfortable. The faith healing was not important. It was not what the Temple was about. . . .

"Black people, you know, have always been attached to the church. . . ."

The subject is a delicate one and I do not pursue it. Huey, she says, will be able to explain it to me much better than she could.

The Oakland Community School occupied a whitewashed barn of a building. A big-leafed, smooth-skinned tree grew in the skylighted entrance. When I arrived, a piano was being played somewhere in the bowels of the building. The end of term was approaching, and some of the children were rehearsing their graduation exercises. Citations hung on the walls of the main office, each one a recognition of the school's excellent record. Huey was not present, but he was expected soon.

The woman who welcomed me was tall and thin and bony. Her name was vaguely familiar, bringing back memories of sixties militancy and hectic courtroom dramas. But I could detect nothing of that now in her manner and speech. She told me more about the school. It was financed by a combination of state and federal grants. It took in children from the age of two and a half. Even at that tender age they were taught to read. The school stopped at the sixth grade, but the staff were hoping that they might be able to extend its reach. Each child was given breakfast and lunch free of charge, as well as whatever medical attention was called for. She took me on a brief tour, apologizing for the messiness of the classrooms, which she ascribed to end-of-term laxity. In the auditorium, where the children were rehearsing their graduation exercises to piano accompaniment, there was a big, framed photograph of Huey, an indication that his personality cult, though greatly modified by circumstances, was not altogether dead. I was told about the long waiting list. Admission was tied to urgency of need.

"But"—my guide laughed, flourishing her arms—"since most of the people we cater to are in desperate need . . ."

Relative to what was required, the Oakland Community School was a drop in the ocean of need. In the sixties, the statistics of black inner-city education painted a frightening picture of human ruin. In Newark, New Jersey, for instance, more than half of adult blacks had not made it to the eighth grade. Overcrowding meant that a quarter of the children in the public system attended double-session schools. One in three blacks was a functional illiterate. Of 13,600 blacks between the ages of sixteen and nineteen, half were not in school. Almost every other black child came from a broken home. Eighty percent of crimes were committed by blacks; the victims too were predominantly black. That was the day before yesterday; that was the situation at a time when America was readying itself to land men on the moon. How much had changed? Today, of the sixty thousand children in San Francisco's public school system, thirty-two thousand come from families dependent on welfare. San Francisco prided itself on its liberalism and its generosity. But even a top official of that city's social-services administration admitted to me that what the welfare system did to its clients could not be described as humane. Its niggardliness consistently denigrated and humiliated the individual. Oakland, a tough, Republican-dominated town, was neither liberal nor generous. It was not hard to imagine the urgency of need faced by the Oakland Community School; the sad quixotism of its ideals.

"We love each child," my guide said. "We try to know every child as an individual. That's the difference between us and the public schools."

The school, she said, was not narrow and sectarian. She compared it with other black schools that flourished in the Bay Area, Chicago and New York, schools that were avowedly racist and separatist in their outlook.

"They even teach the kids Swahili. Swahili! Why Swahili? That's a made-up language of slave traders. A language of oppression. There are so many more beautiful African languages to choose from. Why Swahili, for God's sake?"

I thought of Jim Jones leading his followers through exercises in elementary Russian. Learning Swahili in the Bay Area, Chicago and New York reflected a similar agony; a fantastic wish to escape into a new and uncontaminated world. So, in its way, did the Community School, picking up the wreckage of the streets, loving each of its one hundred and fifty urchins, treating each as an individual—only to send them out, after their graduation exercises, into a society that had no place for them, that would betray them at nearly every turn. So, in her way, did this woman, who suddenly drew my attention to a statuette of the Buddha she kept on a shelf, telling me she was a disciple of Guru Mukhtananda, that meditation on the Eternal had brought her peace and acceptance.

Huey arrived, accompanied by his wife. Newton, wiry and

handsome, walked with a slight limp—the ex–Minister of Defense, ex–People's Warrior, who had once sat on a cane throne, holding a spear, challenging the world to do battle with him. The world had done battle with him; and it had won. That morning there was nothing about him to suggest a flamboyant, revolutionary past. His speech was slow, diffident and thick. His legs dithered as he talked and struggled to string together his ideas. The Panthers remained what they always had been: a community organization, dedicated to education and to lifting the consciousness of the people. The Party had not changed. It was the people, the times that had changed.

"What we have now," he said, his legs dithering, "is only a shadow of the enthusiasm that existed in the sixties."

How did he account for that?

"Thousands of my people were imprisoned. Many of us were killed. Supporters and sympathizers were hounded by the Internal Revenue Service. They used every tactic they could to destroy us. I myself am still facing a tax-evasion suit. . . ."

His eyes clouded over. What was it? Fatigue? Anxiety? Boredom? He mentioned the COINTELPRO operation, the counter-intelligence program organized by the FBI in 1967 to harass, discredit and destroy the radical movements. Not even the Watts Writers Workshop, set up in the aftermath of the Los Angeles riots, had escaped their attentions: its premises were eventually burned down by an *agent provocateur*.

"It was terrifying, the kinds of things that were done, the kinds of things they were planning to do. That repression during the Nixon era came very close to establishing a fascist state." He waved a hand in front of his eyes. "That was where our support went. Right now I'm still having to cope with a possible fifteen years in a state penitentiary because of a frame-up. . . ." It was not easy to survive. The persecution just seemed to go on and on.

He had not foreseen what was going to happen when, together with Bobby Seale, he founded the party in 1966. They had gained a great deal of notoriety very quickly, and this had set up a momentum they had been unable to control. COINTELPRO docu-

ments showed that the police jumped on the bandwagon and took
it upon themselves to open a number of Panther chapters. All the
same, they were the only black organization established in the
sixties that still existed. So they must have been doing something
right. But he would not deny that mistakes had been made.

What kind of mistakes?

He hesitated, searching for language. "What I mean by that is
. . . is that certain conditions exist in each country which are different from that in any other, so that in each country it takes
different means and different measures to make progressive
changes."

In the sixties they had thought they could map out a blueprint
of revolutionary transformation by looking at what had occurred
in certain other countries. Cuba and Algeria had been the favored
models in those days.

"Of course, that was the wrong thing for us to do—not wrong
to look at them as such, but wrong to use them as a blueprint. We
now realize that the conditions in those places are very different
from the conditions you find in America."

In America, the revolutionary had to train himself to be a long-
distance runner because the resources at the disposal of the state
were so powerful, varied and sophisticated. It was not realistic to
have romantic fantasies of staging a Cuban-style or Algerian-style
revolution. Many people had become frustrated because they believed they could have liberation straightaway. When that did not
happen, they began to feel they had been betrayed.

"That was the result of a wrong understanding. There was a
tendency in the sixties to run on ahead. When nothing happened,
many of us became bitter toward the people and turned away
from them to God or whatever. . . ."

It had been a hard-won wisdom, aggravated by the Panthers'
predilection for melodrama—the guns, the uniforms, Huey's
warrior-chief photograph; the empty titles they had assigned
themselves—Minister of Defense, Foreign Minister (a role assumed by Eldridge Cleaver), Field Marshal (a role assumed by
George Jackson) and so on. Surely even in the sixties, the Party

must have known it was engaging in dangerous heroics, inflaming passions and enmities it could neither satisfy nor control?

"That was sabotage," Huey said.

"Sabotage? By whom?"

"By the media. The media deal in sensationalism. They sensationalized us."

"But the media didn't dream up the titles, the uniforms, the guns. Those were your own freely chosen symbols of defiance."

"The guns were not symbolic." Huey looked at me truculently. "The guns were used to patrol the police. They were used to protect our rights which the police were violating."

But were they not an unnecessary provocation of superior forces? Did not the flaunting of weaponry invite martyrdom and disaster?

"When a victim who is little better than a slave decides to demand some dignity for himself and picks up a weapon to enforce that demand because he has been so demeaned, so humiliated . . . I can't say that's provocation. I didn't expect to live. I never expected to go into my thirties. I was arrested, I was shot, I was put through two murder trials, the first one of which carried the gas chamber with it. We had put our lives on the line. The Panthers meant business."

I reminded him of the incident described with relish in his book *Revolutionary Suicide,* telling what happened when Malcolm X's widow paid a brief visit to San Francisco. The Panthers decided they would give the slain hero's wife—"mother of his beautiful children"—a suitably military Black Power welcome at the airport and, while she remained in the city, to act as her bodyguards. "Before leaving Oakland," Huey wrote, "I had told the comrades that we were not going to take any arrests on this trip. If anything happened, I said, we would fight right down to the last man, but we definitely would not give ourselves up to the police." Those who were not prepared to die, he added, should not go. This samurai devotion was intrinsically symbolic, devoid of any concrete revolutionary substance. It was a sentimental but deadly caprice; machismo for the sake of machismo. Yet for this, the leaders of the Party were prepared to fabricate a confrontation with the police and to lay down their lives. Had not a flair for melodrama become irresponsibility of a high order?

"History shows we were not shot down. History shows the Party then grew tenfold."

Nevertheless, was it not folly to risk all for a symbolic gesture? Were they not guilty of playing lethal games with themselves and with the people to whose service they had pledged themselves?

A political movement, Huey said, should never be dependent on one or two or three individuals. Leaders were the sparks that lit the prairie fire—nothing more. In America, television had conditioned the masses into a star syndrome. They felt they could not move unless up front there was a star, a superman. Superman —or Superparty—was supposed to do everything. The Black Panthers had rejected that way of thinking. They had assigned themselves a more modest function: they were organizers, consciousness raisers.

I wondered which was of greater importance—organizing the people or ostentatiously protecting the widow of Malcolm X? In risking themselves and their Party for the latter, hadn't they too shown themselves to be victims of the "star syndrome"? Why the famous cultic photograph of himself? However, I did not ask these questions. The confusions were too deep and too intractable. I asked instead about the grandiloquent titles they had conferred on themselves.

"We took those titles because we were really Field Marshals, Generals and Ministers."

"Were you really?"

He smiled. "Every army has a right to use titles. As I say, we were somewhat romantic, and we believed at the time that we would raise a large army and be able at least to fight until we had a plebiscite and a say in the fate of all our various communities and the power to determine what our destiny would be."

Together with Bobby Seale, he had worked out the ten points of the Party's platform. It had taken them only about twenty minutes to compose.

1. We want freedom. We want power to determine the destiny of our Black Community.
2. We want full employment for our people.
3. We want an end to the robbery by the capitalists of our Black community.
4. We want decent housing, fit for shelter of human beings.
5. We want education for our people that exposes the true nature of this decadent American society. We want education that teaches us our true history and our role in the present-day society.
6. We want all Black men to be exempt from military service.
7. We want an immediate end to POLICE BRUTALITY and MURDER of Black people.
8. We want freedom for all Black men held in federal, state, county and city prisons and jails.
9. We want all Black people when brought to trial to be tried in court by a jury of their peer group or people from their Black communities, as defined by the Constitution of the United States.
10. We want land, bread, housing, education, clothing, justice and peace. And as our major political objective, a United Nations–supervised plebiscite to be held throughout the Black Colony in which only Black colonial subjects will be allowed to participate, for the purpose of determining the will of Black people as to their national destiny.

It is perhaps true to say that none of these demands have been realized; it is perhaps also true to say that none of them were realizable. Only the truly powerless could be so detached from reality, could write a manifesto in twenty minutes that demanded everything.

Huey fought off a circling fly. "In those days we thought of ourselves as being similar to a government in exile. You must know how governments in exile behave, how they arrange a whole system of state administration and sometimes actually institute these in the foreign land where they are. That was how we liked to think of ourselves. We weren't dealing in fantasies any more than those shadow governments. . . ."

I looked at him doubtfully.

"I said not any *more* than they do."

At some point in 1976 (or thereabouts—he is vague about the date), Huey, exiled by the threats of American justice, met Jim Jones in Cuba. (It is interesting to note that Charles Garry, Newton's lawyer, had advised his client to stay on in Cuba—in much the same way that he would later advise Jim Jones to stay on in Guyana.) Jones was accompanied on that trip by about a dozen of the Temple faithful. They described their various welfare and rehabilitational programs and showed him photographs of Jonestown.

"I understood that Jones had successfully politicized his followers and convinced them that some form of socialism was necessary in the United States. It was a socialism based on the uniqueness of the United States. They were not trying to copy some developing country. I thought that was a contribution."

Only one thing had disconcerted him during that meeting: Jones had kept his dark glasses on inside the house.

To what degree had the Panthers supported the People's Temple?

"I don't know exactly what you mean by support."

"Political support. Some kind of loose alliance . . ."

"There was no alliance."

"Moral support, then . . ."

Huey dithered his legs. "Yes—I suppose you could say we gave them moral support."

Was one to assume that the Panthers had condoned Jones's faith-healing exercises?

"I wasn't aware of his faith healing. As far as I knew he was an herb doctor. He told me in Cuba that he didn't believe in any religion, that he only used that as a tactic to organize the religious community."

"You say you believe in consciousness raising. Isn't attracting people by such dubious means the opposite of consciousness raising?"

"I thought he was an herb doctor," Huey insisted. "I saw him one time on television talking about his herbs. They asked him about the faith healing, and his answer was that with his knowledge of psychology, he knew that many of the ailments people had were psychosomatic. So he tried to encourage them to take their own faith and heal themselves. And I know this to be a true fact—that you can be healed by your faith. I know that to be true. I can heal myself of many of my ailments."

However, he drew the line at mysticism. The faith healing he subscribed to was grounded in scientific observation; it had been recognized by orthodox psychologists. He was aware that the techniques of faith healing could become bizarre, but he would not give a blanket condemnation of the art.

What else had he and Jones talked about in Cuba?

"He tried to tell me that I should think of finding some place outside the United States. He didn't think there was any hope for the United States or the Third World. He said he saw suicide as the only way out."

Huey had disagreed. His progressive outlook, he argued back, compelled him to maintain hope and faith in the possibility of a better world, despite all the discouragements.

"He spoke of the tremendous power of the United States. He had the view that concentration camps were imminent for rebellious minorities and dissenters. After seeing those COINTELPRO documents, I can understand his feeling that way. They are terrifying. I *know* there are concentration camps here waiting. So that's not a matter of speculation or paranoia. He was trying to understand the introduction to my book *Revolutionary Suicide*, where I explain what I mean by that concept."

In that introduction, Huey had sought to distinguish between what he called "reactionary" and "revolutionary" suicide. Reactionary suicide was carried out by those who were demeaned and demoralized beyond redemption. This form of suicide did not invariably imply a literal taking away of life. Reactionary suicide could mean the death of the spirit, the flight into liquor and drug addiction. The majority of American blacks had had their spirits slaughtered. Their lives, like their actual deaths, were emblematic of their powerlessness and subjugation. Revolutionary suicide is the exact opposite of this passive moribundity. It begins to occur when the slave rises up and says "no" to his oppressor. The death of such a man is a positive act. It is positive because it springs not out of defeat and self-contempt but out of self-assertion and calculated disobedience. Both his life and his death thereby acquire meaning. The revolutionary, while not actively seeking martyrdom, has to be consciously prepared to die for the revolution—to lay his life on the line. A revolutionary death, Che Guevara had written, is the reality; victory is the dream. Huey notes that and approves. Elsewhere, he refers to one of the major manifestos of Russian nineteenth-century terrorism, *The Revolutionary Catechism*, which begins with the dramatic statement "The Revolutionary is a doomed man." Huey had also given that sentiment the stamp of his approval. Life gave meaning to death. Death gave meaning to life.

A linking of the Revolution with personal doom, forged in the twisted passions of Sergei Nechayev, the most probable author of *The Revolutionary Catechism,* touched up and romanticized by Che Guevara against the mountain scenery of Cuba and Bolivia, picked up by a former Oakland street boy and given another little twist, ends on the lips of Jim Jones in the Guyanese wilderness. What ironic life histories ideas can have! Did Huey know that Sergei Nechayev had also said, "Loving people means driving them into a hail of bullets"? That is to be doubted. But if he had, would he have detected the link between the alluring, romantic notion of revolutionary doom and its squalid stepchild—mass, mindless carnage? Would he have detected its influence in his nonsensical and bloody willingness to kill and be killed in his defense of the widow of Malcolm X? We may blithely enunciate ideas (or quasi ideas), but we cannot control them, we cannot chain them up and prevent them from straying beyond the bounds we have marked out for them. An idea, once loosed into the world, is anybody's plaything.

"I don't think my meaning ever properly got through to Jim Jones," Huey said. "He took the idea and used it in his own way, in a way I didn't intend at all. I can't make any sort of rational picture of what happened in Guyana. Maybe one shouldn't try and approach it in a rational way. Nobody I've met can make sense of it from an objective point of view. And that's my position too—you can't make sense of it."

On November 18, 1978, the very day on which Jim Jones was slaughtering his followers in Guyana, Huey Newton was in Boston, giving a speech to a group of students.

"We, the people," he was telling those students, "are threatened with genocide because racism and fascism are rampant in this country and throughout the world."

The ghost of Jim Jones in Boston on that day found an echo in the ghost of Huey Newton in Jonestown.

"We didn't commit suicide," the Messiah was crying out over Jonestown's final howls of anguish; "we committed an act of revolutionary suicide protesting the conditions of an inhuman world."

Jones had tortured his black followers with nightmare visions of imminent fascist takeover and genocidal doom. He had used them to bind and entrap. But he had not invented those nightmares. The basic groundwork had been done by his black radical precursors—and by their white friends; the requisite conditioning had already taken place by the time Jones appeared on the scene. For years, "fascism" and "genocide" were words on the lips of nearly every black thinker and agitator.

". . . If you don't wake up," Malcolm X told one of his enthusiastic audiences in 1965, "I tell you, they'll be building gas chambers and gas ovens pretty soon—I don't mean those kinds you've got at home in your kitchen. . . . You're in a society that's just as capable of building gas ovens for black people as Hitler's society was. . . ."

For George Jackson, at the close of the sixties, the fascist state was not a threat but an established reality.

"The violence of the ruling class of this country," he was saying, "in the long process of its trend toward authoritarianism and its last and highest state, fascism, cannot be rivaled in its excesses by any other nation on earth today or in history . . . *how can anyone question the existence of a fascist arrangement?*" It was in this same exhortation that Jackson, pronouncing the Revolution temporarily dead, gave his imprimatur to Newton's idea of the inner-city commune, thus providing the basis of one more sympathetic vibration between the People's Temple and the Black Panthers. The communes were to find their raw material among the lumpen proletariat. Revolution could come only from the most debased elements of society.

Angela Davis and her friends talked about fascism and genocide. James Baldwin talked about fascism and genocide. They were bargain-basement political terms, and nearly everyone with pretensions to a radical outlook would make use of them. Long before Jim Jones started to terrorize his following, the blacks, with the assistance of their best white friends, had been terrorizing one another with the rhetoric of mass extermination. Jim Jones, never an original man, was dealing in a common currency. On the day when Huey Newton was talking to those Boston students, the ideological irresponsibilities of a promiscuous decade were coming home to roost in Jonestown.

Huey, if he had tried hard enough, would have been able to make sense of the Guyana massacre.

Had he been taught any lessons by the People's Temple?

"I suppose . . ." Huey paused, groping for words. "I suppose we have to be more careful about the sorts of people and organizations we get involved with in the future. . . . I suppose we'll have to move more slowly. . . ."

I reflected that if they moved any more slowly they were in danger of coming to a standstill.

"I don't believe in utopias," Huey said. "I don't have an ideal kind of state in mind. . . ." His hands fluttered in front of his eyes. "I . . . I think that distribution should be more even. I am not a separatist. I am not a racist. . . ."

He fell silent. The fly continued to buzz around him.

Was that all?

"I told you—I don't believe in utopias. . . . I advocate a type of socialism that would be consistent with the concrete condition, the technological and historical condition, of the American people. . . ."

I watched him fight off the pestering fly.

What Huey seemed to be saying was that he no longer believed in anything.

Truly, there was little left to believe in. All that remained was this school, a drop in the ocean of need, eking out an existence on the altruism of state and federal subsidies and a handful of "survival programs." The Revolution was long dead; so, for all practical purposes, were the Panthers and everything they had stood for. All the militant black voices of the sixties had been effectively silenced. Eldridge Cleaver, a metaphysician of rape, had returned from Algerian exile and declared himself a Born Again Christian —and, later, announced that he was thinking of joining the Unification Church, becoming a Moonie. Rap Brown—"violence is as American as cherry pie"—had converted to Islam and led a secluded life in Atlanta. Stokely Carmichael had settled in Africa, where he dreamed of the restoration of Nkrumahism. Bobby Seale, the coauthor with Newton of the Panthers' ten-point manifesto, was, according to latest report, planning to publish a book titled *Barbecuing with Bobby*. Today, he wears a suit and travels with a briefcase. "Anytime," he is reported as saying in February of 1980, "a Black Panther member like Eldridge Cleaver can come back here and say he's a Born Again Christian, there's not a damn thing wrong with people knowing that I've been cooking for twenty-five years."

Huey was sensible not to believe in utopias.

The sixties, despite the gains that had been made in civil rights, had left the racial structure of American society essentially intact. It was the black middle class who had benefited most from the triumphs of the era. The headlong rush to tokenism could be comic. Daniel Moynihan has described how, in 1964, the personnel executives from the big corporations descended en masse on

Lincoln University, a black college in Pennsylvania, outnumber-
ing their quarry—the black Ph.D.s—two to one. As the well-
known journalist I. F. Stone concluded at the time, suitably qualified blacks were being bought off by the classload. But while this
stampede to get hold of office blacks was going on, the position
of the black masses remained unchanged or became even worse.
Stone expressed it thus: the American Negro, he said, was condemned to live in Egypt, but it was an Egypt that had already
built its pyramids and no longer needed slaves. "Mechanization
on the farm and automation in industry have at last set him free,
but now freedom turns out to be joblessness."

The truth is starker. Joblessness is a euphemism. It would be
more accurate to say that a technologically sophisticated society
has no use for these people. They are redundant. They are good
for nothing. They do not even evoke fellow feeling. One can
think of them as the human equivalent of the radioactive waste
produced by nuclear power plants: sterile and potentially lethal.
What, the ecologists ask, is one to do with this waste? Bury it miles
underground? Shoot it into outer space? Discover some way of
breaking it down and rendering it harmless? The junk people,
the human waste left behind by American history, are no less
negative, no less dangerous a quantity. One sees them on the
streets of midtown Manhattan, carrying glittering noisemaking
machines, dressed to kill, the ugliness and the hatred of the discarded slave glowing in their eyes. You see them in Harlem,
standing drunk or drugged on street corners. What is to be done
with them?

Back in the sixties I. F. Stone shuddered when he heard a
sociologist, commenting on the latest insurrections in Chicago
and Cleveland, say that America had to adopt one of two choices:
either it made the gargantuan effort required for the blacks to
achieve "equality," or it would have to exterminate them. America
has lacked the courage to do either. Instead, it has temporized by
buying off a black middle class and inserting the statutory black
in television commercials—integration is largely a media event.
With regard to the unassimilable *lumpen* hordes, America has

adopted an unspoken policy of containment and neglect, leavened by welfare and summary street executions by the police: a policy quietly endorsed by the celebrated flight from taxes, politics and bureaucrats. It is much nicer to worry about solar energy, the environment and whales. It is much more fascinating to speculate about planetary colonization and to pay Mr. Erhard hundreds of dollars to have one's consciousness raised—usually by being abused as an "asshole" and writhing about on floors in three-star hotels, weeping and shrieking obscenities.

In February of 1980 a horror story was enacted at a New Mexico penitentiary. The prisoners, maddened by brutality, neglect and drugs, went on a rampage. They beheaded one another, incinerated one another, tortured one another. The carnage was unspeakable. Nearly forty prisoners died. It was clear that the men locked up in that jail had ceased to be human. The society did not react. It was as if nothing of consequence had happened. The politicians carried on with their speeches about Afghanistan and Iran. Friends with whom I raised the subject looked bored. *The New York Times* reported the incident, but did not see fit to editorialize about it. Nobody cares what the Morlocks do to one another. They are beyond the pale even of humane curiosity. Junk is junk. Self-centered neutrality—a major legacy of the sixties—can be as chilling and as murderous as an old-fashioned Southern policeman shouting, "To hell with the niggers!" The message may be much more muted. But it is the same message.

In 1975 there was published on the West Coast a futuristic fantasy titled *Ecotopia,* a book that has received the commendation of Ralph Nader. It is imagined that by the year 1999 Northern California, Oregon and Washington have broken away from the rest of the country to set up an independent state run on strictly ecological lines—"ecology," as the rebels say, "in one country." Ecotopia, needless to say, is ruled by feminists. Recycling is the highest good, biodegradability the most sought-after attribute. Ecotopians worship trees, practice ritualized warfare and regulate themselves not by clocks but by the motions of the tides and the cosmic rhythms of sunrise and sunset. They naturally have few hang-ups and give full rein to their feelings. What you think is not half as important as what you feel. Interpersonal relationships are very caring, sincere, supportive and open (promiscuous). When Ecotopians make love—which they seem to do all the time —there occurs a scary sharing of whole beings.

But what has happened to the blacks in this stable-state paradise? They, it turns out, live apart from their environmentalist rulers in what are referred to as Soul Cities, self-governing entities that are remarkably similar to Bantustans. The ecological future, strictly speaking, has no proper place for them. It is interesting that the page or so of the book reluctantly devoted to the Ecotopian blacks is mostly taken up with a description of penological practices. These are very progressive, of course; but however progressive, penology is still penology. Mugging brings harsh penalties in Ecotopia—a five-year sentence without the possibility of parole. In the Soul Cities (you could, I suppose, also call them ghettoes), racial separateness is emphasized by language. The blacks in the twenty-first century speak fluent Swahili and have an acute awareness of their African roots. "We look with horror," writes the narrator, "on the apartheid society of South Africa . . . [but] in Ecotopia the black minority has itself enforced a similar segregation . . . this admission that the races cannot live in harmony is surely one of the most disheartening developments in all of Ecotopia. . . ." Racial separatism may be disheartening, but it is also easy to forget. The narrator quickly abandons the subject to resume his lovemaking and his detailed descriptions of energy gathering from the sun and the sea.

Jim Jones built his movement on the debris of the sixties; on its frustrations, failures and apostasies. When, with his small band of followers, he made his hegira from Indiana to California in 1965, the era was still getting into its stride. Its climactic moments lay ahead. People's Park was yet to be battled over and Berkeley placed under martial law; San Francisco's summer of love was two years away; the Black Panthers did not exist; Angela Davis had not been charged with conspiracy and gunrunning; the feminist onslaught had not begun to make its impact; the Woodstock Festival was four years away; Vietnam was only starting to fester; George Jackson was still alive; Timothy Leary, Herbert Marcuse and Buckminster Fuller were only just becoming widely known; the Beatles had not composed their most famous music, the music that would one day inspire Charles Manson; Ronald Reagan was not yet Governor of California; Patricia Hearst was eleven years old and the Symbionese Liberation Army was not even a dream. In 1965, the sixties were in their infancy.

The world had changed substantially when, in 1972, the People's Temple moved out of its rural lair in Northern California and made San Francisco its headquarters. By then, the student revolt had all but evaporated; Vietnam would soon diminish as a source of torment with the abolition of the draft; Timothy Leary was in deep trouble with the law and Herbert Marcuse had lost much of his influence; Buckminster Fuller never stopped talking but could talk only about the same things; the Beatles had composed their most famous music and the Manson Family had committed its murders; racism was, more or less, abandoned as an issue, its place usurped by the aggressive introversions of feminism and ecology and consciousness raising; the elements of the Symbionese Liberation Army, fag end of the New Left, were gathering in the seedy communes and rooming houses of San Francisco, Berkeley and Oakland—within two years, even that late-blooming dusk of the Revolution would be extinguished. George Jackson was dead. The Black Panthers were in their death throes. Est, initiated by Werner Erhard in October 1971, was scooping up adherents. So were Synanon, the drug and alcoholic rehabilitation group that had turned itself into a religion; the Unification Church; the Hare Krishnas; the Divine Light Mission; the Children of God; Born Again Christianity and apocalyptic Fundamentalism.

Jim Jones was as much a Protestant fundamentalist as he was a "Marxist." The traditions, atmosphere and techniques of Protestant fundamentalism were all present in the People's Temple—

just as they are all present in the ecological movement. The words might have been different, but the spirit was the same.

"You are all guilty," shrieks Rev Jack Impe on television. "You are guilty. You are condemned. You are doomed." No one is righteous anymore. No one does good anymore. Even newborn babies are practiced liars, diseased from head to toe with the old Adamic sins. Satan rules over sinful mankind. Only those who accept Christ will be saved from certain destruction. "When we take a hard, cold, realistic view of conditions and trends," preaches Herbert Armstrong of the Worldwide Church of God, "they do point inevitably to a fast-approaching *world crisis* of combined nuclear war, starvation, uncontrollable disease, epidemics, crime and violence, and the extinction of human life on this planet."

We could be listening to the voice of Jim Jones. All the latest environmental fears are marshaled by Armstrong to prove his point. The air we breathe is poisoning us. So is the water we drink. Super Rat is unconquerable. As fast as new drugs appear, microbes find ways of rendering them ineffective. Autopsies carried out on soldiers in Korea and Vietnam showed their arteries to be in an advanced stage of premature decay. Pestilence will inevitably strike down the teeming cities of the backward, degenerate races who make up the Third World. These afflictions are beyond human solution. Mankind is cursed. We are living in the Last Days. Only those who embrace Christ—and, presumably, the Worldwide Church of God—will be saved from annihilation.

How different is the message of the extreme environmentalists? How different was the message of Jim Jones? To escape the ravages of a sick and hopeless world, you embrace Christ, the divine dictator, who will come to rule with a rod of iron and who will tolerate no dissent. In the case of the People's Temple, you embrace Jones, a semidivine dictator, who rules with a rod of iron and tolerates no dissent. Just how dictatorial Armstrong's Christ will be is nowhere better shown than in His racial plans. Noah's world had ended because of "racial hatreds, racial intermarriages and racial violence caused by man's efforts towards integration

and amalgamation of races, contrary to God's laws." The returned Christ was going to make sure that nothing of the kind
happened again. It was obvious, Armstrong said, that the resur-
rected Noah would be appointed to take charge of a big and
ambitious project whose aim would be the relocation of races and
nations within the boundaries God had set for them. "This will be
a tremendous operation," Armstrong writes enthusiastically. "It
will require great and vast organization, reinforced with *power* to
move whole nations and races. This time, peoples and nations will
move where God has planned for them, and no defiance will be
tolerated."

The Worldwide Church of God is not an obscure or a poor
organization. It claims a membership of one hundred thousand
and has a self-declared annual income of seventy million dollars.
Included among its many missionary activities is the publication
of an up-market, glossy magazine—*Quest*—which pays well and
often features the work of prominent literary figures.

In the utopia that Armstrong describes, after Christ has carried
out His holy bloodbath the survivors will experience no want, no
sickness, no death. Jones too held out such promises to his disciples. It was even hinted that membership in his select band would
confer immortality and that, after the holocaust, they would
emerge to create a new ruling race. Joy, Armstrong says, will
become compulsory in the One Party, One Religion, One Language universal state to be rigorously ruled from the top down.
Jones too had made joy compulsory for his cavorting senior citizens.

"Poverty, ignorance *banished!* Smiles on human faces—faces
that radiate! Wild animals tame! Air pollution, water pollution,
soil pollution *gone!* Crystal pure water to drink; clean, crisp, pure
air to breathe; rich black soil where deserts, mountains and seas
formerly were, producing full-flavored foods, and fantastic *beauty*
in flowers, shrubs, trees." We could be reading one of several
ecstatic descriptions of Jonestown, of Ecotopia. But it isn't Jonestown that is being hymned: it is the theocratic Utopia of the res-
urrected Christ as it takes shape in the imagination of Herbert
Armstrong.

The People's Temple was laid out on the latitudinal and longitudinal grid of the fundamentalist imagination; an imagination obsessed with sin and images of apocalyptic destruction, authoritarian in its innermost impulses, instinctively thinking in terms of the saved and the damned, seeking not to enlighten but to terrorize into obedience. Fundamentalism has no respect for the human personality, because to be human is, by definition, to be sick. It was upon such a framework that Jim Jones, son of the small-town Midwest, grafted his primitive visions of socialist sharing and racial justice. The result was neither racial justice nor socialism but a messianic parody of both.

And they came to him. "I was eighteen years old when I joined the People's Temple," Deborah Blakey wrote in her affidavit. "I had grown up in affluent circumstances in the permissive atmosphere of Berkeley, California. By joining the People's Temple, I hoped to help others and in the process to bring structure and self-discipline to my own life." They came to him—the seekers of structure, the *I Ching* decoders, the Tarot interpreters, the higher-consciousness addicts, the catharsis freaks, the degenerated socialists, those who thirsted for universal justice and wanted utopia "real bad."

The People's Temple rooted itself in disintegration and ruin. It has often been said that the Temple was reared on an idealism which, somehow, became perverted. It would, I think, be more correct to say that the Temple was reared on—or, better still, inherited—an idealism that had already gone wrong, that had already lost its way and been twisted out of shape in the promiscuous chaos of the sixties. Jim Jones was a beachcomber, picking up the flotsam and jetsam washed ashore from the sixties shipwrecks. The "idealism" on which he fed was not virginal but considerably shop-soiled, eaten up with inner decay.

CHAPTER

11

SHE WAS white and she was in her middle twenties.

She had first heard about the People's Temple in 1966 when her grandparents had decided to follow Jim Jones from Indiana to California. They had been seduced by his miracles and by all his talk about freedom and brotherhood. He had opened their eyes to life and to truth. They believed he was God.

When he told them that the world would soon be destroyed in a nuclear holocaust, they did not doubt him. Her grandparents, she said, were solid Midwestern folk. They were property-owning and they were prosperous. She had never thought of them as being anything other than rational, practical, God-fearing people.

In 1966, she went with her mother and brothers to Redwood Valley to spend a two-week vacation with them.

"I was very virginal," she said. She liked to read, to dance, to sew. "I had no political consciousness that I can remember. My raising had been very white and middle-class."

The high school she attended was segregated.

"I was fearful about the black race. I didn't know any black people."

Even so, her mother had always tried to do the proper thing.

"Nigger was a bad word in our house. Mother wouldn't allow it to be used."

Her father, however, did not share her mother's delicate sensibilities. He was a self-made man: he had worked his way up into the middle class.

Redwood Valley was a revelation. It was the first time she had seen black and white people living and working together. Compared with the other churches she had known, the People's Temple had seemed so lighthearted. Jones had said there was no need to be solemn in church. Her grandparents looked healthy and happy. She accompanied them to the Temple services. She listened to the members testifying for hours on end how Jim Jones had changed their lives and made them so happy. Jones had preached about racism and fascism. He said these evils were threatening all human existence. She heard about a cave he had found in the nearby hills. When the nuclear war broke out, the Temple's followers would find shelter in that cave and be saved.

"I had a lot of fun. I had gone up there with a very snobby and arrogant white middle-class attitude. But I made a lot of new friends. I had a good time. So I wanted to stay."

Her mother too had wanted to stay. Jim Jones had told her that one of her brothers who had died had been reincarnated in one of her sons. This had pleased her mother, because she was greatly attached to theories of reincarnation, astrology, ESP and the like.

When she returned to Indiana, she found that she could not readjust to her old friends and their ways.

"I lost all my interest in them. I felt lethargic. I didn't even want to go swimming anymore."

All she wanted to do was return to Redwood Valley and live with her grandparents. Her father would not hear of it. He contacted the FBI and told them that Jim Jones was a Communist. The Bureau did nothing about it. It took many months for the feeling of displacement to wear off.

"I wondered sometimes if Jim Jones was aware of what I was going through. If, you know, he could feel my unhappiness and my longing to return."

In the meantime, she entered Indiana University, taking a course in nursing.

The Watts riots in 1967 had left a deep impression on her.

"It just didn't make any sense to me. I didn't know people could be so angry. Somehow I felt it wasn't the black people's fault. Then I remembered all the things I had heard Jim Jones say in Redwood Valley."

She began to do a lot of reading. Malcolm X. George Jackson. Eldridge Cleaver. Huey Newton. The world seemed an exciting and dangerous place. Hippies were everywhere. Jane Fonda was giving solace and support to the North Vietnamese.

"Nixon, of all people, was President of the United States. Civil rights was a mess. The blacks were rioting everywhere. . . ."

She became infected by the spirit of the age.

"I was young. I felt very powerful. I felt I could do whatever I set my mind to."

She signed up for a course in political science.

But to begin with, she did not join anything. She was not a joiner. She was "into" herself. Hippies were too shaggy, too dirty. Why, wondered the well-brought-up Indiana girl, should anyone want to go around in bare feet?

In 1969, she returned to visit her grandparents in Redwood Valley. There was now a proper church. A church with a swimming pool. Wow!

"What other church had a swimming pool in it?"

She liked swimming, and so that made the Valley seem even nicer.

Still, she was also enjoying college; enjoying the academic broadening of her political consciousness.

Fate intervened: her father's employer transferred him to California.

"Mother was *so* pleased. She was dying to get back to Jim Jones, to be close to him. But she was careful not to say anything about that to Father."

They moved to California. Every weekend they began going up to Ukiah to visit her grandparents.

Now there were no doubts, no hesitations.

"Jim Jones just got to me right away. He was talking about current events, about self-determination, about all the things I was interested in."

He was very political. He was very magical. He awed her.

His miracle working reinforced her faith in him. Once, her grandfather hurt his leg badly in an accident. For a while he had lost all feeling in it. But one day, when Jim Jones walked past him, he felt warmth returning.

How could she fail to be overawed? She had found, at one stroke, both a vehicle for her radical political beliefs and an almighty Messiah, someone who would help her to realize her individual potential.

She believed everything she was told: she believed that he was the greatest healer who had ever lived; she believed that he could do no wrong; she believed that he was God.

"The healings were so fantastic. I saw how he had healed my grandfather. I believed everything. I questioned nothing. He held us with his healing power. He really held us. We surrounded him with our reverence."

It was exhilarating. With the faith healing there went the lectures on socialism, the classless society, the elimination of poverty, the brotherhood of man, the coming nuclear war which they alone would survive. They would come out of that cave in the hills to found a new society and a new race. To that end, she and others of her age were trained in survival techniques. She learned to tie complicated knots, to handle compasses, to make maps, to develop physical endurance, to handle guns. On their military maneuvers, they would pretend passing cars were tanks.

She lost her interest in the outside world.

"We thought of ourselves as the vanguard. We were trained to think that we were the elite. Those who were not with us didn't count. We knew that they were doomed and that only we would be saved."

Jones, she said, explained that he worked at many different levels. He would reach people at any level they were at. His message took on the color of his intellectual surroundings. She did not have much personal contact with him. He was a remote object of her reverence.

Yet though she believed, the passing years brought increasing strain. Jim Jones was becoming ever more demanding.

He began to say that they should be interested in no one and nothing else but him. He must be the sole legitimate object of contemplation, desire and dream. Anyone who did otherwise was a traitor to the cause.

"I became very depressed and withdrawn. I didn't trust anybody. Nobody trusted anybody. There were spies everywhere ready to report on you. There was no privacy. Everything you did and said was dissected and analyzed."

She got a job in San Francisco. She was now twenty-two. Gradually, she started pocketing some of the money she made, instead of handing it all over to the Temple as she was supposed to do.

In the summer of 1973, she was approached by a few friends. They too had had enough; they were planning to "split." Would she join them? It was dangerous, but she agreed. Jim Jones had said any college student who left would be hunted down and killed.

Her mother wanted to know why. Why? Why was she condemning herself to perdition? By that time her father, threatened with divorce if he did not comply, had joined the People's Temple.

She left. She went into hiding, knowing that her life was in danger.

She lost contact with her family. When the time came, her mother, her father, her brothers, her grandparents all went to Guyana.

On one occasion, she managed to get hold of them on the radiotelephone.

They asked her if she was still forging checks; still bombing bridges.

They died without ever being reconciled to her desertion.

She was middle-aged and she was white.

It was her husband who would precipitate one of the climactic incidents of the Ryan mission to Jonestown—he would try to stab the Congressman.

They were both California-bred. He, a machinist from the Bay Area, was over six feet tall and a trained Olympic swimmer. They were both, in her opinion, normal Californians. In the course of time, they had fetched up in the small Northern California town of Willits, not far from Redwood Valley.

"We were searching for some meaning to our lives," she said.

One of the early influences on her thinking was Edgar Cayce. Cayce, a mystic, was born in 1877 in Kentucky. He died in 1945. One of Cayce's predictions was that California would be destroyed by earthquakes. Various groups had been formed to ponder his teachings and prophecies. These had a wide range of reference—from racial strife to reincarnation. She joined one of these Cayce groups.

Of the seven couples in her group, five were eventually to become members of the People's Temple.

It was in 1965, the year of the migration from Indiana, that she had first heard about Jim Jones. Two of the couples in her Cayce group had gone "out of curiosity" to hear the new preacher who had settled in Redwood Valley. They had come back "raving" about Jim Jones. Spurred by their enthusiasm, she and her husband went along to a service one Sunday.

"The power of love was just overwhelming," she said. "It just hit you as you walked through the door."

At that point, they had considered themselves agnostics. Religion, as they had so far experienced it, was hypocritical. She recalled that when he was six years old, their son had suddenly announced that he no longer believed in God.

"If there is a God," he had said, "how can there be people without arms and legs?"

That, to some extent, had echoed their own feelings on the

subject. She regarded herself as somewhat more interested in religious questions than her husband.

"I always wanted to find out more about the Supreme Power out there," she said.

What especially interested her was doctrines of reincarnation. If there was no reference to it in the Bible, that was so because of an oversight. She could think of no other reason for its omission.

In Jim Jones and the People's Temple they felt they had at last found what—unconsciously—they had always been searching for. The Temple preached a political and social philosophy they could understand. It talked about service to those less fortunate than oneself. It talked about justice. It talked about equality. It talked about universal brotherhood. They were bowled over to come across a genuinely integrated church. Jim, in those early days, showed so much love and concern for the Temple children. She liked working with old people; and the Temple had so many of those in its ranks.

Moved by what they had seen and felt, they transferred themselves to Redwood Valley a month after they had attended their first service. What really drew them was the atmosphere of caring, the sense of community, the feeling that one belonged to a large, multiracial family.

The four years between 1966 and 1970 were golden ones.

The old people were so happy. They had their own health clinic; they had their own rest homes where they were tenderly looked after; they spent their days baking cakes and pies. Their happiness was a beauty to behold.

Husband and wife felt that their lives had been given a new meaning.

The People's Temple during those utopian days overflowed with love and devotion. She remembered a drug addict known as Dave. They had taken him into their house. He had called them Mom and Dad.

It was not the welfare services that really attracted people to the Temple. Not in the least. The real attraction came from feeling equal, from the sense of belonging that the Temple provided.

The main goal of the People's Temple, as she saw it, was to assist in the establishment of socialism in the United States.

She had never doubted the genuineness of the healings.

"You could never have told me they were faked—and sometimes I would be standing right next to Jim when he performed them."

After 1970, Utopia began to turn sour.

More and more, Jones began to whip up paranoia, to create a distorted picture of what was going on in the outside world, to fill his defenseless old people and children with fear. That was so easy to do. It was the simplest thing in the world to take newspaper stories out of context and use them to show whatever it was one wanted to show. Every day, if you looked hard enough, you could find something in the newspapers to justify Jones's view of the world. He and the Temple aristocracy assiduously unearthed every reference to the Ku Klux Klan and the Nazis that they could find and constructed out of them a vision of unavoidable genocidal doom. He would display brutalized black children from Watts and other ghettoes to drive his message home. The fenced-in compounds they could see around the San Francisco headquarters were, he said, some of the concentration camps being prepared for ethnic minorities.

But what really upset her more than anything else was the harshness of the discipline. After 1970, the Temple seemed to lose sight of individual need. It abandoned affection and turned to terror.

"I don't know what happened to all that tender loving care. It just disappeared, ran off into the ground."

The main victims were the children. They were mercilessly punished for any infringement of the rules. Their screams were magnified by a microphone put close to their mouths.

"The beatings began to get really bad. No one was allowed to cry."

After a while, she had forgotten how to cry. She had not cried for years. She had had to teach herself how to cry after leaving the Temple.

In 1973, she was moved from Redwood Valley to San Francisco. This happened because she was one of their big earners. The fledgling Guyana settlement, the earthly paradise, was eating up money. By then, she was close to complete disenchantment. But it would take another two years for her to gather up the courage to leave.

In February 1976, she defected. She was threatened with death. Her husband stayed behind. So did her son. Without her consent or knowledge, they shipped him out to Guyana. There he would die. She knew that he had tried on several occasions to run away from Jonestown. Because of that he had spent a lot of time in the "hot box," the punishment cell to which Jonestown consigned its recalcitrant children.

The ideals that had led her to join the People's Temple remained unimpaired.

"I fought with all my heart for a cause that I believed in. I don't regret having done that."

But those ideals were now dormant.

She knew that despite everything, there were many who were still loyal to Jim Jones. Survivors were meeting; trying to re-create and regroup themselves.

"People don't give up their dreams easily."

Grace Stoen was nineteen when she met Timothy Stoen.

She, of Maltese and Mexican ancestry, came from a poor but respectable family.

He came from a prosperous family.

"All my life I felt I had a lot of potential," she said.

But that potential had never been realized in her austere home environment. You did as you were expected to do and asked no questions. Timothy Stoen opened up a whole new world to her.

"He was the only person that ever bought me a book. He would read poetry to me. I felt like Alice in Wonderland. I felt like I was going down the Yellow Brick Road."

Tim was driven by feelings of guilt about everything.

He wanted to change the world.

"There is a man I want you to meet," he said to her one day.

This man, he told her, wanted to change the world too.

She was susceptible to the Temple's message because she had always wanted to do something for the "minority races." The Temple overwhelmed her with its display of racial harmony. She marveled at the way it was able to bring together people from such different classes, cultures and religions.

"I was impressed. I was touched."

What touched and impressed her most of all was the children.

She had never seen so many happy children.

They would come and climb up on your knee; they would hug and kiss you.

Beautiful children.

The spiritual loveliness was matched by the physical loveliness of Redwood Valley.

"The country was so captivating. Just being there mellowed you, made you ready to receive fresh ideas."

In June 1970 she and Timothy Stoen were married.

She had made an agreement with him that they would donate a year of their lives to the Temple. All she had ever desired was a cozy domestic life and children of her own. That was all she had ever wanted.

"I was in love with Tim Stoen. I followed Tim Stoen in because I was in love with him."

She was never, she said, entirely taken in by Jim Jones.

"He was brilliant. He was clever. He was manipulative. But I'm very skeptical. I never believed in his healings. *Never!*"

She had discovered how ready people were to be led. That was frightening. She had watched Jones manipulate the idealism of his white aristocracy and the superstitious nature of his black raw material.

She may not have believed; she may not have been manipulated. But she stayed for six years. Power and privilege fell into her skeptical hands. She was head counselor. She was a record keeper. She collected and passed on to Jones the names of those who were to be punished.

"I was in love with Timothy Stoen," she said.

She was in love; and when the writ of her love for Timothy Stoen no longer ran, she was "brainwashed." A brainwashed skeptic.

The experience had taught her what a great country the United States was. She was prepared to fall down on her knees and kiss the ground. Jim Jones used to say—pointing, for instance, at a fruit tree—that as long as there were starving people in the world, none of them had a right to eat the fruit from that tree.

She no longer accepted that kind of outlook. Such self-denial did not help anyone.

She had not, however, lost all the ideals the Temple had inculcated in her.

She believed in racial brotherhood.

She believed in socialism.

Leaving the Temple, she had once told Jones, would never drive her back into the arms of the pigs. She had meant that.

The People's Temple had, in a sense, taught her everything she knew. It had been her true education.

But she would accept no responsibility for what either she or it had done during their six-year journey down the Yellow Brick Road.

The theme of the symposium was "Making the World Work." It was being sponsored by est, and it was to be chaired by no less a person than Werner Erhard. But the star speaker would be Buckminster Fuller, erstwhile advocate of the revolution of World Studenthood and, of late, an est-ian protégé.

Along all the roads leading to the Berkeley Community Theater, youthful est graduates were holding up directional signs. The symposium, like everything to which est puts its hand, was smoothly and efficiently organized, executed with almost military precision.

The Theater presented a crowded but orderly scene. Smiling but firm-mannered est devotees, their first names prominently exhibited on their breasts, patrolled the aisles. Est seems to have an aversion to last names. I noted the absence of black faces. Blacks, it appeared, were not interested in making the world work. But it was also probable that learning how to make the world work was too expensive a business for them: thirty-five dollars was charged for the privilege of attending the seminar.

A photograph of the cloud-swathed earth was projected onto the stage screen. Periodically, slogans flashed up. Slogans that told us:

• We could all do something . . .

• We were all big enough to be responsible for making a difference in the world . . .

• We were not to be a member of an audience, but to participate, to share . . .

The podium was arrayed with various props: a blackboard, a map of the world, assorted geometric shapes, a geodesic dome—this last Fuller's trademark.

The symposium got under way punctually. Fuller, Erhard and a young relative of Fuller's made their entrance. Prolonged applause greeted their appearance. Gusty, rodeo-style howls and hoots and yahoos resounded through the auditorium. Erhard, dressed with casual impeccability, exuded ease, vigor and complacence. He looked every inch the highly successful encyclopedia salesman he had once been. His manner, charged with camaraderie, was that of the genial host of a TV chat show. The frail Fuller—he is in his seventies—sat on a chair, staring interestedly at Werner.

It was Fuller's young relative, Erhard said, who had first taught him how to interact with Bucky successfully.

Bucky did not intend—nor did he—to provide us with entertainment that day. Nothing was further from their minds. The purpose of the exercise was transformation. He and Bucky were inviting us, giving us an opportunity, to transform ourselves. The symposium was going to be about everybody and everything. Nothing was going to be left out. At a mere thirty-five dollars a head, that was more than a fair bargain.

We were all, Erhard announced, about to participate in the process of making the world work.

No one was too small or too insignificant to take part.

Everyone mattered.

"What can I do to make the world work?" That was the question each and every one of us in that auditorium had to ask himself.

Some bad attitudes were affecting the world. Those bad attitudes could be summed up by one common sentiment: that I will take care of what is mine and you will take care of what is yours.

That, virtually, had become the basis of culture.

I joined the Unification Church in the summer of 1972. I had just finished my third year as a religion student at Princeton, and I was at a point in my life when I was in transition. I came home to Louisville, Kentucky, and I got a job in a tool factory to get out of the cognitive milieu and into the manual milieu; and ran into the movement about two weeks later. A young woman approached me on the campus of the University of Louisville and handed me a flyer. The flyer basically had a schedule of lectures that were going to be delivered in the next couple of days which promised to answer all the questions about life, to put it in a nutshell. I was twenty-one, looking for something to do during the year that I was off, something exhilarating, diverting and yet gratifyingly in line with my ideals. My first reaction to her flyer was amusement. But then I turned to her—I was reading this flyer, I remember the situation quite vividly— and my reaction totally changed because she was looking right into my eyes, this penetrating look, very powerful. I felt embarrassed at being so judgmental, in evaluating her ideas so abruptly. So she persuaded me to come to a lecture. When I saw people gazing intensely into my eyes, anguished over my inability to identify myself emotionally with them, I had to deal internally with the question, why am I different really? How can I take my Ivy League sophistication as any kind of real criterion for human life? How much is that just a product of class? of intellectual development? These other people were located in something which was very intense, very real to them . . .

Why, asked Erhard, should one want to share Bucky Fuller with one's friends?

One would want to share Bucky Fuller with one's friends because he was a universal thinker.

"To be in the presence of such a being," Erhard said, "is a blessing."

Frail Bucky sat motionless in his chair, gazing up tranquilly at Werner.

Whenever he was with Bucky, Werner went on, he was somehow able to get in touch not only with Bucky's wisdom but with his own wisdom. It was incredible the things that could happen when you were around Bucky Fuller.

He invited us all to interact with Bucky in a meaningful way.

We might encounter some problems in doing that. Bucky, he admitted, was not always easy to follow. Even he, Werner, had to confess that sometimes he had difficulty in following Bucky. But we ought not to be unduly confounded by that.

We had to "be" with our confusions; "be" with the things we could not immediately understand.

But eventually, the whole wonderful picture would fall into place.

"*Be* with Bucky," Werner urged, "as he creates the principles by which the world works."

He wanted to encourage us all to stay with our confusions and be with Bucky because if we did that, we would all be rewarded with a breakthrough. When we walked out of the Berkeley Community Theater we would be transformed people.

Bucky, Werner said, had written somewhere that he—Bucky —was just an average human being.

Werner could not agree with that.

Bucky, in his opinion, was a truly wonderful human being.

"I don't ever spend a day with Bucky," he said, "when tears don't come to my eyes."

In fact, just thinking about Bucky often made him cry.

Rows of rapt, solemn faces looked from Werner to Bucky. It was a frightening spectacle.

. . . When I went to Princeton my first objective was to get into politics. I was always idealistically motivated. My freshman year, 1969–1970,

was the year that the lid really blew off the colleges. I was involved in that. I saw the political arena as a real source of remedies for the injustices I saw in the world. During that year, however, I became disillusioned with the Left, because I saw people manipulated. I saw a tiny cadre of people manipulating enormous groups of people who were intensely, but vaguely, concerned about the war. Some were exercising their humanitarian idealism in symbolic gestures that didn't really get hold of their lives—for example, students putting their draft cards on the altar of the chapel as a gesture of defiance and then coming back the next day and picking them up. So I got disillusioned with politics. There was nothing in it that was consistent with my idealism. That's why I went into religion. I felt that I wanted to understand the ultimate symbols of meaning in human life. To me, God was a symbol of what was crucial to people's lives, a symbol of the source of value, of an enduring meaning to life. Love, creativity, death, sin, guilt, community—these are all originally religious concepts . . .

Werner withdrew. Bucky was on his feet.

"What," he said, turning to his young relative, "does the Universe have to do with making the world work?"

His young relative looked suitably confused.

Bucky drew our attention to China's invasion of Vietnam—then the big news story.

"We may have only a few days left," he said.

Sighs of approval rose from the audience; heads nodded sagely. The fundamentalist imagination, feeding on visions of doom, was at work in the Berkeley Community Theater. The people here had not come to learn anything: they had come in search of revelation; they had come to discover how they might save themselves, save mankind, save the world. Being with Bucky was an act of spiritual communion; of worship.

"Do you really have the guts," Bucky asked, "to make yourself go along with the truth as you know it?"

Could we *feel*, for instance, the earth going around the sun?

He was not here to talk about dry intellectual systems. He was here to talk about the Truth. But you could not, ultimately, talk about the Truth. You had to feel it. It was consciousness; it was awareness.

. . . This is a characteristic thing about Americans. We tend to seek resolution. That is because of an implicit, unarticulated utopianism which is deeply embedded in our character. It's very difficult for Americans to live with contradictions. We are not by nature cynical. We've got to resolve tensions; we can't accept them as a part of life. You've got somehow to have people smiling and shaking hands and really meaning it. That's the kind of implicit utopianism I'm talking about. It's not just pie in the sky, it's a deep-rooted emotional quality. When I came in contact with the Moonies, that sort of attitude was my Achilles' heel. They, I saw, had found a resolution. What will happen to me if I tried what they tried? When I began asking myself questions like that, the criteria of evaluation dissolved, the critical faculties dissolved. I went back and graduated from Princeton while I was in the church. "Gary," said a professor there who was a good friend of mine, "it's good to be open-minded, but you can't be so open-minded your brains fall out." I didn't know quite what he was getting at at the time, but since coming out of the church I've realized the importance of maintaining a functioning rational capability. . . .

Bucky's discourse was broad and flowing. He talked about Kepler and Isaac Newton, alloys, tetrahedrons and the First World War. Werner listened with an intent smile, his index finger playing about his chin.

If he had idolized Bucky, he himself had been no less idolized in his time. One of his graduates has described at length the impression Werner made on him when he appeared at the San Francisco Civic Auditorium for the est seminar on Making Relationships Work. Werner and his physical space had been in perfect harmony. His voice had filled the auditorium like the Zarathustra Symphony [*sic*]. On that occasion Werner had said that he would settle for nothing less than a complete transformation; an alteration of substance. When Werner leaned over the lectern, he looked like a falcon. Toward the end, the writer had begun to see him as "a mythic being, someone whose self-conceived mythopoeiac destiny was to 'get the physical universe back to work.' " Making your relationships work could get you into deep waters.

Bucky was talking about fossil fuels, the advent of the motorcar, Spaceship Earth.

"What can the individual do? He can think. Why are humans here? Why are there humans in the universe? We must be here for some very important reason. . . ."

Synergy was mentioned—the bringing together of energy rather than its dispersal. There could be four billion billionaires on the planet. We retreated to ancient Egypt. Life expectancy was nineteen years then; life was seen as one long trial. Levers were invented. Irrigation ditches came into their own. Before, only one man—the Pharaoh—could go to Heaven. Now, we could all go to Heaven. But there was no need to go to Heaven. We could have Heaven right here on Spaceship Earth.

. . . I felt I was working shoulder to shoulder with a chosen few, a handful of people who were really willing to put their lives out for something beyond themselves, and there's no question that they were, they were sacrificing themselves like mad. The sincerity had a kind of dissolving effect. I wanted to have a real solid experience with a group of idealistic people. I was willing to try it out for a year, and when I did, that's when things really started happening to me. . . .

Bucky turned to the props arrayed about the stage.

He drew a rectangle on the blackboard; he divided the rectangle with a diagonal.

Look! Two triangles!

The audience gasped; they started to applaud; they stamped their feet.

He pointed to the Asiatic quarter of the world map.

Look! More than half of humanity lives in that corner!

The audience gasped.

Revelation was in the air.

But I had had enough. I wanted fresh air. Outside, the California sun was hidden. The Technicolor civilization was driven into hiding by a persistent drizzle.

Acknowledgments

GATHERING MATERIAL for this book was not an easy task: the open society of California was often closed against me. I could, if I wished, compile a page of un-acknowledgments. But courtesy makes me refrain. There are, however, several people whose assistance was of great value to me. I would especially like to thank Dr. Clark Kerr and Huey Newton. In addition, I would like to express my gratitude to two San Francisco politicians, Willie Brown and Art Agnos; the San Francisco Social Services Department; Gary Scharfs; Grace Stoen; Stephen Katsaris; George and Kathy Hunter; Lorri Cocke; Wendy Watriss and Frederick Baldwin; Hannibal Williams; Father Floyd Lotito of St. Anthony's Dining Room; The Reverend Austin Ford and the staff of Emmaus House in Atlanta. With greater reserve, I thank Walter Williams and the Human Freedom Center. In Guyana, my thanks to Eusi Kwayana and those lawyers and academics whose names it would be impolitic to mention; and, of course, to Janet Jagan and the dedicated young disciples of the People's Progressive Party. I wish them well. Nor must I forget that wonderfully fair-minded official from the Guyanese Ministry of Information who got me on the aircraft to Jonestown. I wish him well. It is probable that none of the individuals I have mentioned will agree with any of the opinions or judgments expressed in this book. For those, I alone am to blame.   S.N.

Bibliography

Alinsky, Saul D., *Reveille for Radicals*. New York: Vintage, 1969.

Annamunthodo, W., ed., *Malik Guilty—Murder!* San Fernando, Trinidad: Unique Services, 1972.

Armstrong, Herbert W., *The Wonderful World Tomorrow: What It Will Be Like*. Pasadena, Calif.: Worldwide Church of God, 1973.

The Assassination of Representative Leo J. Ryan and the Jonestown Guyana tragedy, Report of a Staff Investigative Group to the Committee on Foreign Affairs, U.S. House of Representatives. Washington, D.C.: Government Printing Office, 1979.

Bach, Richard, *Illusions: The Adventures of a Reluctant Messiah*. New York: Delacorte, 1977.

Baldwin, James, *No Name in the Street*. New York: Dial, 1972.

———, *The Fire Next Time*. New York: Dial, 1963.

Barnes, Jack, *et al.*, *Prospects for Socialism in America*. New York: Pathfinder Press, 1978.

Becker, Ernest, *The Denial of Death*. New York: The Free Press, 1975.

Bergon, Frank, and Papanikolas, Zeese, *Looking Far West: The Search for the American West in History, Myth, and Literature*. New York: Mentor, 1978.

Breitman, George, ed., *Malcolm X Speaks*. New York: Merit, 1965.

Bugliosi, Vincent, *Helter Skelter: The True Story of the Manson Murders*. New York: Norton, 1972.

Callenbach, Ernest, *Ecotopia*. Berkeley, Calif.: Banyan Tree, 1975.

Carmichael, Stokeley, and Hamilton, Charles V., *Black Power: The Politics of Liberation in America*. New York: Random House, 1967.

Carpozi, George, Jr., *The Suicide Cults*. New York: Manor, n.d.

Cleaver, Eldridge, *Soul on Ice.* New York: McGraw-Hill, 1968.

Collymore, Clinton, ed., *This Is Guyana,* a People's Progressive Party booklet, rev. ed. Georgetown, Guyana: New Guyana Co., 1977.

Davis, Angela Y., *et al., If They Come in the Morning.* New York: Signet, 1971.

Declaration of Sophia, address by the leader of the People's National Congress, Prime Minister Forbes Burnham, at a Special Congress to mark the 10th anniversary of the PNC in government. Georgetown, Guyana: Guyana Printers, 1974.

de Tocqueville, Alexis, *Democracy in America,* vols. 1 and 2. New York: Knopf, 1944.

Dunne, John Gregory, *Quintana & Friends.* New York: Dutton, 1978.

Efrein, Laurie, "The Greatest Man in America: 8½ Years with Jim Jones," *The Soho Weekly News,* Jan. 25, 1979.

Farquhar, Francis P., ed., *Up and Down California in 1860–1864, The Journal of William H. Brewer.* Berkeley: University of California Press, 1974.

Fenwick, Dr. Sheridan, *Getting It: The Psychology of est.* New York: Penguin, 1977.

Fitzhugh, George, *Cannibals All! or Slaves Without Masters.* Cambridge, Mass.: Belknap/Harvard, 1973.

Forcade, Thomas King, ed., *Underground Press Anthology.* New York, Ace, 1972.

Fuller, R. Buckminster, *Operating Manual for Spaceship Earth.* New York: Dutton, 1978.

———, *Utopia or Oblivion—The Prospects for Humanity.* New York: Penguin, 1970.

Ginsberg, Allen, *Allen Verbatim: Lectures on Poetry, Politics, Consciousness.* ed. by Gordon Ball. New York: McGraw-Hill, 1975.

Grier, William H., and Cobbs, Price M., *Black Rage.* New York: Basic, 1968.

Guyana Chronicle, special supplement on Jonestown, Dec. 6, 1978.

Hale, Dennis, and Eisen, Jonathan, eds., *The California Dream.* New York: Collier, 171.

Hargrove, Robert A., *est: Making Life Work.* New York: Delacorte, n.d.

Herr, Michael, *Dispatches.* New York: Knopf, 1977.

The I Ching, or Book of Changes. Princeton, N.J.: Princeton University Press, 1979.

Jackson, George, "On Withdrawal," *The Black Panther,* vol. 18, no. 26 (Dec. 2–15) 1978).

———, *Soledad Brother: The Prison Letters of George Jackson.* New York: Coward, 1970.

Jagan, Cheddi, *The West on Trial: The Fight for Guyana's Freedom* rev. ed. Berlin, D.D.R.: Seven Seas Books, 1975.

Jagan, Janet, *An Examination of National Service,* a People's Progressive Party booklet. Georgetown, Guyana: New Guyana Co., 1976.

Kilduff, Marshall, and Javers, Ron, *The Suicide Cult.* New York: Bantam, 1978.

———, and Tracy, Phil, "Inside People's Temple," *New West* magazine, Aug. 1, 1977.

Krause, Charles A., et al., *Guyana Massacre: The Eyewitness Account.* New York: Berkeley, 1978.

Lane, Mark, *The Strongest Poison.* New York: Hawthorn, 1980.

Lang, Anthony, *Synanon Foundation: The People Business.* Cottonwood, Ariz.: Wayside Press, 1978.

Langer, Elinor, "Notes for Next Time: A Memoir of the 1960's," *Working Papers for a New Society,* vol. 1, no. 3 (fall) 1973.

Levering, Bob, untitled article on the People's Temple, *Bay Guardian,* 1977.

McFadden, Cyra, *The Serial: A Year in the Life of Marin County.* New York: Knopf, 1977.

McLellan, Vin, and Avery, Paul, *The Voices of Guns.* New York: Putnam's, 1977.

McWilliams, Carey, *California: The Great Exception.* Santa Barbara, Calif.: Peregrine Smith, 1979.

Mailer, Norman, *The White Negro.* San Francisco: City Lights Books, 1970.

Malcolm X, *The Autobiography of Malcolm X.* New York: Ballantine, 1979.

Mills, Jeannie, *Six Years with God: Life Inside Reverend Jim Jones's Peoples Temple.* New York: A & W Publishers, 1979.

Nechayev, Sergei, "Catechism of the Revolutionist," reprinted in *The Terrorism Reader,* ed. by Walter Laqueur. London: Wildwood House, 1979.

Newton, Huey P., *Revolutionary Suicide.* New York: Harcourt Brace Jovanovich, 1973.

Nordhoff, Charles, *California: for Health, Pleasure and Residence. A Book for Travellers and Settlers.* Berkeley, Calif.: Ten Speed Press, 1973.

Patrick, Ted, *Let Our Children Go!* New York: Dutton, 1976.

People's Forum, the newspaper of the People's Temple, vol. 1, nos. 9, 14 (Sept. 1976, Jan. 1977), vol. 2, nos. 2, 3, 5, 6 (June, July, Oct. 1977, Jan. 1978).

Peterson, Severin, *A Catalog of the Ways People Grow.* New York: Ballantine, 1971.

Piercy, Marge, *Vida.* New York: Summit, 1979.

Redstockings of the Women's Liberation Movement, *Feminist Revolution.* New York: Random House, 1976.

Report of the British Guiana Constitutional Commission. London: Her Majesty's Stationery Office, 1954.

Report of the National Advisory Commission on Civil Disorders. New York: Dutton, 1968.

Rigged Elections in Guyana, a People's Progressive Party booklet. Georgetown, Guyana: New Guyana Co., June 1978.

Rosten, Leo, ed., *Religions of America.* New York: Simon and Schuster, 1975.

Roszak, Theodore, *Person/Planet, The Creative Disintegration of Industrial Society.* New York: Doubleday, 1978.

Sargant, William, *The Mind Possessed: A Physiology of Possession, Mysticism and Faith Healing.* New York: Lippincott, 1974.

Stearn, Jess, *Edgar Cayce—The Sleeping Prophet.* New York: Bantam, 1977.

Stone, I. F., *In a Time of Torment.* New York: Random, 1967.

Stoner, Carroll, and Parke, Jo Anne. *All Gods Children: The Cult Experience —Salvation or Slavery?* New York: Penguin, 1979.

Sugrue, Thomas, *There Is a River: The Story of Edgar Cayce.* New York: Dell, 1978.

Thielmann, Bonnie, *The Broken God.* Elgin, Ill.: David C. Cook, 1979.

Thompson, Hunter S., *Fear and Loathing in Las Vegas.* New York: Random House, 1972.

———, *Hell's Angels.* New York: Random House, 1967.

Tracy, Phil, "More on People's Temple: The Strange Suicides." *New West* magazine, Aug. 15, 1977.

Transcript of Proceedings, Information Meeting on the Cult Phenomenon in the United States. Washington, D.C.: Ace-Federal Reporters, Feb. 5, 1979.

Weiner, Rex, and Stillman, Deanne, *Woodstock Census.* New York: Viking Press, 1979.

Wells, H. G., *The Time Machine.* New York: Bantam, 1979.

Wright, Richard, *American Hunger.* New York: Harper & Row, 1979.

———, *Black Boy.* New York: Harper & Row, 1966.

———, *Uncle Tom's Children.* New York: Harper & Row, 1965.

Index